The Interaction between Europe's Legal Systems

The Interaction between Europe's Legal Systems

Judicial Dialogue and the Creation of Supranational Laws

Giuseppe Martinico

García Pelayo Fellow, Centro de Estudios Políticos y Constitucionales, Spain

Oreste Pollicino

Associate Professor of Comparative Law, Bocconi University, Italy

Edward Elgar

Cheltenham, UK • Northampton, MA, USA

Published by
Edward Elgar Publishing Limited
The Lypiatts
15 Lansdown Road
Cheltenham
Glos GL50 2JA
UK

Edward Elgar Publishing, Inc.
William Pratt House
9 Dewey Court
Northampton
Massachusetts 01060
USA

A catalogue record for this book
is available from the British Library

Library of Congress Control Number: 2012935269

FSC
www.fsc.org
MIX
Paper from
responsible sources
FSC® C018575

ISBN 978 1 84844 678 6

Typeset by Servis Filmsetting Ltd, Stockport, Cheshire
Printed and bound by MPG Books Group, UK

Contents

Abbreviations

CEE	Central and Eastern European
EAW	European Arrest Warrant
EC	European Community (also 'European Charter')
ECHR	European Convention on Human Rights
ECtHR	European Court of Human Rights (the Strasbourg Court)
ECJ	Court of Justice of the European Union (the Luxembourg Court)
EU	European Union
TFEU	Treaty on the Functioning of the European Union
TEU	Treaty on the European Union
WTO	World Trade Organization

Acknowledgements

This book is part of a broader project we have been carrying out for a long time and it represents just the final link of a long chain of publications devoted to the investigation of the domestic impact of EU and ECHR law (G. Martinico and O. Pollicino (eds), *The National Judicial Treatment of the ECHR and EU Laws. A Comparative Constitutional Perspective* (Europa Law Publishing, Groningen, 2010); G. Martinico, 'Il trattamento nazionale dei diritti europei: CEDU e diritto comunitario nell'applicazione dei giudici nazionali', *Rivista Trimestrale di Diritto Pubblico*, 3/2010, 691, and O. Pollicino, *Corti europee e allargamento dell'Europa: evoluzioni giurisprudenziali e riflessi ordinamentali*, in *Il Diritto dell'Unione Europea*, 2009, 1–45 and *L'allargamento ad est dell'Europa e rapporti tra Corti costituzionali e Corti europee. Verso una teoria generale dell'impatto interordinamentale del diritto sovranazionale?* (Giuffrè, Milan, 2010). The first three chapters were written by Giuseppe Martinico and the last four chapters were written by Oreste Pollicino.

We would like to thank Monica Claes, Arthur Dyevre, Jürgen Kurtz, Irmantas Jarukaitis, Cian Murphy, Filippo Fontanelli, Aida Torres Pérez, Patricia Popelier, Ernst-Ulrich Petersmann and Lorenzo Zucca for their comments and Andrea Biondi, Bruno de Witte, Miguel Poiares Maduro and Petros Mavroidis for their support to the project.

This book would have not been possible without the support of our former and present institutions: the Scuola Superiore Sant'Anna, Pisa (Sant'Anna School of Advanced Studies), the European University Institute (Florence) and its Max Weber Programme, the Centro de Estudios Políticos y Constitucionales, Madrid and the Bocconi University (Department of Law). We would like to thank Professors Paolo Carrozza, Giuseppe Franco Ferrari, Cesare Pinelli, Emanuele Rossi, Antonio Ruggeri, András Sajó and Antonio Tizzano for their support.

Deserving of particular mention is the STALS project (www.stals.sssup.it), made possible thanks to the financial support offered by the Scuola Superiore Sant'Anna and issued within the framework of the School's internationalization policy, which generously financed the workshop 'National Judges and Supranational Laws: On the effective application of EC Law and the ECHR' which has proven to be fundamental in the economy of our research.

Finally, parts of this book were written during research periods spent abroad at the Central European University, Budapest, the Tilburg Institute of Comparative and Transnational Law (TICOM), the Netherlands, King's College, London, and the Institute of European and Comparative Law at the University of Oxford (Faculty of Law).

PART I

1. The interaction between Europe's legal systems: an introduction to the investigation

1. GOALS OF THE RESEARCH

This book examines the broad issue of the rapprochement between the EU and ECHR legal systems. While there is a massive amount of literature in terms of monographs, collected volumes and national reports analyzing either the issue of the national application of EC/EU law or that of ECHR norms, a specific comparative analysis that takes into account the national judicial treatment of both laws is still lacking. This volume aims to answer the following research question: Are the EU and ECHR legal systems converging?

By 'convergence' we mean the possibility of encountering those structural principles that have traditionally contributed to the *sui generis* nature of EU law – namely direct effect and primacy – when dealing with the ECHR. This means that we are not going to compare the levels of protection of fundamental rights in these contexts but rather the impact that these two European legal systems have on national legal structures.

In order to answer this research question we are going to compare both the national judicial treatments of these two European legal systems and the interpretative approaches employed by the Strasbourg and Luxembourg Courts in cases that are sensitive for the national constitutional structures. This means that while the first part of this volume is going to focus on how national judges 'apply' EU law and the ECHR, the second part is going to be devoted, instead, to the European Courts, with an analysis of their origins and then of their recent attitudes. The research question of the first part is 'Are national judges treating the ECHR provisions the same way (or, at least, in a less different way than) they treat EU law?' The second part will investigate whether the Luxembourg and Strasbourg Courts have started adopting similar approaches when dealing with some sensitive areas touching the national constitutional structures. Obviously these two dynamics are strongly related and both European Courts have undergone deep transformations in recent years, especially after the enlargements of the EU and the Council of Europe.

This book originates from a very well known issue: according to many scholars, a clear distinction exists between ECHR and EU law, and this was recently pointed out by Lord Hoffmann in his Judicial Studies Board Annual Lecture (2009).[1] Despite such important scholarship, after a detailed analysis of the national and European case law, this conclusion is questioned. On the contrary, at a first glance, at least in our view, it is possible to argue that, in a way, we are already dealing with partial convergence in the application of EU law and the provisions of the ECHR.

Convergence, like comparison, should be understood as a process: this means that the two legal orders under consideration might still present differences without this resulting in the impossibility of noticing some analogies. Moreover, even comparison refers to a process; comparing two 'things' does not mean to conclude that they are identical at the end of the process of comparison or that they were identical at the beginning of the process. Comparing does not exclude the possibility of finding differences.

The research question formulated at the beginning of this chapter does not seek to anticipate our conclusion: our research originates from the analysis of some factors present both at the national and supranational/international level. In judgments like *Omega Spielhallen*, *Schmidberger* and, most recently, *Sayn Wittgenstein* the ECJ seemed to leave 'a margin of appreciation for Member States to maintain national constitutional specificities instead of imposing uniform solutions'.[2] On the other hand,

---

1 'The fact that the 10 original Member States of the Council of Europe subscribed to a statement of human rights in the same terms did not mean that they had agreed to uniformity of the application of those abstract rights in each of their countries, still less in the 47 states which now belong. The situation is quite different from that of the European Economic Community, in which the Member States agreed that it was in their economic interest to have uniform laws on particular matters which were specified as being within European competence. On such matters, the European institutions, including the Court of Justice in Luxembourg, were given a mandate to unify the laws of Europe. The Strasbourg court, on the other hand, has no mandate to unify the laws of Europe on the many subjects which may arguably touch upon human rights . . . The proposition that the Convention is a "living instrument" is the banner under which the Strasbourg court has assumed power to legislate what they consider to be required by "European public order"', Lord Hoffmann, 'The Universality of Human Rights', Judicial Studies Board Annual Lecture, 19 March 2009.

2 C. Timmermans, 'Relationships between the Strasbourg Court and the ECJ', Intervention Round Table CCBE Luxembourg, 20 May 2011, http://www.ccbe.org/fileadmin/user_upload/document/Roundtable_2011_Luxembourg/Timmermans.pdf.

if scholars had already noticed a certain convergence in countries like the Netherlands – where 'there is no fundamental divide between the application of public international law and EC law'[3] – more recently even in contexts like Italy, for instance, national judges have started setting aside national law that conflicts with the ECHR in the absence of a norm comparable to those present in the Netherlands or in France.

The occasion for reflecting on this issue is given by the impact of the respective 'enlargements' of the two international organizations (the EU and the Council of Europe) to include Central and Eastern Europe, a situation which has induced the two European Courts to reconsider, partly at least, their mission.[4] These factors represent the 'issue' that induced us to commence this research.

Finally, one might argue that the accession of the EU to the ECHR will give a definitive answer that will certainly favour convergence in the judicial treatment of these two European laws. We are not so sure about that. On the contrary, looking at the ECJ case law devoted to international treaties concluded by the EC, one can see how the ECJ has sometimes limited the perfect assimilation between 'EC law proper' and 'Community Agreements'.[5] Moreover, recently, the ECJ has extended the WTO exception (lack of direct effect for WTO law norms) to the provisions of some other international law treaties.[6] Cases like *Mox Plant*,[7] then, reveal how the ECJ considers important the reasons connected to its interpretive monopoly and shows scant tolerance for interpretive competitors.

This is just a reminder of how the conclusions in this field are far from being obvious, even after the Reform Treaty, as always in the fascinating 'journey to an unknown destination'[8] represented by European integration.

---

[3] G. Betlem and A. Nollkaemper, 'Giving Effect to Public International Law and European Community Law before Domestic Courts. A Comparative Analysis of the Practice of Consistent Interpretation' (2003) Eur J Intl L 569.

[4] On this, see: W. Sadurski, 'Partnering with Strasbourg: Constitutionalisation of the European Court of Human Rights, the Accession of Central and East European States to the Council of Europe, and the Idea of Pilot Judgments' (2009) Human Rights L Rev 397; O. Pollicino, *L'allargamento ad est dell'Europa e rapporti tra Corti costituzionali e Corti europee. Verso una teoria generale dell'impatto interordinamentale del diritto sovranazionale?* (Giuffrè 2010).

[5] J. Bourgeois, 'The Effects of International Agreements in European Community Law: Are the Dice Cast?' (1984) 82 Michigan L Rev 1250.

[6] See M. Bronckers, 'From "Direct Effect" to "Muted Dialogue": Recent Developments in the European Courts' Case Law on the WTO and Beyond' (2004) J Intl Economic Law 885.

[7] C-459/03 *European Commission v Ireland* (2006) ECR I-4635.

[8] J.H.H. Weiler, 'Journey to an Unknown Destination: A Retrospective and

2. TYPOLOGY OF RESEARCH AND THEORETICAL PREMISES: WHY JUDICIAL INTERACTIONS MATTER IN EUROPEAN CONSTITUTIONAL LAW

This is case law based research; it does not seek to provide an answer to the question of the nature of EU law or the possibility of extending the notion of supranationalism[9] to the ECHR. We are going to deal with a massive number of cases decided by national and European courts.

Why are we going to examine judicial interactions? What do they represent in the economy of this book? One of the starting assumptions of this work is that the interpretive action of judges is fundamental in order to understand the real impact of EU law and the ECHR on the domestic boundaries, as we are going to show in the following chapters. Judges create links between legal orders even in the absence of expressed norms of connections. Suffice it to think of those contexts originally characterized by the absence of a European clause, where judges adapted and reshaped the original wording of their national constitutions in order to provide a legal basis for explaining the authority of EC law.

The Italian case, for instance, is emblematic of this trend. When looking at the original Italian Constitution[10] it is very hard to understand how the guardians of the Constitution have permitted the erosion of competences caused by EC/EU interference. Article11, in fact, 'agrees to limitations of sovereignty where they are necessary to allow for a legal system of peace and justice between nations, provided the principle of reciprocity is guaranteed'.[11] This provision was conceived for Italy's participation in the UN or other limited-power organizations but not for the EU. The

---

Prospective of the European Court of Justice in the Arena of Political Integration' (1993) 31 J Common Market Studies 417.

[9] J.H.H. Weiler, 'The Community System: the Dual Character of Supranationalism' (1981) Ybk Eur Law 267; P. Hay, *Federalism and Supranational Organizations* (University of Illinois Press 1966). For an overview of the different theories of supranationalism, R. Leal-Arcas, 'Theories of Supranationalism in the EU', 2006, http://law.bepress.com/cgi/viewcontent.cgi?Art.=8481&context=expresso&sei-redir=1#search=%22supranationalism%20weiler%22.

[10] Article 11 of the Italian Constitution: 'Italy repudiates war as an instrument offending the liberty of the peoples and as a means for settling international disputes; it agrees to limitations of sovereignty where they are necessary to allow for a legal system of peace and justice between nations, provided the principle of reciprocity is guaranteed; it promotes and encourages international organizations furthering such ends'.

[11] Italian Constitution, Article 11.

latter imposes limitations of sovereignty for goals that go beyond the 'peace and justice between nations' mentioned in Article 11. The Italian Constitutional Court was forced to 'manipulate' the original meaning of Article 11 in order to allow such limitations. At the same time, when looking at Article 101 ('judges are only subject to the law'[12]), it is impossible to find the legal basis of the judge's power of non-application of the national rule contrasting with EU law.

The theoretical framework supporting the need for research like that we are proposing here can be linked to the existence of a multilevel constitutional legal order[13] and of a constitution that is perceived as the outcome of the steady process of comparison and dialectic between interdependent levels of governance (Member States and the EU). Against this background, by European Constitutional law we mean that study committed to the analysis of a European Constitution thus conceived as a *monstrum compositum*, composed of constitutional principles developed at the European (Union) level and complemented by (common) national constitutional principles[14] and by some other 'materials' like, for instance, the principles of the ECHR and the doctrines of the ECtHR.

Although the EU is not (yet) formally part of the ECHR, the Convention has always played a fundamental role in the progressive constitutionalization of the EU, working as a sort of external engine of such a process. Many fundamental judgments of the ECJ are very rich in references to the judgments of the ECtHR or to the provisions of the ECHR, and the Charter of Fundamental Rights of the EU was shaped, in many cases, with the provisions of the Convention in mind.

All this explains why, in the economy of this book, EU law, national law and the ECHR are conceived as the three sources of European constitutional pluralism.[15] The interplay between levels (or poles/sites if we want

---

12 Italian Constitution, Article 101.

13 I. Pernice, 'Multilevel Constitutionalism and the Treaty of Amsterdam: European Constitution Making Revisited?' (1999) CML Rev 703; F. Mayer and I. Pernice, 'La costituzione integrata dell'Europa', in G. Zagrebelsky (ed.), *Diritti e Costituzione nell'Unione Europea* (Laterza) 43, 49; I. Pernice, 'Multilevel Constitutionalism in the European Union', (2002) Eur L Rev 511. On multilevel constitutionalism, see also L. Besselink, *A Composite European Constitution/Een Samengestelde Europese Constitutie* (Europa Law Publishing 2007).

14 See, among others: M. Claes, *The National Courts' Mandate in the European Constitution* (Hart 2006).

15 On constitutional pluralism, see N. MacCormick, 'Beyond the Sovereign State' (1993) 56 MLR 1. See also N. Walker, 'The Idea of Constitutional Pluralism' (2002) 65 MLR 317; M. Poiares Maduro, 'Contrapunctual Law: Europe's Constitutional Pluralism in Action' in N. Walker (ed.). Sovereignty in Transition,

to avoid the word 'level'[16]) renders the idea of the non-simple distinction between the territorial actors' legislative domains. As a matter of fact, one of the most relevant difficulties in the multilevel legal system is represented by the existence of shared legal sources which make the attempt to define legal orders as self-contained regimes very difficult. This is coherent with the effort of providing an integrated and *complex* (i.e. interlaced[17]) reading of the levels, and represents one of the most fascinating challenges for constitutional law scholars.

At the same time, as a consequence of the lack of a precise distinction within the domain of legal production, it is sometimes impossible to resolve the antinomies between different legal levels on the grounds of the prevalence of a legal order (e.g. the national) over another (e.g. the supranational). Moreover, in this context, because of the inextricability of such an intertwined order, many legal conflicts present themselves as *conflicts of norms* (conceived as the outcome of the interpretation of legal provisions[18]) rather than *conflicts of laws*.[19]

One of the most evident differences between the EU and federal experiences is given by the absence of a supremacy clause. This has permitted the ECJ over the years to devise and reshape the content of the primacy principle, giving it an incredible flexibility. On the other hand, multilevel constitutionalism also suffers from the absence of an unambiguous primacy clause. Scholars have identified at least four different meanings of primacy/

(Hart, 2003) 501–37; M. Poiares Maduro, 'Interpreting European Law: Judicial Adjudication in a Context of Constitutional Pluralism' (2007) 2 Eur J Legal Studies, available at: http://ejls.eu/index.php?mode=htmlarticle&filename=./issues/2007-12/MaduroUK.htm. For a comparison between the different visions of constitutional pluralism, see M. Avbelj and J. Komarek (eds), 'Four Visions of Constitutional Pluralism', EUI Working Paper No. 28/2001, available at: http://cadmus.iue.it/dspace/bitstream/1814/9372/1/LAW_2008_21.pdf. For a different concept of pluralism conceived as being in opposition to that of constitutionalism, see N. Krisch, 'Europe's Constitutional Monstrosity' (2005) 25 Oxford J Legal Studies 321. See also: S. Douglas-Scott, *Constitutional Law*, (Harlow Longman, 2002) 523–30.

16 Besselink, *A Composite European Constitution.*

17 G. Martinico, 'Complexity and Cultural Sources of Law in the EU Context: From the Multilevel Constitutionalism to the Constitutional Synallagma' (2007) German L J 205.

18 According to the distinction between statements (*disposizioni*) and norms (*norme*), see, V. Crisafulli, 'Disposizione (e norma)', in Enc. Dir., XIII (Giuffrè 1964) 195 ff.

19 J. Pauwelyn, *Conflict of Norms in Public International Law. How WTO Law Relates to Other Rules of International Law* (Cambridge University Press 2003) 6–8.

supremacy in ECJ case law[20] and the notion of primacy which came from I-6 of the Constitutional Treaty seemed to be different from that used by the ECJ.

A consequence of the impossibility of tracing these principles back to the wording of a univocal primacy clause,[21] for instance, has underscored the role of the judge. Our assumption is that this context exalts the case-by-case judicial approach to solving legal conflicts between rules. The impossibility of operating a distinction between legal orders implies the end of interpretative autonomy for these courts, showing the other side of the sovereignty crisis. Judicial interactions thus represent a privileged perspective for studying the relations between legal orders, especially when looking at the multilevel and pluralistic structure of the European constitutional legal system.[22]

3. WHAT IS THE ROLE OF COMPARISON?

From a methodological viewpoint, the intertwined nature of the European Constitution implies the massive use of comparative law concepts. First of all, in fact, it is not possible to understand the constitutional exchanges between levels without knowing the constitutional features of the horizontal state level. Secondly, the comparative method is one of the most important approaches carried out by the ECJ[23] in the interpretation of EU law despite the few explicit comparative references contained in the judgments of the ECJ. Thirdly, the importance of the comparison is testified by the origin of the common constitutional traditions. Fourthly, the importance of foreign case law in the interpretation of constitutional law in general[24]

---

20 See, e.g, Claes, *The National Courts' Mandate*, 100–101.

21 Scholars have identified at least four different meanings of primacy/supremacy in ECJ case law. Moreover, the notion of primacy enshrined in Article I-6 of the Constitutional Treaty seems to be different from that used by the ECJ. See e.g. Claes, *The National Courts' Mandate*, 100–101. In order to find a solution to this ambiguity, some scholars have devised a 'law of laws'; see T. Eijsbouts and L. Besselink, 'Editorial: "The Law of Laws" – Overcoming Pluralism' (2008) Eur Constitutional L Rev 395.

22 G. Martinico, 'Judging in the Multilevel Legal Order: Exploring the Techniques of "Hidden Dialogue"', (2010) 21 King's L J, 257.

23 A. Torres Pérez, *Conflicts of Rights in the European Union* (Oxford University Press 2009) 141–79.

24 S. Choudhry, 'Globalization in Search of Justification: Towards a Theory of Comparative Constitutional Interpretation' (1999) 74 Indiana L J 821; A. Slaughter, 'A Typology of Transjudicial Communication' (1994) 29 U. Richmond

provides us with another element: the emergence of constitutional flaws and exchanges in the contemporary global scenery.

The literature on the possible uses (and misuses) of comparative law in European (not only legal) studies is massive. Here we would like to recall that the idea of comparison as a third way in European studies was sponsored by the 'Integration through Law Scholarship' project,[25] in order to analyze European integration in the light of the federal principle. That experiment did not neglect the peculiarity of the EU dimension because in their essays the participating scholars 'applied' a dynamic notion of federalism (Friedrich,[26] Elazar[27]). In doing so they understand federalism as a federalizing process, and federal principle, as a concept overcomes the classic distinction between federation, confederation and consortium.[28]

Obviously all these considerations touch the level, we would say, of the external comparison (i.e. the possibility to compare the EU as such to constitutional experiences of States that do not belong to the EU, like the US for instance) while we are going to insist on the 'internal' side of European constitutional law (and, as we said, the EU level is just a piece of this body of norms and principles). However, references to the 'external' comparison will not be missing when we deal with the complicated issue of the de facto rapprochement between the effects of EU law and that of the ECHR. Our

---

L Rev 99; A. Lollini, 'Legal Argumentation Based on Foreign Law. An Example from Case Law of the South African Constitutional Court', (2007) Utrecht L Rev 3: 60.

[25] M. Cappelletti, M. Seccombe and J.H.H. Weiler, *Integration through Law: Europe and the American Federal Experience* (1985).

[26] C.J. Friedrich, *Trends of Federalism in Theory and Practice* (New York 1968).

[27] D. Elazar, *Idee e forme del federalismo* (Mondadori 1995).

[28] In 1994 Renaud Dehousse wrote about the lack of a comparative approach in European studies, stressing the benefits and the difficulties (the problem of the level of analysis) of comparison in this field. The refusal to make a comparison implies the 'absolutization' of the EU level and the consecutive denial of the European multilevel and pluralistic structure: 'In many respects, the situation of Community lawyers is similar to that of a scholar who would have confined himself to the study of his domestic legal system. Comparative research, with its corollary of relativism, may help him to challenge the assumptions rooted in his own legal system and counteract the "tendency of ultrasophisticated analysis and quasi-scholasticism which arises when generations of scholars continue to examine the same fundamental documents within a purely national context". In other words, one could argue that comparative research is indispensable if Community law is to move to a more advanced level of scholarship'. R. Dehousse, 'Comparing National and EC Law: The Problem of Level of Analysis' (1994) Am J Comparative Law 761, 764.

attention to comparative data does not thus imply a lack of attention to the peculiar features of European integration.[29]

Starting from these considerations, our analysis proposes a 'multiple' comparison. In the first part of this work we will focus on the national level, analyzing the relevant constitutional provisions conceived or adopted for describing the effect of European laws within national boundaries. In the second part we are going to expand our perspective, taking into account the interactions between national and European levels, namely moving from the formal parameter (the constitutional provisions) to the law in action.

National (ordinary) judges have a fundamental role in the application of European laws and this implies the necessity to go beyond the positivist frame. This will be fundamental in order to investigate whether national actors use European laws. As we will see, despite the high degree of fragmentation and great variety in terms of the national constitutional clauses adopted by Member States to grant a basis to the ECHR and EU law, the case law of the different countries shows a certain homogeneity with regard to the effects and authority of EU law and the ECHR respectively.

Starting with EU law, a good example of this is the progressive diffusion of the 'counter-limits' or *Solange* doctrine in the jurisprudence of different constitutional courts in spite of the absence, in many cases, of provisions like 24 of the German Basic Law or Article 5, Chapter X, Paragraph 1 of the Swedish Instrument of Government. These, *expressis verbis*, condition the German and Swedish membership of the EU in respect of some fundamental values protected by the national constitution. By the 'counter-limits' (*controlimiti*[30]) formula we mean those national fundamental principles which have been raised – like impenetrable barriers – against the penetration of EU law by the national constitutional courts. The 'counter-limits' are conceived as a form of 'contrepoid au pouvoir communautaire',[31] an ultimate barrier to the full application of EU law, an intangible nucleus of national constitutional sovereignty.[32] The counter-limits doctrine ('*dottrina*

---

[29] For a different viewpoint see I. Ward, *A Critical Introduction to European Law* (Butterworths 1996) 176 ff.

[30] This formula was introduced in Italian scholarly debate by P. Barile, 'Ancora su diritto comunitario e diritto interno' in *Studi per il XX anniversario dell'Assemblea costituente*, VI (Florence 1969) 49.

[31] About the notion of *contrepoids au pouvoir*, see: B. Manin, 'Frontières, freins et contrepoids – La séparation des pouvoirs dans le débat constitutionnel américain de 1787' (1994) *Revue française de sciences politiques* 257; T. Georgopoulos. 'The Checks and Balances Doctrine in Member States as a Rule of EC Law: The Cases of France and Germany' (2003) 9 Eur L J 530.

[32] It is very interesting to notice that the notion of counter-limits implies a sort of constitutional and moral superiority of the national legal orders with

dei controlimiti') was de facto conceived in case 183/73 by the Italian Constitutional Court and (with some differences) in *Solange I* by the German *Bundesverfassungsgericht*.[33] Many constitutional courts accepted it in the following years the French *Conseil Constitutionnel* in 2004[34] and the *Tribunal Constitucional* in Spain,[35] but before them[36] the English High Court admitted the primacy of EU law by preserving a hard core of principles. One of the most interesting cases is the Danish *Carlsen*,[37] where the Supreme Court specified the possible dynamics of such a declaration.[38] More recently the decisions of the Polish[39] and German Constitutional Courts[40] (but see also the decisions of the Cypriot[41] and Czech[42] judges)

---

regard to the supranational level. This form of constitutional superiority is usually justified by the existence of the democratic deficit which characterizes the EU. See, for example, *Solange I* (*BVerfGE* 37, S. 271 ff.): 'the Community still lacks a democratically legitimated parliament directly elected by general suffrage which possesses legislative powers and to which the Community organs empowered to legislate are fully responsible on a political level.'

33 *BVerfGE* 37, S. 271 ff., in http://www.bundesverfassungsgericht.de/en/index.html.

34 But see also *Conseil d'État, dec. Sarran*, 30 October 1998; *Cour de Cassation, dec. Fraisse*, 2 June 2000; *Conseil d'État, dec. SNIP*, 3 December 2001. In addition see: Conseil Constitutionel 2004-496-497-498-499 DC 2004-505 DC.

35 *Tribunal Constitucional, declaracìon* 1/2004. About this point, see V. Ferreres Comella, 'La Constitución española', 80–89, and A. Saiz Arnaiz, 'De primacia, supremazia y derechos fundamentales en la Europa integrada: la Declaración del Tribunal Constitucional de 13 diciembre de 2004 y el Tratado por el que establece una Constitución para Europa', both in A. Saiz Arnaiz and V. Ferreres Comella (eds), *Constitución española y constitución europea* (Centro deEstudios Políticos y Constitucionales, 2005), 51–75.

36 *McWhirter and Gouriet v Secretary of State for Foreign Affairs* (2003) EWCA civ 384. On this point see A. Biondi, 'Principio di supremazia e "Costituzione" inglese. I due casi "Martiri del sistema metrico" e "McWhirter and Gouriet"', in www.forumcostituzionale.it/site/index3.php?option=com_content&task=view&id=101&Itemid=82.

37 *Højesteret*, *Carlsen v Rasmussen* (1999) 3 CMLR 854.

38 According to the *Carlsen* doctrine, if there is a doubt about the consistency of the EC act with the Constitution, the constitutional court could raise the question by asking the ECJ to clarify the exact meaning of the norm. If the ECJ does not convince them of the compatibility, they could 'apply' the counter-limits theory. Such a vision demonstrates that the constitutional courts have the last word even though they have accepted the preliminary ruling.

39 *Trybunał konstytucyjny*, P 1/05, in http://www.trybunal.gov.pl/eng/index.htm.

40 *BVerfG, 2 BvR* 2236/04, in http://www.bundesverfassungsgericht.de/en/index.html.

41 Ανώτατο Δικαστήριο, 294/2005, in www.cylaw.org.

42 *Ústavní Soud*, Pl. ÚS 66/04, in http://test.concourt.cz/angl_verze/cases.html.

have recalled the question of the ultimate barriers in the field of the European arrest warrant. This kind of comparison is therefore functional to the selection of those fundamental principles which had been opposed by the constitutional courts and which the ECJ later showed itself willing to accept in order to overcome the national courts' criticisms.

The second type of comparison we are going to develop is the vertical one (i.e. between Member States and the EU) in order to show the progressive communitarization of those constitutional principles that the constitutional courts have been opposing to the ECJ for many years.

The European Union is a complex legal order, since it stems from the interlacing between national and supranational legal systems.[43] This implies the existence of shared legal sources (see the common constitutional traditions that are inferred from the national constitutional materials) and many principles of EU law find their 'roots' in the national legal traditions. Against this background the EU is indebted to national constitutional orders since they gave the EU new blood by favouring the circulation of principles and practices that have shaped and reshaped the substance of the Treaties. Such a situation is the outcome of a convergence between the starting positions held by the ECJ (monism) and the national constitutional courts (dualism) in the first years of European integration.

Progressively the ECJ has seemed to get the point by incorporating the concept of fundamental rights as a premise of the primacy of EU law, and new important provisions have been introduced in the Treaties, namely former Articles 6 and 7 of the EUT. Despite this convergence, tension between the ECJ and the constitutional courts has not been lacking because of the progressive expansion of the ECJ's activity in national fields. Moreover, the product of this convergence gave birth to new kinds of conflicts among interpreters, conflicts due to the existence of legal sources (the principles concerning the protection of fundamental rights) that are now shared by the ECJ and the national constitutional courts: such a scenario has produced a dynamics of interpretive competition.

The ECJ has progressively started acknowledging an important role to the national constitutional materials in its decisions. This 'partial' appropriation of the fundamental rights discourse by the ECJ emerges in a long series of judgments, and it is most evident in cases such as *Omega*[44] and *Dynamic Medien*.[45] As some authors have pointed out, from examining those cases one can perceive a certain concern over the

---

43 Martinico, 'Complexity and Cultural Sources of Law'.

44 C-36/02 *Omega* (2004) ECR I-9609.

45 C-244/06 *Dynamic Medien* (2008) ECR I-505.

'*octroyée* methodology of construing common constitutional traditions'.[46] Nevertheless, this convergence is not total, as cases like *Viking*[47] and *Laval*[48] demonstrate.

From the point of view of positive law, confirmation of such convergence can be seen in 4 of the EUT (post-Lisbon scenario) which codifies the respect paid by member states to the constitutional structure (whose core corresponds to the member states' fundamental principles, i.e. the counter-limits). As a result, the respect for the constitutional structure is governed by an EU provision and thus is under the ECJ's jurisdiction: in this sense we write of communitarization of the counter-limits.[49] All this shows the presence of an overlapping zone between levels which is namely what we have called European constitutional law.

A similar situation already exists between the EU legal order and the ECHR system as, for instance, demonstrated by the progressive influence played by the Strasbourg Court over the Luxembourg Court[50] and, on a more formalistic level, by the explanations to the Charter of Fundamental Rights of the EU which refer to the doctrine of the ECtHR and the provisions of the ECHR to a very great extent.[51]

This opens the door for the third type of comparison adopted in this volume: that between the ECHR and EU legal systems or, better, that between the approaches used by the respective courts.

---

46 M. Dani, 'Tracking Judicial Dialogue – The Scope for Preliminary Rulings from the Italian Constitutional Court', Jean Monnet Working Paper, 10/2008, available at http://centers.law.nyu.edu/jeanmonnet/papers/08/081001.html. See also the reactions to the *Mangold* case (C-144/04, *Mangold* (2005) ECR I-9981): Roman Herzog and Lüder Gerken, '(Comment) Stop the European Court of Justice', http://euobserver.com/9/26714. This piece is the translation of an article originally published in German: 'Stoppt den Europäischen Gerichtshof', *Frankfurter Allgemeine Zeitung*, 8 September 2008.

47 C-438/05 *The International Transport Workers' Federation and The Finnish Seamen's Union* (2007) ECR I-10779 and C-341/05 *Laval un Partneri Ltd /Svenska Byggnadsarbetareförbundet* (2007) ECR I-11767.

48 *Laval.*

49 A. Ruggeri, '"Tradizioni costituzionali comuni" e "controlimiti", tra teoria delle fonti e teoria dell'interpretazione' (2003) 1, Dir. Pub. Comp. e Eur, 102–120.

50 See S. Douglas-Scott, 'A Tale of Two Courts: Luxembourg, Strasbourg and the Growing European Human Rights Acquis' (2006) CML Rev 629; See also K. Kuhnert, '*Bosphorus* Double Standards in European Human Rights Protection?' (2006) 2 Utrecht L Rev, 177 and ECtHR, *Bosphorus Hava v Ireland*, judgment of 30 June 2005.

51 On this see: G. Martinico, 'Interpretation as Constitutional Disagreement. On Some (Political) Attempts to Hijack the European Integration Process', in R Toniatti (ed.) *The Law Maker's Interpretation. How the Law Controls Interpretation* (Wolf Legal Publisher, forthcoming).

When looking at the recent history of integration it seems possible to detect an embryonic rapprochement between EU law and ECHR law. Indeed, the enlargements of the Council of Europe and of the European Union have caused two opposite reactions in the Strasbourg and Luxembourg Courts: the Strasbourg Court has accelerated, acting as a quasi-constitutional court, while the ECJ has sometimes drawn back by referring to a 'compromise' – a softened version of primacy. Such a double process makes the two supranational courts more similar with regard to their own idea of the impact of the respective case law on the domestic legal orders.[52] At the same time, judgments like *Lautsi II*[53] or *Elchinov*,[54] *Zambrano*[55] and *Cordero Alonso*[56] show how there is no clear trend in the approach of these two courts to the domestic constitutional structures. We are going to deal with these judicial trends in the second part of this volume.

4. STRUCTURE OF THE WORK

This book reflects the double side of our investigation: in the first part of the volume we will study the 'vertical' (hypothesized) convergence between EU law and the ECHR, focusing on national judges, while in the second our focus will be the progressive 'horizontal' (hypothesized) convergence between the Luxembourg and Strasbourg Courts. In both cases a fundamental role is played by the ECJ case law on fundamental rights, which has allowed the birth of a common axiological platform between the EU and the member states, and the EU and the ECHR.

---

[52] For an overview on the impact of the ECHR on the domestic legal orders see: H. Keller and A. Stone Sweet (eds), *A Europe of Rights: The Impact of the ECHR on National Legal Systems* (Oxford University Press 2008); G. Martinico and O. Pollicino (eds), *The National Judicial Treatment of the ECHR and EU Laws. A Comparative Constitutional Perspective* (Europa Law Publishing 2010).

[53] Case of *Lautsi and others v Italy* (Application no. 30814/06), http://www.echr.coe.int/echr/resources/hudoc/lautsi_and_others_v__italy.pdf.

[54] C-173/09, *Elchinov*, www.curia.europa.eu. On Elchinov, see: M. Eliantonio and C. Backes, 'Taking Constitutionalization One Step Too Far? The Need for Revision of the Rheinmühlen Case Law in the Light of the AG Opinion and the ECJ's Ruling in *Elchinov*', Maastricht Faculty of Law Working Paper, 2010/9, http://papers.ssrn.com/sol3/papers.cfm?abstract_id=1722631.

[55] C-34/09, *Gerardo Ruiz Zambrano v Office national de l'emploi* (ONEM), http://curia.europa.eu/jurisp/cgi-bin/form.pl?lang=EN&Submit=rechercher&numaff=C-34/09.

[56] C-81/05 *Cordero Alonso* (2006) ECR I-7569.

Convergence does not obviously mean perfect coincidence but it describes a process of mutual rapprochement between legal entities characterized by different aims at the origins. Despite the judicial conflicts that sometimes exist between judicial actors, our impression is that we are dealing with a sort of cooperative climate between judges who prefer to guarantee the coherence between legal systems (in the name of the protection of those fundamental rights which represent the common axiological field in the multilevel context), especially through the development of informal ways of dialogue, which recall the international public law experience of judicial comity and judicial deference.

In this sense it is possible to compare judgments such as *Bosphorus*[57] to the famous *Solange* I case. As we know, the *Solange* method[58] implies the recognition of a 'reserve jurisdiction' for domestic courts and the acknowledgment to EC law of a sort of limited primacy: such primacy is guaranteed as long as it does not affect the national constitutional fundamental principles (the 'counter-limits'). Looking at the relationship between the constitutional courts and the ECJ one could notice some common points shared between the *Solange* method and comity, *Solange* being a way to find a solution to the matter of jurisdictional competition induced by the fragmentation of law.[59]

According to Lavranos – who tried to extend the definition of the 'as long as' method to other inter-jurisdictional relations beyond the EU[60] – the '*Solange* method' is thus defined as a tool for determining the scope of the 'reserve jurisdiction' of one court in relation to the existing jurisdiction of another court. Applying this *Solange* method results in refraining from exercising an existing jurisdiction of one court in favour of an existing jurisdiction of another court.[61]

---

57 *Bosphorus Hava v Ireland.*

58 On the *Solange* method see Ni. Lavranos, 'Towards a Solange-Method between International Courts and Tribunals?' in Y. Shany and T. Broude, *The Shifting Allocation of Authority in International Law: Considering Sovereignty, Supremacy and Subsidiarity* (Hart 2008) 217.

59 N. Lavranos, 'From the analysis above it can be concluded that the Solange-method can help to reduce the chance of conflicting or diverging rulings, and thus the potential for fragmentation of fundamental rights in Europe is contained. Similarly, a wider application of the Solange-method by all international courts and tribunals could equally reduce the risk of fragmentation of international law', Lavranos, 'Towards a Solange-Method', 232.

60 See N. Lavranos, 'Regulating Competing Jurisdictions among International Courts and Tribunals' (2008) Heidelberg J Intl L, 575.

61 Lavranos, 'Towards a Solange-Method', 219.

In the *Bosphorus*[62] case, the ECtHR refused to review an EC regulation implementing a UN Security Council resolution, although the content of such an EC act was restrictive of the property right. The conclusion reached by the Strasbourg Court was inspired by the conviction of the comparability between the system of safeguarding fundamental rights which is guaranteed at the EU level and that provided by the ECHR. In *Bosphorus* the ECtHR used the same formula ('as long as') adopted by the German Constitutional Court in *Solange* to introduce a sort of presumption of comparability preventing a clash between jurisdictions. [63]

In the above mentioned cases, courts, despite the *prima facie* impression of judicial clash, preferred to act as cooperative actors and in this sense we conclude for the possible birth of a cooperative constitutionalism, which is the outcome of a process of 'integration through rights'.[64]

Again, this confirms the importance of judicial interactions (maybe we could say judicial dialogue) in these dynamics and the existence of a circulation of models (interpretative techniques, approaches, styles) among judges.

---

62 *Bosphorus Hava v Ireland.*

63 'Paradoxically, the safeguard of core rights, far from being the reason for the application of the counter-limit doctrine, was used as a harmonizing platform, and both tribunals sacrificed their own particular conception to pledge allegiance to the Court of Justice, or to support it.' F. Fontanelli in G. Martinico and F. Fontanelli, 'The Hidden Dialogue: When Judicial Competitors Collaborate' (2008) 8.3 Global Jurist.

64 L. Scheeck, 'The Relationship between the European Courts and Integration through Human Rights' (2005) *Zeitschrift für ausländisches öffentliches Recht und Völkerrecht* 837.

2. The formal parameter

1. NATIONAL JUDGES AND SUPRANATIONAL LAWS: GOALS AND STRUCTURE OF THIS PART OF THE VOLUME

The aim of this section is to answer the question: 'Are national judges extending the structural principles of EU law (primacy and direct effect) to the European Convention on Human Rights'?

In this part, comprising Chapters 2 and 3, we do not intend to examine the broader issue of the rapprochement between the legal systems of the EU and the European Convention on Human Rights (ECHR), but to concentrate on how national judges treat the ECHR compared with how they treat EU norms. Here we investigate the similarities and differences between the national judicial treatment of the ECHR and EU laws in the context of some selected constitutional experiences. We examine whether or not national judges treat the ECHR and EU law in the same manner, and the extent to which they facilitate the convergence of these laws. In this respect the goal of the part is to study the judicial application of the ECHR and EU law to analyse the vertical relationship between the national judges (both constitutional and ordinary judges) and these forms of external laws. In the economy of this part, our investigation is limited to the vertical dimension of convergence.

We have structured this part in two chapters. The present chapter offers a first look at the 'constitutional variety' existing in terms of constitutional provisions devoted to the impact of the ECHR and EU law on the national systems. In the next chapter (Chapter 3) we will move to analyse the relevant case law of the domestic judges and offer some concluding remarks on the convergence issue.

Looking at the constitutional provisions governing the effects of the ECHR and EU norms on the domestic orders, one can easily appreciate the variety of ways to conceive of the relation between the constitutional levels. Something of a gap exists between the formal status of the ECHR norms and their real value and nature: we would like to frame such a gap by distinguishing between a 'static' approach (limited to the superficial analysis of what national constitutions say) and a 'dynamic' one (focused on the analysis of the real binding force of these laws as inferred by the study of the judgments).[1] Keeping this structure in mind we are going to start with the formal provisions governing the relation between national and international/supranational laws.

2. CONSTITUTIONAL VARIETY: THE FORMAL PROVISIONS

(A) A First Look at the Relationship between the ECHR and National Laws

In a recent book, Keller and Stone Sweet[2] underscored the variety of national constitutional provisions regarding the ECHR. Indeed, looking at these provisions (and those applicable to EU law) one easily appreciates the diversity of national approaches with respect to the domestic authority of European laws:

1. Firstly, some constitutions reserve a particular status to EU law, distinguishing it from 'normal' public international law. An example is Italy, where Article 117 of the Constitution states: 'Legislative power belongs to the state and the regions in accordance with the constitution and within the limits set by European Union law and international obligations'. Accordingly, many commentators[3] have stressed the distinction between the limits of the EU and international obligations. This idea was also supported by the Italian *Corte Costituzionale* in the two judgments nos. 348 and 349/2007, as we will see in the next chapter.
2. Second, some constitutions acknowledge the special status of international human rights treaties (or some thereof). In Spain and Portugal (see, respectively, Article 10 of the Spanish Constitution and Article 16 of the Portuguese Constitution) such declarations provide an interpretative support for constitutional human rights provisions.

---

[1] For the same approach, see the book devoted to the ECHR: L. Montanari, *I diritti dell'uomo nell'area europea fra fonti internazionali e fonti interne* (Giappichelli 2002) and O. Pollicino, *L'allargamento ad est dell'Europa e rapporti tra Corti costituzionali e Corti europee. Verso una teoria generale dell'impatto interordinamentale del diritto sovranazionale?* (Giuffrè 2010).

[2] H. Keller and A. Stone Sweet (eds), *A Europe of Rights: The Impact of the ECHR on National Legal Systems* (Oxford University Press 2008).

[3] For instance, C. Pinelli, 'I limiti generali alla potestà legislativa statale e regionale e i rapporti con l'ordinamento comunitario', V *Foro italiano* (2001), 194.

3. Thirdly, some constitutions seem not to distinguish between international and EU law.

According to another classification[4], the ECHR's status in the domestic order may be summarized as follows:

1. Some constitutions are characterized by the acknowledgement of a constitutional rank given to the ECHR in the domestic legal order, for example, Austria and the Netherlands (essentially monist states).
2. In some States, instead, the ECHR has a super-legislative ranking (e.g. France, Belgium, Spain and Portugal).
3. In other states, finally, the ECHR has a legislative ranking (United Kingdom). Countries like Italy and Germany seemingly belong in the third group (if one reads their constitutions) but local Constitutional Courts clarified that the ECHR has a special force that exceeds the normal constitutional discipline of international norms.

Despite these differences, it has been noted[5] that European jurisdictions are progressively nearing on the 'position' of the ECHR in the hierarchy of sources. This convergence is the final outcome of different national pathways; sometimes national legislators must be credited, in other circumstances it is rather Constitutional or Supreme Courts, or even ordinary judges. This is irrespective of the formal position set out in the constitution, or of the dualism or monism classification.[6]

ECHR is a generally acknowledged supra-legislative force, but its relationship with constitutional supremacy is more controversial, as we will see in the next chapter.

(B) A First Look at the Relationship between EU law and National laws

A similar variety can also be found in the domestic treatment of EU law. One can identify several 'strategies' used to ensure EU law's primacy:

1. Some States embrace a monist vision of the relationship between orders, implicating the unconditional acceptance of EU law (the Netherlands, Belgium, Luxembourg). In the Netherlands, for example,

---

4 For example, Montanari, *I diritti*.

5 Keller and Stone Sweet (eds), *A Europe of Rights*, 677–711, 685–86.

6 This conclusion is also supported by Keller and Stone Sweet (eds), *A Europe of Rights*, 677–711, 685–86.

Article 94 of the Basic Law – according to a generally accepted interpretation – provides that international law is not only part of, but is also superior to, any domestic law. The same applies to EU law.

2. Other States expressly constitutionalize a set of limits to European integration (Germany, Sweden). The German text is particularly meaningful, because it seemingly codifies the German Constitutional Court's doctrine of the *Solange* saga.[7]
3. The constitutions of other States, be they monist or dualist – for different reasons – do not include any express 'European clause' (Italy, until the constitutional reform of 2001,[8] the UK, if only for 'structural reasons'). For instance, since its decision No. 183/1973[9] and until 2001, the Italian Constitutional Court only referred to Article 11: 'Italy . . . agrees to limitations of sovereignty where they are necessary to allow a legal system of peace and justice between nations, provided the principle of reciprocity is guaranteed'. This provision was originally conceived to justify Italy's membership to the United Nations. EU membership, in fact, imposes limitations of sovereignty for goals that clearly go beyond 'peace and justice between nations'. Thus, the Court was forced to 'manipulate' the original meaning of Article 11 in order to allow for further sovereignty limitations. Before 1992, something similar had happened in Germany, where the Constitutional Court interpreted Article 24 of the *Grundgesetz* (on participation in international organizations) to explain the penetration of EU law. This is what still happens in Spain, where Article 93 of the Constitution does not mention the European Union.
4. A group of '*souverainist*'[10] legal orders which proudly reaffirm the sovereignty of the constitution (Hungary, Poland and the Baltic States[11]) with regard to international and supranational integration.[12] Some of

---

7 *BVerfGE* 37, S. 271 ff., in http://www.bundesverfassungsgericht.de/en/index.html.

8 Amending Article 117.

9 Italian Constitutional Court judgment no. 183/1973, available at www.cortecostituzionale.it.

10 A. Albi, 'Estonia's Constitution and the EU: How and to What Extent to Amend It?' *Juridica International* (2002) 39.

11 See the report by I. Jarukaitis, 'Report on Estonia, Latvia and Lithuania', in G. Martinico and O. Pollicino (eds), *The National Judicial Treatment of the ECHR and EU Laws. A Comparative Constitutional Perspective* (Europa Law 2010) 167.

12 For a different schematization, see: F. Palermo, 'Nuove occasioni (mancate) per una clausola europea nella Costituzione italiana. Alcune osservazioni critiche' (2003) *Diritto pubblico comparato ed europeo* 1539–51; M. Claes, 'Le "clausole europee" nelle costituzioni nazionali' (2005) *Quaderni Costituzionali* 283–320.

them qualify as '*souverainist*' only at first glance, since constitutional provisions declaring the constitution's supremacy are sometime balanced by the pledge of compliance with international obligations (e.g. see Article 9[13] and Article 8 of the Polish Constitution). In these cases, however, national Constitutional Courts emphasized the '*souveranism*' of the constitution, to confirm its full primacy.[14]

The above is just one of the possible categorizations of the constitutional frameworks in the Member States but, despite such variety, as the literature has pointed out,[15] and although judicial resistance is not absent, EU law is applied in all the Member States in a uniform way. In fact, primacy and direct effect have been accepted by all the national courts.[16]

3. THE CONSTITUTIONAL PROVISIONS: A DETAILED ANALYSIS

After having recalled the most important schematizations provided by the scholarship with regard to the constitutional clauses adopted or reshaped by national courts to explain the authority of the European laws, it is necessary to test these schematizations by providing a detailed analysis of the relevant constitutional provisions. This way, after having carefully studied the formal 'parameter', we will move to the 'law in action' and see how national judges have applied these provisions.

Austria

Austria[17] seems to be a case of constitutional incorporation of the ECHR, the Convention there having 'the status of a provision of the national

---

13 Article 9: 'The Republic of Poland shall respect international law binding upon it'.

14 See the judgment of the Polish Constitutional Tribunal on the Lisbon Treaty (No. K 32/09, http://www.trybunal.gov.pl/eng/summaries/documents/K_32_09_EN.pdf). On Poland: Kowalik-Bańczyk, 'Report on Poland', in G. Martinico and O. Pollicino (eds), *The National Judicial Treatment supra*, 327, at 330.

15 M. Claes, *The National Courts' Mandate in the European Constitution* (Hart 2006).

16 Martinico and Pollicino (eds), *The National Judicial Treatment of the ECHR and EU Laws*.

17 On Austria, see: D. Thurnherr, 'The Reception Process in Austria and Switzerland', in Keller and Stone Sweet (eds) *A Europe of Rights*, 311–93.

Constitution'.[18] Article 50, Paragraph 3, of the Austrian Constitution[19] distinguishes between the international treaties having a constitutional relevance and those presenting a legislative relevance. Should these treaties modify or complement the Constitution they may only be concluded following the procedure set up by Article 50, Paragraph 3. Moreover 'in a vote of sanction adopted pursuant to Paragraph (1)', such treaties or such provisions as are contained in treaties shall be explicitly specified as 'constitutionally modifying';[20] this way this system creates a connection between the content of the Treaty and the form chosen to give it effect.[21]

The ECHR was concluded by the procedure established under Article 50 but without such a declaration: as a consequence the Austrian Constitutional Court originally argued that the ECHR did not have constitutional status.[22] Soon afterwards, a constitutional Act was passed

---

18 M. Janis, R. Kay and A. Bradley (eds), *European Human Rights Law* (Oxford University Press 1996), 448.

19 Article 50 Austrian Constitution: '(1) Political treaties, and others in so far as their contents modify or complement existent laws, may only be concluded with the sanction of the House of Representatives.

(2) At the time of giving its sanction to a treaty which falls under Paragraph (1), the House of Representatives can decide that the treaty in question shall be implemented by the issue of laws.

(3) The provisions of Article 42 (1) to (4) and, should constitutional law be modified or complemented by the treaty, the provisions of Article 44 (1) apply analogously to resolutions of the House of Representatives in accordance with Paragraphs (1) and (2). In a vote of sanction adopted pursuant to Paragraph (1), such treaties or such provisions as are contained in treaties shall be explicitly specified as 'constitutionally modifying'.

20 Ibid. '(1) Political treaties, and others in so far as their contents modify or complement existent laws and do not fall under Article 16 Paragraph 1, may only be concluded with sanction of the National Council. In so far as such treaties settle matters within the autonomous sphere of competence of the Laender, they require in addition the approval of the Federal Council.

(2) At the time of giving its sanction to a treaty which falls under Paragraph 1 above, the National Council can vote that the treaty in question shall be implemented by the issue of laws.

(3) Article 42 Paragraphs 1 to 4 inclusive and, should constitutional law be modified or complemented by the treaty, Article 44 Paragraphs 1 and 2 shall be analogously applied to resolutions of the National Council in accordance with Paragraphs 1 and 2 above. In a vote of sanction adopted pursuant to Paragraph 1 above, such treaties or such provisions as are contained in treaties shall be explicitly specified as "modifying the constitution".'

21 H. Hausmaninger, *The Austrian Legal System* (Kluwer Law International 1998), 24.

22 Drzemczewsky, *European Human Rights Convention in Domestic Law*, 94; Montanari, *I diritti*, 59.

modifying the Constitution and acknowledging the constitutional value of the ECHR[23] and later the Constitutional Court acknowledged the interpretative value of such clause, giving it a retroactive effect.[24] As a consequence, today it is possible to say that the ECHR 'has the rank of directly applicable federal constitutional law'.[25]

Confirmation of the constitutional status of the ECHR is derived from the complementary nature of this document (with regard to the constitutional text). This is the real criterion to evaluate its ranking in the legal sources of the national system despite the procedure followed to incorporate them, and that explains why the ECHR had, de facto, a constitutional rank even before 1964.[26]

As for EU law, the path chosen was completely different compared with that adopted for the ECHR since Austria accepted, in a silent manner and without any explicit reference to the structural principles of EU law, the basic features of the EU legal order[27].

Since the Accession Treaty was considered as implying or involving a sort

---

23 Article II BVG (BGBl 1964/59).

24 'The ECHR has a double status in Austria. In addition to its character as an international treaty, it has been transformed, on the domestic level, into a law with the rank of a constitutional act. This has a twofold implication. First, the ECHR grants individual rights that are directly actionable before all courts and authorities. Given their status as constitutional law, these rights may be relied upon before the CC', P. Cede, 'Report on Austria and Germany', in Martinico and Pollicino (eds), *The National Judicial Treatment of the ECHR and EU Laws*, 63.

25 Ohlinger, 'Austria and Article 6', 286.

26 Montanari, *I diritti*, 62.

27 'Austria's accession to the EU occurred at a time where the principles of direct effect and supremacy of EU law over domestic law, including norms of constitutional rank, were undisputed and well established in the case law of the ECJ. However, neither the Accession Treaty nor the domestic legislation adopted to implement Austria's accession contain any specific reference to the question of status, effects and rank of EU law. The constitutional "entrance door" for the effects of EU law in the Austrian legal order is the constitutional act setting the framework for the conclusion of Austria's Accession Treaty ["'Bundesverfassungsgesetz über den Beitritt Österreichs zur Europäischen Union"', Federal Constitutional Act on the Accession of Austria to the European Union, Federal Law Gazette (Austria) No. 744/1994.]. Rather than achieving the internal reception by a positive constitutional rule allowing for EU law to apply or investing it with a certain rank, the mechanism chosen by Austria can be described as an act of "retreat", on behalf of the domestic constitutional order, so as to "open up" the domestic legal system to the influence of EU law. The domestic legislator can be said to have implicitly acknowledged the specific features of EU law, namely its autonomous source, its direct effect and its primacy over national law, including constitutional law', Cede, 'Report on Austria and Germany', 60–61.

of 'total revision' like that mentioned in Article 44, p. 2[28] of the Austrian Constitution, a referendum was called. Austria followed this scheme, according to which any revision of the Treaties should be evaluated as conducive to a potential total revision in order to decide whether to use the referendum or not. In case of revision, Treaties adopted without a referendum might be subjected to the control of the Austrian Constitutional Court.[29]

The Baltic States

The Baltic States acknowledge – directly or indirectly – the basis for their participation in international organizations. They share a strong '*souverainist*' character[30] and all three countries, Lithuania,[31] Estonia[32] – which also provides for the precedence of international law over national acts – and Latvia[33] consider ratified international treaties as part of the internal legal system, adopting 'a monist approach towards international treaties'.[34] Such provisions were used to support the ratification of the

---

28 Article 44 of the Austrian Constitution: '(2) Any total revision of the Federal Constitution shall upon conclusion of the procedure pursuant to Article 42 but before its authentication by the Federal President be submitted to a referendum by the entire nation, whereas any partial revision requires this only if one third of the members of the House of Representatives or the Senate so demands'.

29 'It follows from these considerations that, within the "hierarchy" of norms, EU law takes precedence over all domestic norms, including constitutional norms, as far as it is not adopted ultra vires and does not exceed the permissible exception from the basic principles of domestic constitutional law. Future amendments of primary law (treaties) adopted without a domestic referendum will be subject to review by the Constitutional Court (Verfassungsgerichtshof, hereafter: CC), and may be annulled if contrary to the basic principles', Cede, 'Report on Austria and Germany' cit, 61.

30 A. Albi, 'Estonia's Constitution and the EU: How and to What Extent to Amend It?' (2002) Juridica International 39–48.

31 Lithuanian Constitution, Article 138, p. 3: 'International treaties ratified by the Seimas of the Republic of Lithuania shall be a constituent part of the legal system of the Republic of Lithuania'. See also Articles 135 and 136.

32 Estonian Constitution, Article 3: 'Universally recognised principles and rules of international law are an inseparable part of the Estonian legal system'; Article 123 Paragraph 2: 'If Estonian laws or other acts are in conflict with foreign treaties ratified by the Parliament, the Articles of the foreign treaty shall be applied'.

33 Latvian Constitution, Article 89: 'The State shall recognise and protect fundamental human rights in accordance with this Constitution, laws and international agreements binding upon Latvia.' Article 68: 'All international agreements, which settle matters that may be decided by the legislative process, shall require ratification by the Saeima'.

34 Jarukaitis 'Report on Estonia, Latvia and Lithuania', 172.

ECHR while a different story occurred with regard to the accession to the EU.[35]

Estonia decided not to modify the main body of its Constitution when entering the EU. Rather, an act provided with constitutional relevance, called the Constitution of Estonia Supplementing Act, was approved by a referendum on 14 September 2003.

As for Latvia, it amended Articles 68 and 79[36] of the Constitution by introducing specific mention of the EU.

Finally, in Lithuania, like in Estonia, a special Constitution Act ('the Constitutional Act on the Membership of the Republic of Lithuania in the European Union') was passed without modifying the main body of the Constitution after the formal accession of the country to the EU.[37]

---

35 'Thus, the ECHR was ratified as an ordinary treaty from the point of view of the letter of the Constitutions of the Baltic states. Differently from the ratification of the ECHR, the prospective accession to the EU in general and the relationship between EU and national law in particular generated wide and lengthy discussions in all Baltic states long before 1 May 2004', ibid., 173.

36 Article 68: 'Upon entering into international agreements, Latvia, with the purpose of strengthening democracy, may delegate a part of its State institution competencies to international institutions. The Saeima may ratify international agreements in which a part of State institution competencies are delegated to international institutions in sittings in which at least two-thirds of the members of the Saeima participate, and a two-thirds majority vote of the members present is necessary for ratification. Membership of Latvia in the European Union shall be decided by a national referendum, which is proposed by the Saeima. Substantial changes in the terms regarding the membership of Latvia in the European Union shall be decided by a national referendum if such referendum is requested by at least one-half of the members of the Saeima'. Article 79: '. . . A draft law decision regarding membership of Latvia in the European Union or substantial changes in the terms regarding such membership submitted for national referendum shall be deemed adopted if the number of voters is at least half of the number of electors as participated in the previous Saeima election and if the majority has voted in favour of the draft law, membership of Latvia in the European Union or substantial changes in the terms regarding such membership'.

37 'Still, the Constitutional Act on the Membership of the Republic of Lithuania in the European Union was adopted already after Lithuania acceded to the EU, i.e., on 13 July 2004 and came into force one month later. On the one hand, it means that Lithuania's membership in the EU lacked an explicit constitutional basis for more than two months and the Constitutional Court had to repair faults of political process', Jarukaitis, 'Report on Estonia, Latvia and Lithuania', 175.

Belgium

Originally the Belgian Constitution[38] did not mention the issue of the relationship between national and supranational law. Article 33 of the Constitution instead, provided that 'tous les pouvoirs émanent de la nation', not leaving any room apparently for sources of power other than the nation. In 1970 a new Article (namely Article 34) was added: 'The exercising of specific powers can be assigned by a treaty or by a law to institutions of public international law'.

When deciding about the possible participation of Belgium in an international organization, the Belgian authorities are bound by the Constitution and the Constitutional Court, among its competences, has the power to review an Act of the Parliament giving assent to an international treaty.[39] The wording of the Constitution presents some special references to EU law, namely at Article 168,[40] and seems to distinguish between international and supranational commitments (like the Italian Constitution at Article 117, as we will see).[41]

However, as we will see in the next chapter, over the years the Belgian *Cour d'Arbitrage* (now *Cour Constitutionnelle*) has de facto distinguished between the ECHR/EU law and other international treaties, and hence some scholars consider both of these two European laws as 'supranational'.[42]

Bulgaria

As Fartunova pointed out: 'The European Convention for the Protection of Human Rights and Fundamental freedoms and the European Union law are a turning point in the building of the Bulgarian legal system.'[43]

---

[38] H. Bribosia, 'Report on Belgium', in Slaughter, Stone Sweet and Weiler (eds), *The European Court* 3–39; B. de Witte, 'Do Not Mention the Word: Sovereignty in Two Europhile Countries, Belgium and the Netherlands' in N. Walker (ed.), *Sovereignty in Transition* (Hart 2003) 351.

[39] Article 3 Special Law on the Constitutional Court.

[40] Article 168 of the Belgian Constitution: 'The Houses are informed from the beginning of negotiations concerning any revision of the treaties establishing the European Community in addition to treaties and acts which may have modified or completed the latter. They are aware of the planned treaty prior to signature'.

[41] See, for instance, Article 77, Paragraph 7 and Article 169.

[42] For instance, see P. Popelier, 'Report on Belgium' in Martinico and Pollicino (eds), *The National Judicial Treatment of the ECHR and EU Laws*, 84.

[43] 'Indeed, the signature of this Convention in February 1992 and its ratification on September 7th of the same year by Bulgaria and the accession of Bulgaria

More generally, Article 5 of the Constitution seems to acknowledge a general precedence of international treaties over national law[44] but, at the same time, grants supremacy to the Constitution, recognizing, from a formal point of view, a super-primary but also sub-constitutional rank to the European laws (EU law and the ECHR).

Cyprus

In Cyprus, Article 169, p. 3,[45] of the Constitution acknowledges the precedence of international treaties over domestic law with the exception of the Constitution, which is conceived as the supreme law of the land, as emphasized by Kyriakou.[46] The entry of Cyprus into the EU did not need constitutional reform since the adhesion Treaty was ratified through the procedure governed by Article 169. The Constitution of 1960 does not make

---

to the European Union on January 1st, 2007 had notable consequences not only on the evolution of the Bulgarian legal system, but also on the functions of the national jurisdictions. The European sources enjoy a particular status within the Bulgarian legal order as specified in the Constitution of July 12th, 1991. Their integration in the Bulgarian normative system is expressly stated in Article 5, Paragraph 4, chapter I, of the Constitution which reads: "International treaties which have been ratified in accordance with the constitutional procedure, promulgated and having come into force with respect to the Republic of Bulgaria, shall be part of the legislation of the State. They shall have primacy over any conflicting provision of the domestic legislation."', M. Fartunova, 'Report on Bulgaria', in Martinico and Pollicino (eds), *The National Judicial Treatment of the ECHR and EU Laws*, 103.

44 Article 5 of the Bulgarian Constitution: '(1) The Constitution is the supreme law, and no other law shall contravene it.

(2) The provisions of the Constitution shall apply directly.

(3) No one shall be convicted for action or inaction which at the time it was committed did not constitute a crime.

(4) Any international instruments which have been ratified by the constitutionally established procedure, promulgated, and come into force with respect to the Republic of Bulgaria, shall be considered part of the domestic legislation of the country. They shall supersede any domestic legislation stipulating otherwise.

(5) All legislative acts shall be promulgated and shall come into force three days after the date of their promulgation unless otherwise envisaged by the acts themselves'.

45 Article 169.3: 'Treaties, conventions and agreements concluded in accordance with the foregoing provisions of this Article shall have, as from their publication in the official Gazette of the Republic, superior force to any municipal law on condition that such treaties, conventions and agreements are applied by the other party thereto'. See Markides, 'Cyprus'.

46 N. Kyriakou, 'Report on Cyprus' in Martinico and Pollicino (eds), *The National Judicial Treatment of the ECHR and EU Laws*, 154.

any provision for the transfer of sovereignty to international organizations and, given the letter of Article 179, p. 1,[47] which points out the supremacy of the Constitution, one could wonder about the coexistence between EU law primacy and such a supremacy. Nevertheless, as Emiliou pointed out, Article 179 does not belong to the 'basic provisions' of the Constitution and thus it might be amended according to the procedure of Article 182.[48]

Besides that, it is necessary to recall Article 61[49] which acknowledges the general legislative competence in all matters to the domestic Chamber of Representatives without leaving, apparently at least, any room for other co-legislators.[50] Going beyond the formal text, today the direct applicability of the EU law is unanimously acknowledged and more recently the Constitution was amended at Article 1 (A) stating that: 'No provision in the Constitution can be deemed as overriding any legislation, acts or measures enacted or taken by the Republic which are obligatory as a member state of the European Union, nor does it hinder Regulations, Directives or other binding provisions or measures of a legislative nature enacted by the European Union from having legal force in the Republic'.

---

[47] Article 179. '1. This Constitution shall be the supreme law of the Republic.

2. No law or decision of the House of Representatives or of any of the Communal Chambers and no act or decision of any organ, authority or person in the Republic exercising executive power or any administrative function shall in any way be repugnant to, or inconsistent with, any of the provisions of this Constitution.'

[48] Emiliou, 'Cyprus', 306. See Article 182. '1. The Articles or parts of Articles of this Constitution set out in Annex III hereto which have been incorporated from the Zurich Agreement dated 11th February, 1959, are the basic Articles of this Constitution and cannot, in any way, be amended, whether by way of variation, addition or repeal.

2. Subject to Paragraph 1 of this Article any provision of this Constitution may be amended, whether by way of variation, addition or repeal, as provided in Paragraph 3 of this Article.

3. Such amendment shall be made by a law passed by a majority vote comprising at least two-thirds of the total number of the Representatives belonging to the Greek Community and at least two-thirds of the total number of the Representatives belonging to the Turkish Community.'

[49] Article 61 of the Constitution of Cyprus: 'The legislative power of the Republic shall be exercised by the House of Representatives in all matters except those expressly reserved to the Communal Chambers under this Constitution.'

[50] Emiliou, 'Cyprus', 306. Scholars have also identified some possible areas of conflict between domestic and EC law in Article 54, Paragraph 1, for instance, devoted to the competences of the Communal Chamber, Article 61, p. 1, devoted to the competences of the House of Representatives, Article 136 regarding the jurisdiction of the Supreme Constitutional Court, Article 152 regarding the judiciary and the already mentioned Article 169.

This is a very open clause which was passed after the evolution of the EU law system in the field of the human rights protection.

Czech Republic and Slovakia

In the Constitution of the Czech Republic, the relevant provisions are Article 1, Paragraphs. 2[51] and 10,[52] and Article 10a,[53] but none of these provisions mentions the EU.[54] Before the Czech Euro amendment, Articles 10 and 87 of the Constitution[55] distinguished between international treaties in general and international human rights treaties, giving the latter a super-primary rank and leaving unanswered the question of whether international human rights treaties belonged to the constitutional block. At the same time Article 87, Paragraph 1,[56] of the Constitution empowered the Constitutional Court to declare the unconstitutionality of laws conflicting

---

[51] Article 1, Paragraph 2, of the Czech Constitution: 'The Czech Republic shall observe its obligations resulting from international law'.

[52] Article 10 of the Czech Constitution: 'Promulgated treaties, to the ratification of which Parliament has given its consent and by which the Czech Republic is bound, form a part of the legal order; if a treaty provides something other than that which a statute provides, the treaty shall apply'.

[53] Article 10a of the Czech Constitution: '(1) Certain powers of Czech Republic authorities may be transferred by treaty to an international organization or institution'.

(2) The ratification of a treaty under Paragraph 1 requires the consent of Parliament, unless a constitutional act provides that such ratification requires the approval obtained in a referendum'.

[54] With the exceptions of the provisions touching the issue of the referendum for the accession to the EU: Articles 62 and 87, 'None of the new provisions, however, expressly referred to the future Czech membership in the European Union. Thus the question quickly arose: which provision precisely "opens the gate" for European Union law? One view held that it is Article 10 CC that granted the authorization by providing for international treaties being part of the Czech legal order. A competing opinion held that the actual support for the application of Community law is provided by the competence clause of Article 10a CC, which states that certain powers of the Czech Republic authorities may be transferred by treaty to an international organization or institution.' M. Bobek and D. Kosař, 'Report on the Czech Republic and Slovakia', in Martinico and Pollicino (eds), *The National Judicial Treatment of the ECHR and EU Laws*. 120.

[55] Article 10 (previous version) of the Czech Constitution: 'Ratified and promulgated international accords on human rights and fundamental freedoms, to which the Czech Republic has committed itself, are immediately binding and are superior to law'.

[56] Article 87, Paragraph 1 (previous version) of the Czech Constitution: '(1) The Constitutional Court resolves: (a) the nullification of laws or their individual provisions if they are in contradiction with a constitutional law or an interna-

with the Constitution but also those conflicting with international human rights treaties.

After the Czech Euro amendment,[57] the new Article 10 of the Constitution abandoned such a distinction and now acknowledges to all international treaties a super-primary but still sub-constitutional rank,[58] at least, from a formal point of view, as we will see in the next chapter.

Another element to be taken into account is the new Article 87, Paragraph 2, which provides: 'Prior to the ratification of a treaty under Article 10a or Article 49, the Constitutional Court shall further have jurisdiction to decide concerning the treaty's conformity with the constitutional order. A treaty may not be ratified prior to the Constitutional Court giving judgment'. Article 89, Paragraph 3, of the Constitution specifies that: 'A decision of the Constitutional Court whereby, in accordance with Section 87, Subsection 2, unconformity of an international agreement with the constitutional order is pronounced, prevents ratification of the agreement until such unconformity is eliminated.' These provisions could be read both as a confirmation of the superiority of the Constitution and as a confirmation of the superiority of the international treaties.

Like the Czech Republic, in Slovakia also a distinction between 'normal' international treaties and international human rights treaties was present in the Constitution. The Slovakian model differed from the Czech pattern because it also provided for a sort of 'conditionally prioritized treaties'[59] since it specified that '[i]nternational treaties on human rights [. . .] [ratified and promulgated by the Slovak Republic] have priority over statutes, insofar as [these treaties] provide for *greater protection of basic rights* . . .'.[60] The Slovak Euro amendment[61] changed the picture only slightly by amending Article 7, Paragraph 5[62] and Article 154 c. (1).[63] Article 127,

tional agreement under Article 10 [international human rights treaties]'. Pollicino, *L'allargamento ad est*, 104.

57 Constitutional Act 395/2001 Coll.

58 See Bobek and Kosař, 'Report on the Czech Republic and Slovakia', 133.

59 Ibid., 134.

60 Article 11 of the Slovakian Constitution (previous version).

61 Constitutional Act no. 90/2001 Coll.

62 Article 7, Paragraph 5, of the Slovak Constitution: '(5) International treaties on human rights and fundamental freedoms and international treaties for whose exercise a law is not necessary, and international treaties which directly confer rights or impose duties on natural persons or legal persons and which were ratified and promulgated in the way laid down by a law shall have precedence over laws'.

63 Article 154c(1) of the Slovak Constitution: 'International treaties on human

Paragraph 2,[64] was also introduced in order to permit individual constitutional complaints based on the ECHR.

It should be also taken into account that Article 93 excludes referenda on fundamental rights.[65] As for EU law, the Euro amendment introduced Article 7[66] in the fundamental text of Slovakia and acknowledged the superiority of EU law over (primary) national law *expressis verbis*.

France

In France there are no specific constitutional provisions devoted to human rights treaties. All the provisions of Title VI of the Constitution, regarding the mechanism for the entry into force of international treaties, are applicable to the ECHR. The super-primary value of international treaties

---

rights and fundamental freedoms which the Slovak Republic has ratified and were promulgated in the manner laid down by a law before taking effect of this constitutional act, shall be a part of its legal order and shall have precedence over laws if they provide a greater scope of constitutional rights and freedoms'.

64 Article 127 of the Slovak Constitution: '(2) If the Constitutional Court accepts a complaint, it shall hold in its decision that the rights or freedoms according to Paragraph 1 were infringed by a valid decision, measure or by other action and it shall cancel such a decision, measure or other action. If the infringement of rights or freedoms according to Paragraph 1 emerges from inactivity, the Constitutional Court may order the one who has infringed these rights or freedoms to act in the matter. The Constitutional Court may at the same time remand the matter for further proceedings, prohibit continuing in the infringement of fundamental rights and freedoms or human rights and fundamental freedoms resulting from the international treaty which has been ratified by the Slovak Republic and promulgated in the manner laid down by a law, or if possible, to order the one who has infringed the rights or freedoms according to paragraph 1 to reinstate the status before the infringement'.

65 Article 93 of the Slovakian Constitution: '(1) A constitutional law on joining a union with other states or the secession from it, shall be confirmed by a referendum.

(2) A referendum may also be used to decide on other crucial issues of the public interest.

(3) No issues of fundamental rights, freedoms, taxes, duties or state budget may be decided by a referendum'.

66 Article7, Paragraph 2, of the Slovakian Constitution: 'The Slovak Republic may, by an international treaty, which was ratified and promulgated in the way laid down by a law, or on the basis of such treaty, transfer the exercise of a part of its powers to the European Communities and the European Union. Legally binding acts of the European Communities and of the European Union shall have precedence over laws of the Slovak Republic. The transposition of legally binding acts which require implementation shall be realized through a law or a regulation of the Government according to Article 120, Paragraph 2'.

in the domestic system can be inferred by reading Articles 54 and 55[67] together: the latter provides for the superiority of ratified treaties over national acts, while the former governs the preventive control of compatibility between international treaties and the Constitution (entrusted to the *Conseil Constitutionnel*). Article 55 empowers national ordinary judges to carry out the control of '*conventionnalité*' in order to verify the consistency of national law with the texts of international treaties.

As was already pointed out, human rights treaties do not have particular status according to the Constitution; the only difference between them and other international treaties is the exclusion of the applicability of the reciprocity clause for them because of their multilateral character and, above all, because of their nature.[68] At the time of the entry into force of the first European Treaties in the 1950s, the old 1946 Constitution was still in force: its Article 26 provided that international treaties regularly ratified and published have a particular legal binding force, since it was not possible to abrogate them by means of ordinary national laws.[69] As we saw above, international treaties have a super-legislative force under the 1958 Constitution.

In 1992 a constitutional reform was passed in order to introduce a new title (title XV) entirely devoted to the participation of France in the EC and EU.

It has been argued that in France the ECHR plays the role of a shadow constitution.[70] That might be explained taking into account the open nature of the Constitution which admits integration, as the case law of the *Conseil Constitutionnel* on the *bloc de constitutionnalité* has confirmed over the years. The first step of this route is represented by decision no. 88-1082

---

67 Article 54: 'If the Constitutional Council, on a referral from the President of the Republic, from the Prime Minister, from the President of one or the other Houses, or from sixty Members of the National Assembly or sixty Senators, has held that an international undertaking contains a clause contrary to the Constitution, authorization to ratify or approve the international undertaking involved may be given only after amending the Constitution'.

Article 55: 'Treaties or agreements duly ratified or approved shall, upon publication, prevail over Acts of Parliament, subject, with respect to each agreement or treaty, to its application by the other party'.

68 L. Dubouis, 'La portée des instruments internationaux de protection des droits de l'homme dans l'ordre juridique français', in E. Smith and R. Badinter (eds), *Les droits de l'homme dans le droits national en France et en Norvège* (1990), 131 ff. Montanari, *I diritti*, 84.

69 See Claes, *The National Courts' Mandate*, 50–51.

70 H. Keller and A. Stone Sweet, 'Assessing the Impact of the ECHR on National Legal Systems' in Keller and Stone Sweet (eds), *A Europe of Rights*, 677, 686.

DC of 21 October 1988,[71] where the *Conseil* gave direct application to the ECHR by integrating it in the '*bloc de constitutionnalité*', conceiving that as an element to be taken into account in the evaluation of the 'constitutional validity of norms'.[72] Two years later the *Conseil* reminded the legislature of the duty of 'respecter les engagements internationaux souscrits par la France et les libertés et droits fondamentaux de valeur constitutionnelle reconnus à tous ceux qui résident sur le territoire de la République'.[73]

Finally, it is useful to recall the recent reform concerning the control of constitutionality which resulted in the very famous *Melki* 'saga', involving the *Cour de Cassation*, the *Conseil Constitutionnel* and the ECJ.[74] The case originates from the reform introduced in France by Article 61-1 of the French Constitution by which the *incidenter* control of constitutionality was introduced.[75] This provision was implemented by Institutional Act No. 2009-1523, which amended Ordinance No. 58-1067 of 7 November 1958. After this reform, Article 23–5 Paragraph 2, of the Ordinance provided for the priority of the question of constitutionality over the review concerning conformity with EU law and international treaties.[76] We will return to this decision in the next chapter.

---

[71] In Rec., 1988, p. 183.

[72] See M. Calamo Specchia, 'Il Conseil constitutionnel e le Corti europee: dall'indifferenza al dialogo?' in G. Franco Ferrari (ed.), *Corti costituzionali e Corti europee* (ESI 2006), 343.

[73] See Calamo Specchia, 'Il Conseil constitutionnel e le Corti europee', 343.

[74] ECJ, C-188/10, available at http://curia.europa.eu/jurisp/cgi-bin/form.pl?lang=en&Submit=Rechercher&alldocs=alldocs&docj=docj&docop=docop&docor=docor&docjo=docjo&numaff=C-188/10&datefs=&datefe=&nomusuel=&domaine=&mots=&resmax=100.

[75] Article 61-1: 'If, during proceedings in progress before a court of law, it is claimed that a statutory provision infringes the rights and freedoms guaranteed by the Constitution, the matter may be referred by the *Conseil d'État* or by the *Cour de Cassation* to the Constitutional Council, within a determined period. An Institutional Act shall determine the conditions for the application of the present Article'. On this, see F. Fabbrini, 'Kelsen in Paris: France's Constitutional Reform and the Introduction of *a posteriori* Constitutional Review of Legislation', (2008) German L J 1297.

[76] In all events, the *Conseil d'État* or *Cour de Cassation* must, when asked to rule on arguments claiming firstly that a provision infringes the rights and freedoms guaranteed by the Constitution, and secondly that it runs counter to the international commitments entered into by France, rule in priority on the transmitting to the Constitutional Council of the application for a priority preliminary ruling on the issue of constitutionality.

Germany

In Germany an important norm to understand the effects of international agreements within the national boundaries is represented by Article 59.2 of the *Grundgesetz*.[77] Another fundamental provision is Article 24[78] concerning the transfer of sovereign powers to international organizations; it was used as the basis for explaining the authority of EC law at the beginning of the German membership. However in 1992 there was an important constitutional reform regarding the transfer of sovereignty to the international organizations and the involvement of the *Länder* in the process of creation of EU law through the *Bundesrat*. This constitutional reform amended Article 23 of the *Grundgesetz*, which now represents the *Grundnorm* as for the relation between national and supranational law.[79]

---

[77] 'Treaties that regulate the political relations of the Federation or relate to subjects of federal legislation shall require the consent or participation, in the form of a federal law, of the bodies responsible in such a case for the enactment of federal law. In the case of executive agreements the provisions concerning the federal administration shall apply mutatis mutandis'. In Germany the primary value of the ECHR is also mentioned in Article 2, 1 of the federal Ratification Act dated 7 August 1952, Bundesgesetzblatt, II, 1952, 685.

[78] '(1) The Federation may by a law transfer sovereign powers to international organizations.

(1a) Insofar as the Länder are competent to exercise state powers and to perform state functions, they may, with the consent of the Federal Government, transfer sovereign powers to transfrontier institutions in neighboring regions.

(2) With a view to maintaining peace, the Federation may enter into a system of mutual collective security; in doing so it shall consent to such limitations upon its sovereign powers as will bring about and secure a lasting peace in Europe and among the nations of the world.

(3) For the settlement of disputes between states, the Federation shall accede to agreements providing for general, comprehensive, and compulsory international arbitration'.

[79] 'With a view to establishing a united Europe, the Federal Republic of Germany shall participate in the development of the European Union that is committed to democratic, social, and federal principles, to the rule of law, and to the principle of subsidiarity, and that guarantees a level of protection of basic rights essentially comparable to that afforded by this Basic Law. To this end the Federation may transfer sovereign powers by a law with the consent of the Bundesrat. The establishment of the European Union, as well as changes in its treaty foundations and comparable regulations that amend or supplement this Basic Law, or make such amendments or supplements possible, shall be subject to paragraphs (2) and (3) of Article 79.

(2) The Bundestag and, through the Bundesrat, the Länder shall participate in matters concerning the European Union. The Federal Government shall keep the

Given the importance of the case law of the Federal Constitutional Court for understanding the effects and strength of EU law and international agreements, all the relevant details concerning the issue at stake will be treated in the next chapter.

Greece

In Greece the ECHR has a super-legislative value thanks to Article 28[80]

Bundestag and the Bundesrat informed, comprehensively and at the earliest possible time.

(3) Before participating in legislative acts of the European Union, the Federal Government shall provide the Bundestag with an opportunity to state its position. The Federal Government shall take the position of the Bundestag into account during the negotiations. Details shall be regulated by a law.

(4) The Bundesrat shall participate in the decision-making process of the Federation insofar as it would have been competent to do so in a comparable domestic matter, or insofar as the subject falls within the domestic competence of the Länder.

(5) Insofar as, in an area within the exclusive competence of the Federation, interests of the Länder are affected, and in other matters, insofar as the Federation has legislative power, the Federal Government shall take the position of the Bundesrat into account. To the extent that the legislative powers of the Länder, the structure of Land authorities, or Land administrative procedures are primarily affected, the position of the Bundesrat shall be given the greatest possible respect in determining the Federation's position consistent with the responsibility of the Federation for the nation as a whole. In matters that may result in increased expenditures or reduced revenues for the Federation, the consent of the Federal Government shall be required.

(6) When legislative powers exclusive to the Länder are primarily affected, the exercise of the rights belonging to the Federal Republic of Germany as a member state of the European Union shall be delegated to a representative of the Länder designated by the Bundesrat. These rights shall be exercised with the participation and concurrence of the Federal Government; their exercise shall be consistent with the responsibility of the Federation for the nation as a whole.

(7) Details respecting paragraphs (4) through (6) of this Article shall be regulated by a law requiring the consent of the Bundesrat'.

80 Article 28: '1. The generally recognised rules of international law, as well as international conventions as of the time they are ratified by statute and become operative according to their respective conditions, shall be an integral part of domestic Greek law and shall prevail over any contrary provision of the law. The rules of international law and of international conventions shall be applicable to aliens only under the condition of reciprocity.

2. Authorities provided by the Constitution may by treaty or agreement be vested in agencies of international organizations, when this serves an important national interest and promotes cooperation with other States. A majority of three-fifths of the total number of Members of Parliament shall be necessary to vote the law ratifying the treaty or agreement.

of the Constitution and Article 93.4[81] regarding the diffuse control of constitutionality operated by the national ordinary judges. According to some authors[82], with the combination of Articles 28 and 93: 'Mutatis mutandis, the supra-legislative effect that Article 28 GC grants to international law allows courts to control the compatibility of domestic acts with Greece's international obligations.'

The accession to the EU in Greece[83] was based on Article 28 of the Constitution (the object of constitutional amendment in 1986)[84] which provides for the superiority of public international law sources over domestic ones but which also subordinates the application of the Constitution.

Hungary

The Hungarian legal system seems to be characterized by a strong dualist tradition, although the Constitutional Court Act empowers the Constitutional Court to review the validity of a national act with the

---

3. Greece shall freely proceed by law passed by an absolute majority of the total number of Members of Parliament to limit the exercise of national sovereignty, insofar as this is dictated by an important national interest, does not infringe upon the rights of man and the foundations of democratic government and is effected on the basis of the principles of equality and under the condition of reciprocity'.

[81] Article 93.4 Const: 'The courts shall be bound not to apply a statute whose content is contrary to the Constitution'.

[82] V. Tzevelekos and S. Vetsika, 'Report on Greece' in Martinico and Pollicino (eds), *The National Judicial Treatment of the ECHR and EU Laws*, 230.

[83] See Dimitrios Evrigenis, 'Legal and Constitutional Implications of Greek Accession to the European Communities' [1980] CML Rev 157–69; A. Celotto and T. Groppi, 'Diritto UE e diritto nazionale: primauté vs controlimiti' [2004] *Riv. it. dir. pubb. comunitario* 1309.

[84] Article 28, Const: '1. The generally recognised rules of international law, as well as international conventions as of the time they are ratified by statute and become operative according to their respective conditions, shall be an integral part of domestic Greek law and shall prevail over any contrary provision of the law. The rules of international law and of international conventions shall be applicable to aliens only under the condition of reciprocity.

2. Authorities provided by the Constitution may by treaty or agreement be vested in agencies of international organizations, when this serves an important national interest and promotes cooperation with other States. A majority of three-fifths of the total number of Members of Parliament shall be necessary to vote the law ratifying the treaty or agreement.

3. Greece shall freely proceed by law passed by an absolute majority of the total number of Members of Parliament to limit the exercise of national sovereignty, insofar as this is dictated by an important national interest, does not infringe upon the rights of man and the foundations of democratic government and is effected on the basis of the principles of equality and under the condition of reciprocity'.

possibility of taking into account international treaties promulgated into the domestic order.[85] At the same time international treaties have to be consistent with the Constitution (defined at Article 77 as the supreme law of the Republic).[86]

The Hungarian legal order expressly distinguishes between EU law and international law at Article 2A[87] of the Constitution, which was introduced after the constitutional reform of 2002 together with other provisions, including Article 6.[88] Article 2A conditions the EU membership to the protection of fundamental rights and the respect of national competences.[89]

In the new Hungarian Constitution, Article E[90] is the successor to the

---

85 Constitutional Court Act, Section 1 (c), Section 45 (1).

86 Article 77 of the Hungarian Constitution: '(1) This Constitution is the supreme law of the Republic of Hungary.

(2) This Constitution and laws and statutes established in accordance with this Constitution are equally binding for everybody of the country'.

87 Article 2 A of the Hungarian Constitution: '(1) By virtue of treaty, the Republic of Hungary, in its capacity as a Member State of the European Union, may exercise certain constitutional powers jointly with other Member States to the extent necessary in connection with the rights and obligations conferred by the treaties on the foundation of the European Union and the European Communities (hereinafter referred to as 'European Union'); these powers may be exercised independently and by way of the institutions of the European Union.

(2) The ratification and promulgation of the treaty referred to in Subsection (1) shall be subject to a two-thirds majority vote of the Parliament'.

88 Article 6, p. 4 of the Hungarian Constitution, 'The Republic of Hungary shall take an active part in establishing a European unity in order to achieve freedom, well-being and security for the peoples of Europe'.

89 'As regards the protection of fundamental rights, Article 2/A of the Constitution stipulates that only "competencies resulting from the Constitution" may be exercised together with the other Member States, or by the Community institutions. Undoubtedly, this is a *nemo plus iuris* rule: it provides that the exercise of powers by the Union is subject to the same constitutional barriers as are applicable to the Republic of Hungary and its organs. Since the organs of the Republic lack the power to violate fundamental rights of the individuals, no such power can be transferred to the EU. As regards the scope of competencies transferred to the EU, Article 2/A(1) of the Constitution provides that only those powers may be exercised by the EU that are necessary to exercise the rights and fulfil the obligations resulting from the founding treaties. This language makes it clear that Article 2/A does not legitimize those sovereign acts of the EU that are not founded on a competence resulting from the treaties. Ultra vires acts are therefore not covered by the integration clause.' P. Sonnevend, 'Report on Hungary' in Martinico and Pollicino (eds), *The National Judicial Treatment of the ECHR and EU Laws*, 256.

90 Article E of the new Hungarian Constitution '(1) In order to enhance the liberty, prosperity and security of European nations, Hungary shall contribute to the creation of European unity.

former Article 2A and Paragraph 6(4), without any substantial changes. Paragraph (3) of Article E seems to be really new, but its function is only to make an exception for EU law from the new exhaustive listing of sources of law in Article T, even though this exception was not necessary, as it could be deduced from Paragraph (2) of Article E.[91]

Italy

Italy is usually seen as a country characterized by a strong dualist tradition, according to which the international and national legal systems are conceived of as autonomous. There are two fundamental provisions in the Italian Constitution regarding the relationship between international and domestic law; Articles 10[92] and 11.[93] These two Articles provide the first important distinction existing in this field in Italy: the distinction between the general rules of international law and international treaties. As for the

---

(2) With a view to participating in the European Union as a member state, Hungary may exercise some of its competences arising from the Fundamental Law jointly with other member states through the institutions of the European Union under an international agreement, to the extent required for the exercise of the rights and the fulfilment of the obligations arising from the Founding Treaties.

(3) The law of the European Union may stipulate a generally binding rule of conduct subject to the conditions set out in Paragraph (2).

(4) The authorisation to recognise the binding nature of an international agreement referred to in Paragraph (2) shall require a two-thirds majority of the votes of the Members of Parliament.' http://verfassungsblog.de/wp-content/uploads/2011/03/Draft-of-Fundamental-Law-of-14-March-2011_RP.pdf.

[91] To conclude on this point it is interesting to recall the resolution of the European Parliament which invited Hungary to amend its new Constitution in order to make it consistent with the position expressed on this point by the Venice Commission and of the ECtHR (Application No 30141/04, *Schalk and Kopf v Austria* on same sex marriages). The resolution focuses on the content of the Preamble and 'on serious setbacks in the fields of the rule of law and human rights'.

[92] 'The Italian legal system conforms to the generally recognised principles of international law.

The legal status of foreigners is regulated by law in conformity with international provisions and treaties.

A foreigner who, in his home country, is denied the actual exercise of the democratic freedoms guaranteed by the Italian constitution shall be entitled to the right of asylum under the conditions established by law.

A foreigner may not be extradited for a political offence'.

[93] 'Italy rejects war as an instrument of aggression against the freedom of other peoples and as a means for the settlement of international disputes. Italy agrees, on conditions of equality with other States, to the limitations of sovereignty that may be necessary to a world order ensuring peace and justice among the Nations. Italy promotes and encourages international organisations furthering such ends'.

former, Article 10 provides for an automatic procedure of adoption, in the sense that such norms are directly incorporated into the Italian system.

According to Italian scholars, the general rules of international law (which would correspond to customary international law) belong to the constitutional level.[94] According to some scholars, the international customary law existing before the entry into force of the Italian Constitution could prevail over the constitutional provisions (because of the application of the chronological criterion) but this does not apply with regard to the principles belonging to the untouchable core recalled by Article 139 of the Constitution[95] (this untouchable core, according to judgment 1146/1988, also includes the supreme principles included in the first part of the Italian Constitution.[96])

As for international treaties, it is necessary for there to be a national act transforming the international act into national law. The intervention of the national legislature is not required for all treaties, since Article 80 provides for the necessity of legislation enabling the ratification only with reference to some particular treaties.[97] The procedure of ratification is also governed by Article 87, which empowers the President of the Republic to ratify international treaties. When the intervention of parliament is required, it intervenes with a normal legislative statute. According to the majority of scholars, this confers a primary force in the national hierarchy of law to norms derived from international treaties. Despite that, the Italian Constitution recognizes a particular force to laws related to international obligations. Article 75, Paragraph 2 (devoted to the referendum), states: 'No referendum may be held on a law regulating taxes, the budget, amnesty or pardon, or a law ratifying an international treaty'.

Apart from Articles 10 and 11, another fundamental provision is entrenched in Article 117[98] which will be discussed below. What we would like to specify here is that, because of the dualist tradition, international

---

[94] G. de Vergottini, *Diritto costituzionale* (Cedam 2004), 32.

[95] 'The form of Republic shall not be a matter for constitutional amendment'.

[96] For an overview of the debate, see: A. Cassese, 'Commento Article10 della Costituzione', in G. Branca (ed.), *Commentario della Costituzione*, vol. *Principi fondamentali*. Articles 1–12 (Zanichelli 1975) 485, 502. According to Quadri, the automatic procedure shall be applied to the international treaties but this remains a minority view. This theory was based on the fact that one of the general rules of international law is given by the principle *pacta sunt servanda*. R. Quadri, *Diritto internazionale pubblico* (Naples 1989), 64.

[97] 'Parliament shall authorise by law the ratification of such international treaties as have a political nature, require arbitration or a legal settlement, entail change of borders, spending or new legislation'.

[98] Other relevant provisions in this field are given by Article 26: 'Extradition of

treaties acquire the strength of the domestic statute adopted for their incorporation. This explains why, from the beginning, both the ECHR and EC law were considered as primary sources in the Italian legal system.

Another important feature of the Italian legal order is the fact that, unlike in other countries like Portugal and Spain, no specific status is accorded to treaties devoted to human rights. This is another important point to be kept in mind when analysing the Italian Constitutional Court's judicial developments in this field.

The Italian Constitution's new Article 117, Paragraph 1, expressly codifies the limit that supra-national obligations represent for domestic law by providing that: 'Legislative power belongs to the State and the regions in accordance with the constitution and within the limits set by European Union law and international obligations.' Looking at the judicial parameter, we will see that this provision provoked interesting innovations in the Italian Constitutional Court's case law. Soon after the reform, the interpretation of this provision created a division among scholars.[99] According to some, Article 117, Paragraph 1, would simply codify the pre-existing situation: it would grant a sort of *a posteriori* assent to European primacy[100] as it was developed by the ECJ and accepted across the European Community. Other scholars, on the other hand, emphasized the importance of the constitutional status given to the European primacy, and asserted that Article 117 paved the way for the acceptance of the Italian monist thesis.[101]

Luxembourg

Article 49 *bis* of the Luxembourg Constitution provides for the possibility to transfer sovereignty to international institutions.[102] According to the

a citizen may be granted only if it is expressly envisaged by international conventions'. In any case, extradition may not be permitted for political offences.

99 For an overview, see R. Chieppa, 'Nuove prospettive per il controllo di compatibilità comunitaria da parte della Corte costituzionale', (2007) *Il Diritto dell'Unione Europea* 493, 499 ff; A. Ruggeri, 'Riforma del titolo V e giudizi di 'comunitarietà' delle leggi' (2007), http://www.associazionedeicostituzionalisti.it/dottrina/ordinamentieuropei/ruggeri.html.

100 Cesare Pinelli, 'I limiti generali alla potestà legislativa statale e regionale e i rapporti con l'ordinamento comunitario' (2001) 5 *Foro italiano* 194.

101 F. Paterniti, 'La riforma dell'Article 117, 1° co. della Costituzione e le nuove prospettive dei rapporti tra ordinamento giuridico nazionale e Unione Europea' (2004) *Giur. Cost.*, no. 2, 2101; Alessandro Pajno, 'Il rispetto dei vincoli derivanti dall'ordinamento comunitario come limite alla potestà legislativa nel nuovo Titolo V della Costituzione' (2003) *Le Istituzioni del federalismo*, 814.

102 Article 49 *bis*: 'The exercise of the powers reserved by the Constitution to

scholarship,[103] a super primary vale should be acknowledged to international treaties although 'the Constitution is silent on the question of the status and primacy of treaty law in the domestic legal order, including the ECHR. Therefore, this question was dealt with by the courts in their case law'.[104]

Malta

As for Malta, the ECHR was incorporated with the European Convention Act (19 August 1987) and the Act itself provides for the superiority of the rights included in the Convention on national law, which is void in case of contrast with them.

Another fundamental provision is given by Article 65, which is devoted to the powers of the Parliament and provides: 'Subject to the provisions of this Constitution, Parliament may make laws for the peace, order and good government of Malta in conformity with full respect for human rights, generally accepted principles of international law and Malta's international and regional obligations, in particular those assumed by the treaty of accession to the European Union signed in Athens on the 16th April, 2003.' This provision seems to give a particular super-primary value to the international law of human rights and, above all, to EU law.

The Netherlands

The Dutch model is based on Articles 91 and 93 of the *Grondwet*[105] but the most evident signal of the remarkable openness of the domestic order to international law is given by Article 90, according to which: 'the

---

the legislature, executive, and judiciary may be temporarily vested by treaty in institutions governed by international law'.

[103] Claes, *The National Courts' Mandate*.

[104] E. Mak, 'Report on the Netherlands and Luxembourg' in Martinico and Pollicino (eds), *The National Judicial Treatment of the ECHR and EU Laws*, 309.

[105] Article 91 provides: 'The Kingdom shall not be bound by treaties, nor shall such treaties be denounced without the prior approval of the Parliament. The cases in which approval is not required shall be specified by Act of Parliament. The manner in which approval shall be granted shall be laid down by Act of Parliament, which may provide for the possibility of tacit approval. Any provisions of a treaty that conflict with the Constitution or which lead to conflicts with it may be approved by the Chambers of the Parliament only if at least two-thirds of the votes cast are in favour'. Article 93, instead, provides: 'Provisions of treaties and of resolutions by international institutions, which may be binding on all persons by virtue of their contents, shall become binding after they have been published'.

Government shall promote the development of the international rule of law'. Starting from this, Grewe[106] argued that the Dutch system is the only really monist one in Europe, since it would recognize the prevalence of the international legal order over the national one. Further confirmation of that is represented by Article 94, according to which: 'Statutory regulations in force within the Kingdom shall not be applicable if such application is in conflict with provisions of treaties that are binding on all persons or of resolutions by international institutions.'

According to some authors,[107] the original Dutch formulation[108] should be understood as referable to constitutional provisions as well.[109] In any case, thanks to Article 94, the national judges are empowered to control the consistency of domestic law with the ECHR and it is very interesting to notice how in this country the judges are not allowed to control the constitutionality of the laws, according to Article 120 of the Constitution.[110]

In the Netherlands[111], since specific provisions on the EU do not exist, all that we saw above concerning international law applies to EU law, and on this basis some scholars have argued that the primacy of EU law is accepted and tolerated by the Dutch *Grondwet*.[112]

---

106 C. Grewe, 'La question de l'effet direct de la Convention et les résistences nationales', in P. Tavernier, *Quelle Europe pour les droits de l'homme?* (Bruylant 1996), 157 ff.

107 Van Dijk, 'Dutch experience', 137; Montanari, *I diritti*, 65.

108 Article 94 'Binnen het Koninkrijk geldende wettelijke voorschriften vinden geen toepassing, indien deze toepassing niet verenigbaar is met een ieder verbindende bepalingen van verdragen en van besluiten van volkenrechtelijke organisaties'.

109 See Van Dijk, 'Dutch experience', 137; Montanari, *I diritti*, 65.

110 Article 120 of the Dutch Grondwet: 'The constitutionality of Acts of Parliament and treaties shall not be reviewed by the courts'. On the possibility to introduce the review of legislation in the Netherlands see: G. van der Schyff, 'Constitutional Review by the Judiciary in the Netherlands: A Bridge Too Far?' (2010) German L J 275. 'Through this filter of "moderate monism", the ECHR has obtained great influence in the Dutch legal system. A major reason for this is the constitutional prohibition of judicial review regarding the constitutionality of Acts of Parliament. In order to provide sufficient protection of fundamental rights in individual cases, the Dutch courts have developed the review of conventionality', Mak, 'Report on the Netherlands and Luxembourg', 307.

Moreover: 'Thus, the status of the ECHR in the Dutch legal order can be derived from the Constitution on the basis of the general provisions concerning the implementation of treaty law. However, the status of EC law cannot be directly derived from the Constitution', ibid.

111 On the Netherlands, see: Claes and de Witte, 'Report on the Netherlands'; de Witte, 'Do Not Mention the Word'.

112 C. Kortmann, 'Reports on the Netherlands', in *FIDE Conference, Droit communautaire et Constitutions nationales*, London, 2002, 6.

The Nordic Countries

The Nordic countries incorporated the ECHR only in the 1990s although they were among the first countries to sign the ECHR. Because of the absence of a Constitutional Court in many of these countries the control on the compatibility between international treaties and the Constitution is carried out by political bodies belonging to the legislature or the executive, and in all these countries the ECHR was incorporated by means of an ordinary statute of parliament.

However, in Sweden, Article 23 of Chapter 2[113] of the Instrument of Government acknowledges a special force to the ECHR since no provision conflicting with it may be promulgated. According to some authors, this implies a constitutional status for the ECHR but the question is still debated.[114] As for EU law in Sweden, the accession occurred in 1995 after a consultative referendum. Chapter X of the Instrument of Government, at Article 6, provides that the Parliament may transfer sovereignty to the EU but respecting the fundamental rights. Transfer of sovereignty may occur in two ways: 'The Riksdag may approve a transfer of authority by means of a decision supported by at least three fourths of those voting. The Riksdag's decision may also be taken in accordance with the procedure prescribed for the enactment of fundamental law.'[115]

As for Denmark, Section 20 of the Constitution[116] requires a statute approved by the majority of five-sixths of members of the *Folketing* for the transfer of sovereignty to international authorities, in case of

---

113 Article 19 of Chapter 2 of the Instrument of Government: 'No act of law or other provision may be adopted which contravenes Sweden's undertakings under the European Convention for the Protection of Human Rights and Fundamental Freedoms'.

114 On this debate, see: I. Cameron, 'The Swedish Experience of the European Convention on Human Rights Since Incorporation' (1999) ICLQ, 20.

115 Article 6 of Chapter X of the Instrument of Government.

116 Section 20 of the Danish Constitution: '(1) Powers vested in the authorities of the Realm under this Constitutional Act may, to such extent as shall be provided by statute, be delegated to international authorities set up by mutual agreement with other states for the promotion of international rules of law and cooperation.

(2) For the enactment of a Bill dealing with the above, a majority of five-sixths of the members of the Folketing shall be required. If this majority is not obtained, whereas the majority required for the passing of ordinary Bills is obtained, and if the Government maintains it, the Bill shall be submitted to the electorate for approval or rejection in accordance with the rules for referenda laid down in section 42'.

failure to achieve such a majority the approval of the statute requires the referendum.

In Finland the relationship between domestic and international law is based on a dualist approach according to which no treaty can be considered as a part of the land law, the interposition of a national statute being necessary in order to give the treaty effect.[117] According to Ojanen, such an approach is also codified in the Constitution, where Section 94 requires the approval of the Parliament for those international obligations 'that contain provisions of a legislative nature, are otherwise significant, or otherwise require approval by the Parliament under this Constitution'. Concerning EU law, as Ojanen pointed out, the Treaty of Accession was incorporated into Finnish law through an exceptive enactment[118] which was approved by the Parliament with a two-thirds majority in Parliament[119].

The same author wrote about a Finnish 'minimalist approach' to the issue of the relation with the EU law, since only in Chapter VIII is there a set of provisions devoted to the distribution of powers in the field of EU affairs and to the participation of the Parliament in such affairs. Nevertheless such a conclusion is questionable since Finland has an expressed counter-limits clause, contained in Section 94 of the Constitution,[120] although such a clause refers to the international cooperation of the

---

[117] T. Ojanen, 'The Impact of EU Membership on Finnish Constitutional Law' (2004) Eur Public Law 531, 532.

[118] Act No. 1540 of 1994. Other exceptive enactments were approved in order to accept the amendments to the Treaties operated with the Amsterdam and Nice and Lisbon Treaties.

[119] 'The Treaty of Accession of 1994 was in conflict with the Constitution of Finland, the major reason simply being the incompatibility of the transfer of powers to the EU with the sovereignty of Finland. However, an amendment to the Constitution to enable the accession was not found necessary, because it was possible to take advantage of the institution of exceptive enactments. Accordingly, the Treaty of Accession was incorporated into Finnish law through an exceptive enactment (Act No 1540 of 1994) which was approved by a two-thirds majority in Parliament. In addition, Parliament consented to the ratification of the Treaty of Accession by a simple majority decision', 'The Impact of EU Membership on Finnish Constitutional Law' (2004) Eur Public Law 531, 537.

[120] Section 94 of the Finnish Constitution: 'The acceptance of the Parliament is required for such treaties and other international obligations that contain provisions of a legislative nature, are otherwise significant, or otherwise require approval by the Parliament under this Constitution. The acceptance of the Parliament is required also for the denouncement of such obligations.

A decision concerning the acceptance of an international obligation or the denouncement of it is made by a majority of the votes cast. However, if the proposal concerns the Constitution or an alteration of the national borders, the decision shall be made by at least two thirds of the votes cast.

country in general. This 'connection' allows us to share that view according to which the Finnish system – a system that knows 'exceptive enactments' (Sect. 73 Constitution)[121] – does not permit violations of fundamental rights.[122] Under the Constitution there is a parliamentary body empowered to undertake preventive constitutional control of legislation, called the Constitutional Law Committee;[123] this body also plays an important role in questions related to Finnish membership of the EU.

All the structural EU law principles have been acknowledged by scholarship has been confirmed by the Constitutional Law Committee with the condition not to weaken the human rights protection provided by the Constitution. Here one can notice the importance of the counter-limits clause provided by Article 94.

Poland

In Poland, Article 9 of the Constitution provides that 'The Republic of Poland shall respect international law binding upon it'. Moreover international agreements are listed in Article 87[124] among the binding legal sources. Ratified international agreements shall be 'applied directly, unless its application depends on the enactment of a statute' (Article 91(1)) and according to Article 91 (2) they have priority over national statutes in case

---

An international obligation shall not endanger the democratic foundations of the Constitution'.

[121] Sect. 73: 'A proposal on the enactment, amendment or repeal of the Constitution or on the enactment of a limited derogation of the Constitution shall in the second reading be left in abeyance, by a majority of the votes cast, until the first parliamentary session following parliamentary elections. The proposal shall then, once the Committee has issued its report, be adopted without material alterations in one reading in a plenary session by a decision supported by at least two thirds of the votes cast. However, the proposal may be declared urgent by a decision that has been supported by at least five sixths of the votes cast. In this event, the proposal is not left in abeyance and it can be adopted by a decision supported by at least two thirds of the votes cast'.

[122] Celotto and Groppi, 'Diritto', 1323.

[123] Section 74 of the Finnish Constitution: 'The Constitutional Law Committee shall issue statements on the constitutionality of legislative proposals and other matters brought for its consideration, as well as on their relation to international human rights treaties'.

[124] Article 87 of the Polish Constitution: 'The sources of universally binding law of the Republic of Poland shall be: the Constitution, statutes, ratified international agreements, and regulations.

Enactments of local law issued by the operation of organs shall be a source of universally binding law of the Republic of Poland in the territory of the organ issuing such enactments'.

of conflict with the exception of the Constitution.[125] The same provisions can be used for reading the status of EU law provisions together with what is ruled by Article 90 of the Constitution.[126] Another Article to be taken into account is Article 9[127] which grants a sort of interpretative favour to the international law provisions.

Article 188 of the Constitution empowers the Polish Constitutional Tribunal to adjudicate the conformity of national laws with the international agreement ratified and, at the same time, to check the conformity of international agreements with the Constitution, seen as the supreme law of the land.[128] Finally, Article 193 of the Constitution empowers national courts to raise *incidenter* questions to the Constitutional Tribunal in case of conflict with a ratified international agreement or statute, 'if the answer to such a question is decisive for the determination of an issue pending before such court'.[129]

---

125 K. Kowalik-Bańczyk, 'Report on Poland', in Martinico and Pollicino (eds), *The National Judicial Treatment of the ECHR and EU Laws*, 330.

126 Article 90 of the Polish Constitution: '1. The Republic of Poland may, by virtue of international agreements, delegate to an international organization or international institution the competence of organs of State authority in relation to certain matters.

2. A statute, granting consent for ratification of an international agreement referred to in Paragraph 1, shall be passed by the Sejm by a two-thirds majority vote in the presence of at least half of the statutory number of Deputies, and by the Senate by a two-thirds majority vote in the presence of at least half of the statutory number of Senators.

3. Granting of consent for ratification of such agreement may also be passed by a nationwide referendum in accordance with the provisions of Article 125.

4. Any resolution in respect of the choice of procedure for granting consent to ratification shall be taken by the Sejm by an absolute majority vote taken in the presence of at least half of the statutory number of Deputies'.

127 Article 9 'The Republic of Poland shall respect international law binding upon it'.

128 Article 188 of the Polish Constitution: 'The Constitutional Tribunal shall adjudicate regarding the following matters: the conformity of statutes and international agreements to the Constitution; the conformity of a statute to ratified international agreements whose ratification required prior consent granted by statute; the conformity of legal provisions issued by central State organs to the Constitution, ratified international agreements and statutes; the conformity to the Constitution of the purposes or activities of political parties; complaints concerning constitutional infringements, as specified in Article 79, Paragraph 1'.

129 Article 193 of the Polish Constitution: 'Any court may refer a question of law to the Constitutional Tribunal as to the conformity of a normative act to the Constitution, ratified international agreements or statute, if the answer to such question of law will determine an issue currently before such court'.

Portugal

The Portuguese[130] case is characterized by a super-legislative relevance granted to treaties. The Portuguese Constitution, at Article 278, p. 1, provides for a prior review of constitutionality concerning compatibility between the Constitution and international treaties.[131] In case of conflict between an international treaty and the Constitution, the treaty shall only be ratified if the Assembly of the Republic passes it by a special majority.[132]

According to the literature, the particular force of treaties in the domestic legal order can be inferred from Article 8[133] of the Portuguese Constitution. Indeed in Portugal the combination of Articles 204[134] and 8 of the Constitution empowers national judges to disapply national law conflicting with constitutional and international law. Nevertheless the most important confirmation of the special ranking reserved to human rights treaties in this country is Article 16 of the Constitution,[135] which

---

130 On Portugal, J. Madureira, 'Portugal', in Blackburn and Polakiewicz (eds), *Fundamental Rights in Europe*, 681.

131 Article 278: '1. The President of the Republic may ask the Constitutional Court to conduct a prior review of the constitutionality of any rule laid down by an international treaty that is submitted to him for ratification, by any decree that is sent to him for enactment as a law or executive law, or by any international agreement, the decree passing which is sent to him for signature'.

132 Article 279.4 Const. 'If the Constitutional Court pronounces the unconstitutionality of any rule contained in a treaty, the said treaty shall only be ratified if the Assembly of the Republic passes it by a majority that is at least equal to two thirds of all Members present and greater than an absolute majority of all the Members in full exercise of their office'.

133 Article 8: '1. The rules and principles of general or common international law shall form an integral part of Portuguese law.

2. The rules set out in duly ratified or passed international agreements shall come into force in Portuguese internal law once they have been officially published, and shall remain so for as long as they are internationally binding on the Portuguese state.

3. Rules issued by the competent bodies of international organisations to which Portugal belongs shall come directly into force in Portuguese internal law, on condition that this is laid down in the respective constituent treaties.

4. The provisions of the treaties that govern the European Union and the rules issued by its institutions in the exercise of their respective responsibilities shall apply in Portuguese internal law in accordance with Union law and with respect for the fundamental principles of a democratic state based on the rule of law'.

134 Article 204 of the Portuguese Constitution: 'In matters that are brought to trial, the courts shall not apply rules that contravene the provisions of this Constitution or the principles enshrined therein'.

135 Article 16: '1. The fundamental rights enshrined in this Constitution shall

recognizes a complementary role to international human rights treaties while the second paragraph, which acknowledges an interpretative role to the Universal Declaration of Human Rights alone, seems to exclude an extension to other conventions like the ECHR. Moreover in 1982 an expressed attempt to insert the ECHR into the text of the Constitution was rejected, but the issue is not yet clear because of the existence of a judgment of the Portuguese Constitutional Court where it used the ECHR besides the Universal Declaration[136] as we will see in the next chapter.

After the constitutional revision of 1989, Article 7 of the Portuguese Constitution[137] provides: 'Portugal shall make every effort to reinforce the European identity and to strengthen the European states' actions in favour of democracy, peace, economic progress and justice in the relations between peoples'.

In 1992, for the ratification of the EUT, a new revision occurred, hence a new paragraph was added to Article 7 reading: 'Subject to reciprocity and to respect for the fundamental principles of a democratic state based on the rule of law and for the principle of subsidiarity, and with a view to the achievement of the economic, social and territorial cohesion of an area of freedom, security and justice and the definition and implementation of a common external, security and defence policy, Portugal may enter into agreements for the exercise jointly, in cooperation or by the Union's institutions, of the powers needed to construct and deepen the European Union.'

Beside that, it is worth mentioning also Article 8, p. 4, according to which 'the provisions of the treaties that govern the European Union and the rules issued by its institutions in the exercise of their respective responsibilities shall apply in Portuguese internal law in accordance with Union law and with respect for the fundamental principles of a democratic state based on the rule of law'.

---

not exclude such other rights as may be laid down by law and in the applicable rules of international law.

2. The provisions of this Constitution and of laws concerning fundamental rights shall be interpreted and construed in accordance with the Universal Declaration of Human Rights'.

[136] The episode is mentioned by Montanari, *I diritti*, 112. See also E. Cavagna and E. Monteiro, *Iberian Peninsula: Spain and Portugal*, in M. Delmas-Marty (ed.), *The European Convention for the Protection of Human Rights. International Protection versus National Restrictions* (Martinus Nijhoff) 171.

[137] On Portugal, see: M. Poiares Maduro, 'EU Law and National Constitutions. Portuguese Report', Report for the XX FIDE Conference, London, 2002.

Romania

Romania is characterized by a dualist approach as Article 11 of the Constitution shows.[138] Article 20 of the Constitution provides for the priority of international human rights treaties (including the ECHR) over national law. In general the supremacy of the Constitution over international treaties seems to be guaranteed by Article 11, p. 3 of the Constitution, concerning the case of contrast between a treaty and a constitutional provision and requiring amendment of the Constitution for the ratification of the international agreement in that case.

Slovenia

Article 8[139] of the Slovenian Constitution, read together with Article 153,[140] acknowledges the prevalence of international agreements properly ratified over national law. A new provision was introduced after the constitutional reform of 2003 aimed at governing the transfer of sovereignty to international organizations: Article 3a,[141] which gives EU law a particular status. The ECHR is conceived, like all other international treaties, as a

---

[138] Article 11 of the Constitution of Romania: '(1) The Romanian State pledges to fulfil as such and in good faith its obligations as deriving from the treaties it is a party to.

(2) Treaties ratified by Parliament, according to the law, are part of national law.

(3) If a treaty in Romania is to become a party to comprises provisions contrary to the Constitution, its ratification shall only take place after the revision of the Constitution.'

[139] Article 8 of the Slovenian Constitution: 'Laws and other regulations must comply with generally accepted principles of international law and with treaties that are binding on Slovenia. Ratified and published treaties shall be applied directly'.

[140] Article 153 of the Slovenian Constitution: 'Laws, regulations, and other general legal acts must be in conformity with the Constitution.

Laws must be in conformity with generally accepted principles of international law and with valid treaties ratified by the National Assembly, whereas regulations and other general legal acts must also be in conformity with other ratified treaties.

Regulations and other general legal acts must be in conformity with the Constitution and laws.

Individual legal acts and actions of state authorities, local community authorities, and bearers of public authority must be based on a law or regulation adopted pursuant to law'.

[141] Article 3A: '(1) Pursuant to a treaty ratified by the National Assembly by a two-thirds majority vote of all deputies, Slovenia may transfer the exercise of part of its sovereign rights to international organisations which are based on respect for human rights and fundamental freedoms, democracy and the principles of the

super-primary but still sub-constitutional source,[142] and in general it can be traced back to the scope of Article 8 of the Constitution.[143]

Spain

> The special nature of ECHR and EU law is not expressly reflected in the Constitution. Two constitutional clauses, Articles 10.2 and 93, are particularly relevant in this field, even though neither explicitly refers to the ECHR or the EU. . . . The ECHR, like all international human rights treaties, enjoys a particular status in Spain, thanks to Article 10, p. 2, of the Constitution.[144]

For Spain, the constitutional problems regarding EU adhesion were challenged based on the original provisions of the 1978 Constitution, which does not include any specific provisions for European primacy, Article 93 of the Constitution[145] being just a procedural clause, as we will see in the next chapter.

---

rule of law and may enter into a defensive alliance with states which are based on respect for these values.

(2) Before ratifying a treaty referred to in the preceding paragraph, the National Assembly may call a referendum. A proposal is passed in the referendum if a majority of those voting have cast valid votes in favour of the same. The National Assembly is bound by the result of such referendum. If such referendum has been held, a referendum regarding the law on the ratification of the treaty concerned may not be called.

(3) Legal acts and decisions adopted within international organisations to which Slovenia has transferred the exercise of part of its sovereign rights shall be applied in Slovenia in accordance with the legal regulation of these organisations.

(4) In procedures for the adoption of legal acts and decisions in international organisations to which Slovenia has transferred the exercise of part of its sovereign rights, the Government shall promptly inform the National Assembly of proposals for such acts and decisions as well as of its own activities. The National Assembly may adopt positions thereon, which the Government shall take into consideration in its activities. The relationship between the National Assembly and the Government arising from this paragraph shall be regulated in detail by a law adopted by a two-thirds majority vote of deputies present'.

[142] Article 153 of the Slovenian Constitution: 'Laws must be in conformity with generally accepted principles of international law and with valid treaties ratified by the National Assembly, whereas regulations and other general legal acts must also be in conformity with other ratified treaties.'

[143] Article 8 of the Slovenian Constitution: 'Laws and other regulations must comply with generally accepted principles of international law and with treaties that are binding on Slovenia. Ratified and published treaties shall be applied directly.'

[144] A. Torres Perez, 'Report on Spain', in Martinico and Pollicino (eds), *The National Judicial Treatment of the ECHR and EU Laws*, 460. On Spain, see also M. Candela Soriano, 'The Reception Process in Spain and Italy', 393.

[145] Article 93 of the Spanish Constitution: 'By means of an organic law,

Other relevant provisions are Article 63, p. 2[146] of the Constitution, which empowers the King to express 'the consent of the State to obligate itself internationally through treaties in conformity with the Constitution and the laws' and Article 96 of the Constitution which reads that: 'Validly concluded international treaties, once officially published in Spain, shall be part of the internal legal system. Their provisions may only be repealed, amended or suspended in the manner provided for in the treaties themselves or in accordance with the general rules of international law. (2) The procedure provided for in section 94 for entering into international treaties and agreements shall be used for denouncing them'.

As we will see in the next chapter, the meaning of the second provision (especially its first paragraph) is still debated among scholars. According to some of them, this Article would imply the possibility for the national judges to disapply national law conflicting with international treaties duly ratified and concluded by Spain.

Finally, as mentioned, Article 93 of the Constitution has been used as the provision enabling Spanish participation in the EU, but we will return to this issue in the next chapter.

The United Kingdom and Ireland

In the United Kingdom the ECHR was incorporated in 1998 by means of the well known Human Rights Act which actually provides for a sort of selective incorporation of the rights of the ECHR (the so called 'Convention rights') and which acknowledges the necessity for the national judges to take into account also the case-law of ECtHR when interpreting these rights. Section 3[147] provides for the necessity to interpret domestic law 'so far as is possible' in a way consistent with the Convention rights.

---

authorization may be established for the conclusion of treaties which attribute to an international organization or institution the exercise of competences derived from the Constitution. It is the responsibility of the Parliament or the Government, depending on the cases, to guarantee compliance with these treaties and the resolutions emanating from the international or supranational organizations who have been entitled by this cession'.

146 Article 63, p. 2 of the Spanish Constitution: '(2) It is incumbent on the King to express the consent of the State to obligate itself internationally through treaties in conformity with the Constitution and the laws'.

147 Section 3 '(1) So far as it is possible to do so, primary legislation and subordinate legislation must be read and given effect in a way which is compatible with the Convention rights.

(2) This section—

(a) applies to primary legislation and subordinate legislation whenever enacted;

In case of contrast between the primary legislation and the Convention rights, the judges are not allowed to disapply national provisions but they shall adopt a 'declaration of incompatibility' which does not influence the validity and the efficacy of the law. After such a declaration 'if a Minister of the Crown considers that there are compelling reasons for proceeding . . . he may by order make such amendments to the legislation as he considers necessary to remove the incompatibility' (Section 10).[148]

It is difficult to understand the exact nature of the Human Rights Act in the domestic legal system: the possibility to remove incompatibility between the Convention rights and primary legislation seems to give it a sort of super-primary value but from a formal point of view the Human Rights Act is a normal piece of legislation. The situation will be partly solved by the case law as we will see in the next chapter.

As for EU law the fundamental provisions are included in the 1972 European Communities Act. The UK legal order also presents a monist approach in that general international law is seen as a part of the national law; the same applies to EC law after the approval of the European Communities Act. Section 2 of the Act regulates the general implementation of treaties.[149] Last July (2011) the new European Union Act 2011 received royal assent. This Act presents two important innovations,

---

(b) does not affect the validity, continuing operation or enforcement of any incompatible primary legislation; and

(c) does not affect the validity, continuing operation or enforcement of any incompatible subordinate legislation if (disregarding any possibility of revocation) primary legislation prevents removal of the incompatibility'.

[148] A. Wilfred Bradley and K. D. Ewing, *Constitutional and Administrative Law* (Longman 2007), 436. Another important provision is included in Section 19, according to which: 'A Minister of the Crown in charge of a Bill in either House of Parliament must, before Second Reading of the Bill—

(a) make a statement to the effect that in his view the provisions of the Bill are compatible with the Convention rights ("a statement of compatibility"); or

(b) make a statement to the effect that although he is unable to make a statement of compatibility the government nevertheless wishes the House to proceed with the Bill.

(2) The statement must be in writing and be published in such manner as the Minister making it considers appropriate.'

[149] Article 2.1 'All such rights, powers, liabilities, obligations and restrictions from time to time created or arising by or under the Treaties, and all such remedies and procedures from time to time provided for by or under the Treaties, as in accordance with the Treaties are without further enactment to be given legal effect or used in the United Kingdom shall be recognised and available in law, and be enforced, allowed and followed accordingly; and the expression "enforceable Community right" and similar expressions shall be read as referring to one to which this subsection applies'.

represented by section 18, devoted to the so-called 'sovereignty' clause; and the instrument of 'referendum locks' introduced in sections 2, 3 and 6.[150]

As Gordon pointed out, 'the final text of the provision enacted in the EUA is no "sovereignty" clause at all; instead, section 18 simply confirms the narrower point that the status of EU law within the UK is ultimately dependant on its continuing statutory basis. In other words, section 18 maintains that EU law is effective and supreme over other domestic norms because an Act of Parliament, the European Communities Act 1972, makes it so'.[151]

As for the second main innovation, it aims at introducing a 'referendum lock' on any further transfers of power from the UK to the European Union.

Basically, the Act provides that 'certain decisions can only be lawfully authorised by an Act of Parliament which makes the subsequent effectiveness of the decision contingent on whether it has been approved by a majority of the electorate voting in a referendum. The range of situations in which the EUA requires a referendum to be held to authorise action to be taken in relation to the EU is remarkably broad'.[152]

In the Republic of Ireland the primacy of EU law finds its confirmation in Article 29, p. 10 of the Constitution, according to which: 'No provision of this Constitution invalidates law enacted, acts done or measures adopted by the State necessitated by the obligations of membership of the Communities, or prevents laws enacted or acts done or measures adopted by the Communities or the institutions thereof, from having the force of law in the State.'

Thus, since this provision acknowledges the EC law's unconditioned prevalence over the Constitution's provisions, domestic constitutional law has been described as 'neutralized'.[153] However, at a closer look, the Irish

---

[150] On this Act see: P. Craig, 'The European Union Act 2011: Locks, limits and legality' (2011) Common Market Law Review 1915–44.

[151] M. Gordon, 'The European Union Act 2011', http://ukconstitutionallaw.org/2012/01/12/mike-gordon-the-european-union-act-2011/. The original wording was: 'Status of EU law dependent on continuing statutory basis. It is only by virtue of an Act of Parliament that directly applicable or directly effective EU law (that is, the rights, powers, liabilities, obligations, restrictions, remedies and procedures referred to in section 2(1) of the European Communities Act 1972) falls to be recognised and available in law in the United Kingdom'.

[152] P. Yowell, 'EU Act 2011: Law and Politics', http://ukconstitutionallaw.org/2012/01/19/paul-yowell-eu-act-2011-law-and-politics/.See Section 4 for a list of decisions attracting a referendum.

[153] A. Celotto and T. Groppi, 'Diritti UE e diritto nazionale: primauté vs controlimiti' (2004) *Rivista italiana di diritto pubblico comunitario*, 1309, 1337.

legal system poses at least two conditions for EU law primacy, showing respectively a formal nature and a substantive content, as we will see in the next chapter. First of all, according to the dualist vision of the relationship between domestic and external law,[154] a national act is necessary for the incorporation of the European Treaties. Secondly, those rights granted by the Constitution – defined as 'antecedent and superior to all positive law'[155] – should be understood as prevalent over EU law.

Finally, Ireland was for a long time the only participant member of the ECHR that did not incorporate the ECHR. The Irish system is dualist, pursuant to Article 29.6 of the Constitution.[156] In a 1960 decision of the Supreme Court, Chief Justice Maguire[157] stressed how the national judges are not empowered to give the ECHR effect if it is in contrast with domestic law. This can be explained looking at Article 15.2.1 of the Constitution,[158] which acknowledges the monopoly of the national legislature in law-making power.

The ECHR was finally incorporated in Ireland by the European Convention on Human Rights Act 2003. The incorporation provoked a general debate about the compatibility of certain areas of domestic law (like criminal, family and immigration law) with the ECHR although, according to some scholars, 'the ECHR now functions as a supplement to national rights protection'.[159] However, this does not guarantee a constitutional status to the ECHR.[160]

---

154 D. Morgan, *Lineamenti di diritto costituzionale irlandese* (Giappichelli 1998), 243.

155 Irish Constitution, Article 41: '1 The State recognises the Family as the natural primary and fundamental unit group of Society, and as a moral institution possessing inalienable and imprescriptible rights, antecedent and superior to all positive law'; Irish Constitution Article 43: '1° The State acknowledges that man, in virtue of his rational being, has the natural right, antecedent to positive law, to the private ownership of external goods'.

156 Article 29.6 of the Irish Constitution: 'No international agreement shall be part of the domestic law of the State save as may be determined by the Oireachtas'.

157 Irish Supreme Court, *O'Laighleis* (1960).

158 Article 15.2.1: 'The sole and exclusive power of making laws for the State is hereby vested in the Oireachtas: no other legislative authority has power to make laws for the State'.

159 A. Stone Sweet, 'On the Constitutionalisation of the Convention: The European Court of Human Rights as a Constitutional Court', available at http://works.bepress.com/cgi/viewcontent.cgi?Article=1032&context=alec_stone_sweet.

160 'The European Convention on Human Rights Act 2003 effectively mirrors the [UK] Human Rights Act 1998 in imposing an interpretive obligation on the Irish courts when considering domestic legislation. The sub-constitutional nature of incorporation is emphasised by the long title, which described the legislation

As we will see, even in recent times, instances of collision between the Irish legal system and the ECHR have not been lacking.

4. INTERIM FINDINGS

After having recalled the most important schematizations given by the scholarship and after a detailed analysis of all the European legal provisions (or better, the national clauses adopted for explaining the authority of EU law and the ECHR within the national boundaries), one can confirm the great variety existing, from a formal point of view, in Europe. However, as mentioned at the beginning of this chapter, this variety does not have a decisive impact on or offer a decisive answer to the question of the comparative strength of the European laws within the national boundaries, a major role being played in this field by judges, as we will see in the next chapter.

as 'to enable further effect to be given, subject to the Constitution' to certain provisions of the ECHR. The title affirms the historic Irish claim that the ECHR protections were already present within the domestic legal order and reiterates that the Constitution remains the principal legal authority in the state.' C. Murphy, 'Report on the UK and Ireland', in Martinico and Pollicino (eds), *The National Judicial Treatment of the ECHR and EU Laws*, 490.

3. The law in action

1. GOALS AND STRUCTURE OF THE CHAPTER

Having recalled the constitutional framework in Chapter 2, and following the scheme anticipated in Chapter 1, we are going to provide a detailed analysis of the relevant domestic case laws, taking into account not only the decisions given by the Constitutional and Supreme Courts but also trying to go beyond them, touching the application of European law in litigation before common judges (i.e. administrative and ordinary judges). Finally, in the very last part of this chapter we are going to stress those elements that we perceive as shared in the national judicial treatment of the ECHR and EU law.

2. LAW IN ACTION: EUROPEAN LAWS BEFORE (NATIONAL) COURTS

Austria

In Austria, the Constitution seemingly does not allow the Constitutional Court to review national legislation under EU law and, in fact, the respect of the Simmenthal doctrine is entrusted to the common judges. This is different from the national treatment of the ECHR, since the ECHR, as we specified in Chapter 2, belongs to the constitutional block and this implies that the competence to review national statutes under the ECHR is part of the business of the Constitutional Court.[1] Especially since the 1980s, the system has been deeply influenced by the ECHR and it is possible to appreciate such an influence in the case law of the Austrian Constitutional Court.[2]

In case of conflict between national law and the ECHR, if this issue cannot be solved by means of a consistent interpretation, such a conflict can give rise to a question of constitutionality and the Austrian

1 Cede, 'Report on Austria and Germany', 66.
2 Ibid.

Constitutional Court in this case could take into account the interpretation provided by the Strasbourg Court.[3] In any case, as the scholarship has pointed out, openness to the ECHR cannot lead to a violation of the Constitution.[4] Some authors[5] have also compared the *Görgülü* judgment to the *Miltner* case[6] whereby the Austrian Constitutional Court has pointed out the possibility of departing from the case law of the ECtHR if this would lead to a violation of the Constitution.

The Austrian Constitutional Court has also indicated it considers the refusal to raise the preliminary ruling by national common judges as a violation of the right of the lawful judge.[7] Unlike in Germany, the Austrian Constitutional Court in this case does not have the competence to review the decisions of the other common judges in case of refusal to raise the preliminary question.

The primacy of EU law over national law is respected and the Austrian Constitutional Court is among those constitutional guardians that considers itself as a judge under Article 267 of the TFUE.[8] The Austrian *Verfassungsgerichtshof*[9] first referred a preliminary question in 1999, just four years after Austria's accession, and today it is the second most active constitutional court, close behind the Belgian one.

---

[3] VfSlg. 14.696/1996 or 15.129/1998.

[4] 'In this case, even though the Convention has constitutional rank, the contrary rule of constitutional law would have to prevail by virtue of its lex specialis character', Cede, 'Report on Austria and Germany', 70. On this point see the slightly different picture given by L. Montanari, *I diritti dell'uomo nell'area europea fra fonti internazionali e fonti interne* (Giappichelli 2002).

[5] N. Krisch, 'The Open Architecture of European Human Rights Law' [2008] MLR 183.

[6] Austrian Constitutional Court, Judgment of 14 October 1987, Miltner, VfSlg 11500/1987, available via http://www.ris.bka.gv.at/vfgh/.

[7] VfSlg. 14.390/1995: 'A national authority that would refrain, in violation of Article 177 paragraph 3 EC from referring a question of interpretation of Community law to the ECJ would violate the lawful order of competences which includes Art 177 EC. The authority would deprive the parties of the proceedings from their lawful judge insofar as it answers itself a question of Community law the answer to which is reserved to the ECJ'. Reported by Cede, 'Report on Austria and Germany', 69.

[8] *VfGH*, 10 March 1999, B 2251/97, B 2594/97, available at www.vfgh.gv.at/cms/vfgh-site.

[9] On the Austrian case, see U. Jedliczka, 'The Austrian Constitutional Court and the European Court of Justice' [2008] J Intl Constitutional Law 4:301.

The Baltic States

The Baltic States represent the most evident example of the gap between the formal wording of the Constitution (which in each of these countries is supposed to be '*souverainiste*') and the reality of the law in action.

The EHCR is deemed a source of inspiration and even for the reconstruction[10] of national (including constitutional) law, and was cited by constitutional courts of these countries even before their accession to the ECHR.[11] This applies to Lithuania but also to Latvia, where the Court has *expressis verbis* accepted itself as bound by the case law of the Strasbourg Court[12] even when it interprets its own Constitution.[13] The same applies to Estonia, where the Supreme Court expressly acknowledged the priority of the ECHR over national law,[14] also recognizing the duty to follow the case law of the ECtHR.[15] This is understandable considering that the ECHR and the case law of the Strasbourg Court were used as a model when drafting the Constitutions.

As for EU law, again, Baltic courts started citing it before accession.[16] The case law of the ECJ and the provisions of the Charter of Fundamental Rights of the EU have been used for a long time in Estonia and Latvia,[17] and something similar occurred in Lithuania.[18] The Constitutional (or in Estonia, Supreme) Courts soon had the chance to express their views on

---

[10] Constitutional Court of Lithuania, Ruling of 8 May 2000. All the cases reported in this section have been cited by I. Jarukaitis, 'Report on Estonia, Latvia and Lithuania' in Martinico and Pollicino (eds), *The National Judicial Treatment of the ECHR and EU Laws*.

[11] For the Lithuanian context, see, for instance, the Ruling of 28 May 2008; the Ruling of 7 January 2008; the Ruling of 29 December 2004. Constitutional Court of Latvia see Judgment of 29 October 2009; the Judgment of 5 November 2008; the Judgment of 11 April 2006 in case no. 2005-24-01. Constitutional Review Chamber of the Supreme Court of Estonia, No. 3-4-1-2-01 of 3 May 2001.

[12] Constitutional Court of Latvia, Judgment of 30 August 2000 No. 2000-03-01.

[13] Constitutional Court of Latvia, Judgment No. 2006-03-0106, adopted 23 November 2006.

[14] Supreme Court of Estonia, Judgment of 6 January 2004 in case No. 3-1-3-13-03.

[15] Judgment of the Constitutional Review Chamber of the Supreme Court of Estonia, 30 December 2008 in case No. 3-4-1-12-08.

[16] Supreme Court of Estonia, Judgment of 30 September 1994, No. III-4/A-5/94.

[17] Supreme Court of Estonia, Judgment of 17 February 2003 in case No. 3-4-1-1-03; Supreme Court of Estonia, Judgment of the Supreme Court of 21 January 2004 in case No. 3-4-1-7-03.

[18] Constitutional Court of Lithuania, Ruling of 9 December 1998; Constitutional Court of Lithuania Ruling of 14 March 2002.

the relation between the Constitution and EU law, dealing with some constitutional complaints concerning the procedure followed for the accession, but all the Courts rejected these complaints on procedural grounds.[19] The only exception is that of a case before the Latvian Constitutional Court, concerning the Lisbon Treaty, which gave rise to a judgment on the merits where the Court decided that Parliament had acted in a proper way.[20]

As to Lithuania:

> Differently from Estonia and Latvia there were no direct constitutional challenges to Lithuania's membership in the EU or the further steps of deeper integration. Despite the belated adoption of the Constitutional Act concerning Lithuania's membership in the EU, neither the Accession Treaty/ratifying law, nor some other pieces of national legislation dealing with European issues (e.g. elections of the European Parliament, the issue of non-publication of some pieces of EU legislation in Lithuanian language, the constitutionality of ratification of the EU Constitutional Treaty or the Lisbon Treaty) were challenged before the Constitutional Court.[21]

The Constitutional Court in any case decided to point out how the Constitutional Act had confirmed Lithuania's membership of the EU, having thus a mere codificatory value.[22] In 2006 the Lithuanian Court stated:

> the Constitution consolidates not only the principle that in cases when national legal acts establish the legal regulation which competes with that established in an international treaty, then the international treaty is to be applied, but also, in regard to European Union law, establishes expressis verbis the collision rule, which consolidates the priority of application of European Union legal acts in the cases where the provisions of the European Union arising from the founding Treaties of the European Union compete with the legal regulation established in Lithuanian national legal acts (regardless of what their legal power is), save the Constitution itself.[23]

This was an ambivalent judgment whereby the Court emphasized the special nature of EU law and, according to some authors,[24] established the priority of the Constitution. Nevertheless, in all its successive judgments,

---

[19] Jarukaitis, 'Report on Estonia, Latvia and Lithuania', 181.

[20] Constitutional Court of Latvia, Judgment of 7 April 2009.

[21] Jarukaitis, 'Report on Estonia, Latvia and Lithuania', 182.

[22] Constitutional Court of Lithuania, Ruling of 13 December 2004.

[23] Constitutional Court of Lithuania, Ruling of 14 March 2006, as cited by Jarukaitis, 'Report on Estonia, Latvia and Lithuania', 184.

[24] For an overview of the debate, see: Jarukaitis, 'Report on Estonia, Latvia and Lithuania', 185 ff.

the Constitutional Court has attempted to guarantee the coexistence between constitutional supremacy and the primacy of EU law, by indicating that it considers the case law of the ECJ and the CFI (Court of First Instance) as a source of inspiration.[25] Moreover, the same Constitutional Court in 2007 joined the club of constitutional courts that accept the preliminary ruling mechanism.[26]

The Constitutional Court of Latvia has had various opportunities to dwell on the impact of EU law on the Latvian Constitution as well.[27] In a ruling given in 2008 it stated that: 'upon ratification of the Treaty on Accession of Latvia to the European Union, the European Union law has become an integral part of the Latvian legal system. Therefore, legal acts of the European Union and interpretation provided by [the] case law of the European Court of Justice should be taken into account when applying national law.'

However, according to the Court such openness to EU law is not boundless: 'Latvian law must be interpreted so as to avoid any conflicts with the obligations of Latvia towards the European Union, unless the fundamental principles incorporated in the Satversme are affected.'[28] Another link in this chain is represented by the judgment concerning the domestic act ratifying the Lisbon Treaty[29] but in that case the Constitutional Court said that there was no breach of the Constitution.

In the Baltic constitutional experience, Estonia seems to be characterized by the greatest constitutional openness, since no limits to EU integration seem to emerge from our analysis of the case law of the Estonian Supreme Court. In 2005 it pointed out that there were no constitutional grounds for declaring the unconstitutionality of a national law conflicting with EU law[30] and this induced the parliament to amend the Rules of the Parliament and the Constitutional Review Act in order to set up a special procedure permitting it to request the Supreme Court for a non-binding opinion about the interpretation of the Estonian Constitution with regard to EU law.[31] The Opinion of the Court paved the way for the amendment of the Estonian Constitution in order to make it consistent with EU law.

---

25 Constitutional Court of Lithuania, Ruling of 21 December 2006.

26 Constitutional Court of Lithuania, Decision of 8 May 2007.

27 Constitutional Court of Latvia, Judgment of 7 July 2004 No. 2004-01-06.

28 Constitutional Court of Latvia, Judgment of 17 January 2008 No. 2007-11-03 as cited by Jarukaitis, 'Report on Estonia, Latvia and Lithuania', 190.

29 Constitutional Court of Latvia, Judgment of 7 April 2009 No. 2008-35-01.

30 Supreme Court of Estonia, Judgment of 19 April 2005 No. 3-4-1-1-5.

31 Opinion of the Constitutional Review Chamber of the Supreme Court of Estonia of 11 May 2006, No. 3-4-1-3-06.

That is why many authors describe Estonia as an example of the superiority of EU law even over the Constitution.[32]

The Supreme Courts in Lithuania and Latvia started using EU law even before the accession, adopting the technique of consistent interpretation as the privileged tool for avoiding conflict between EU law and the Constitution and acknowledging the principles of direct effect[33] and primacy, while the preliminary ruling has seldom been used by these Courts.[34]

Belgium

In Belgium, in order to find a constitutional basis for EU law, and similarly to what happened in Italy and Germany before the respective constitutional amendments, there has been an evident readjustment of the constitutional text by national courts with regard to Article 34 of the Constitution.[35]

The *Franco Suisse Le Ski* judgment in 1971 was the first important turning point in the Belgian case law since it enabled the *Cour de Cassation* to recognize the primacy of self-executing international law (including EC law) over national law.[36] Courts are empowered to review national statutes that are not consistent with international treaties while more disputed is the possibility of applying such a rule to cases of conflict with provisions belonging to the constitutional level.[37] This possibility has been endorsed by the *Cour de Cassation* in a case concerning the ECHR[38] and then supported by ordinary courts.[39] In the *Orfinger* case[40] the Council of State also accepted the precedence of international over national law, including the Constitution.

In Belgium courts normally use and cite the ECHR and EU law, and the preliminary ruling mechanism is also used by the *Cour Constitutionnelle*

---

32 See the authors cited by Jarukaitis, 'Report on Estonia, Latvia and Lithuania', 190 ff.

33 Supreme Administrative Court of Lithuania in case No. A17-1137/2007, Judgment of 11 May 2007; the Supreme Court of Latvia in case No. SKA-234/2008, Judgment of 3 June 2008.

34 Jarukaitis, 'Report on Estonia, Latvia and Lithuania', 201 ff.

35 M. Claes, *The National Courts' Mandate in the European Constitution* (Hart 2006), 508.

36 Cass. 27 May 1971, *Pas.* 1971, I, 886.

37 For this debate, see: P. Popelier, 'Report on Belgium', in Martinico and Pollicino (eds), *The National Judicial Treatment of the ECHR and EU Laws*, 87–88.

38 Cass. 16 November 2004 [2005] *CDPK* 610.

39 Popelier, 'Report on Belgium', 88.

40 Council of State, *Orfinger* No. 62.922, 5 November 1996.

which holds the record for preliminary references from constitutional courts so far.[41] The *Cour Constitutionnelle* has also accepted the precedence of international law[42] and it considers the rights included in the ECHR as indirectly guaranteed by Articles 10 and 11 of the Constitution.[43] This way it de facto enlarged the parameter although it also emphasized that it is not competent in cases of complaints regarding the direct and sole violation of the ECHR.[44] The *Cour Constitutionnelle* 'accepts ECJ rulings requiring the Constitutional Court to depart from constitutional principles for the allocation of powers to the federal government and the federated entities, in so far as the law at stake extends to situations which exceed the purely Belgian scope'.[45]

Beside this indirect form of review of national law in light of international law, the *Cour Constitutionnelle* also uses the technique of consistent interpretation, taking into account the case law of both the European courts and demonstrating itself ready even to adapt its previous case law if necessary.[46] However, as scholars have pointed out, the issue of the national judicial treatment of EU law is much more complicated, and there has been no lack of tension between the Constitutional Court and the Court of Cassation in regards to this complexity.[47]

---

41 'Thus, the Constitutional Court of Belgium broke at least three records. Among national constitutional courts it is the court that has referred most questions to the ECJ (five); moreover it is the first to have made preliminary references on the validity of EU law (*Money Laundering*) as well as on the validity of EU law (*Advocaten voor de Wereld*)', T. Vandamme, 'Prochain Arrêt: La Belgique! Explaining Recent Preliminary References of the Belgian Constitutional Court' (2008) Eur Constitutional Law Rev 127–48, 128. From the 2008 Annual Report, one can remark that the number of references raised since 1952 is very high (12): http://curia.europa.eu/jcms/jcms/Jo2_7000/annual-report.

42 Const. Court of Belgium (at that time *Court d'Arbitrage*) No. 70, 14 December 1988. In this case it seemed to accept the prevalence of international law even on the constitutional sources.

43 Popelier, 'Report on Belgium', 89.

44 CA 95/2001

45 Const. Court No. 11/2009, 21 January 2009. Popelier, 'Report on Belgium', 89.

46 For instance, Const. Court No. 81/2007, 7 June 2007.

47 'The Constitutional Court however does not entirely follow the Court of Cassation in its open stance towards international law. Unlike the Court of Cassation it does not unconditionally adopt the international perspective. The Constitutional Court gives preliminary rulings concerning Parliamentary Acts holding assent to an international treaty even long after the treaty has entered into force. As mentioned above, it is no longer competent to do so in the case of a[n] EU treaty or the ECHR. Before this legislative intervention the Constitutional Court did not hesitate to recognize its competence even in the case of supranational

According to some authors this would imply the prevalence of the Constitution over international and EU law,[48] but the issue is still debated.[49] The issue regarding the possibility of reviewing Belgian parliamentary acts that transpose or execute supranational law, depending on the margin of discretion left to the national legislature, is also very complicated.[50] In one case[51] the Belgian Constitutional Court seemed to admit such a possibility: where it seemed to depart from the ECJ's case law[52] first, and then annulled the national provision implementing a directive on the grounds of conflict with the Constitution and the ECHR[53] but this case has been described as very particular, if not extraordinary, in its nature.[54]

---

treaties, however it avoided a substantial assessment on other grounds'. Popelier, 'Report on Belgium', 90. See Const. Court No. 16/94, 18 October 1994.

48 'When the *Cour d'arbitrage* was set up, it introduced a limit to the supremacy of international treaties: they would only be supreme over national law on condition that they could stand the constitutionality test: treaties infringing upon the Constitution – the highest norm of the land – would not take precedence', Claes, *The National Courts' Mandate*, 261. See the authors cited by Popelier, 'Report on Belgium', 90.

49 'In any case the Constitutional Court has never openly expressed the primacy of the Constitution over international law. Instead it has merely assessed whether the Constitution allowed Belgium to join the international treaty at the time of access. If this is the case, the international treaty is binding, even though afterwards international or constitutional developments make it contrary to the Constitution', Popelier, 'Report on Belgium', 90.

50 'In case the Directive does not give discretionary power to the national legislator, the review of implementing laws may come down to the review of the EU Directive in the light of the Constitution. In most cases the Constitutional Court refers to the EU Directive to reject the claim that the implementing law is discriminatory. In other cases the Court refers a validity question to the ECJ. If the ECJ upholds the Directive, the implementing law will subsist as well, even if it runs counter to the Constitution', Popelier, 'Report on Belgium', 91.

51 Const. Court No 10/2008, 23 January 2008, www.courconstitutionnelle.be.

52 ECJ C-305/05, *Ordre des barreaux francophones et germanophone* [2007] ECR I-5305.

53 'It is clear however that the Constitutional Court in this case has chosen for the full protection of a fundamental right, protected not only by the Constitution but also by the ECHR. Hence in the end the matter does not concern so much the relation EU law and constitutional law, but the relation EU law and the ECHR', Popelier, 'Report on Belgium', 91.

54 Finally, in order to give a complete overview of the possible interactions between EU law and national constitutional law, it is interesting to analyse the Chartry case. (ECJ C-457/09, available at http://curia.europa.eu/jurisp/cgi-bin/form.pl?lang=en&Submit=Rechercher&alldocs=alldocs&docj=docj&docop=docop&docor=docor&docjo=docjo&numaff=C-457/09&datefs=&datefe=&nomusuel=&domaine=&mots=&resmax=100). Special law of 12 July 2009 amended

Bulgaria

As we saw in the previous chapter, Article 5 of the Bulgarian Constitution seems to recognize a general precedence of international law (including

---

Article 26 of special law of 6 January 1989 regulating the Cour d'Arbitrage (now the Cour Constitutionelle). Basically, the Belgian legislation now provides that, in case of a conflict between one of the acts listed by Article 134 of the Constitution and a fundamental right guaranteed by Title II of the Constitution or by an EU law or international provision, the national judges shall first of all refer to the Belgian Constitutional Court the question concerning the conflict between the normative act and Title II of the Constitution. This way this provision seems to imply a priority granted to the question of constitutionality. Doubting this mechanism, in Chartry the *a quo* (Belgian) judge referred the following preliminary question to the ECJ: 'Do Article 6 [EU] and Article 234 [EC] preclude national legislation, such as the Law of 12 July 2009 amending Article 26 of the Law [on the Constitutional Court], from requiring the national court to make a reference to the Constitutional Court for a preliminary ruling, if it finds that a citizen taxpayer has been deprived of the effective judicial protection guaranteed by Article 6 of the European Convention for the Protection of Human Rights and Fundamental Freedoms, as incorporated into Community law, by another national law, [namely] Article 49 of the Law . . . of 9 July 2004, without that national court being able to ensure immediately the direct [effect] of Community law [in the] proceedings before it and without being able also to carry out a review of its compliance with the Convention where the Constitutional Court has recognised the compatibility of the national legislation with the fundamental rights guaranteed by Title II of the [Belgian] Constitution?'

This preliminary question was badly formulated since it implied the incorporation into EU law of the ECHR, while this is still far from being accomplished. It was very easy for the ECJ to avoid the 'trap' of a judicial clash with the Belgian Constitutional Court. Since the question raised by the national judge in this case did not regard the EU law provisions *stricto sensu* conceived, the Luxembourg Court concluded that it was not competent to deal with the preliminary question. In doing so, the ECJ recalled Article 51 of the Charter of Fundamental Rights of the EU, recalling how the Charter is 'addressed to the institutions and bodies of the Union with due regard for the principle of subsidiarity and to the Member States only when they are implementing Union law'. A similar interpretation of Article 51 has been used by the ECJ in the *McB* case, where it interpreted Article 51 of the Charter in a very restrictive way, by showing great deference towards the Member States' legislation and competences. C-400/10 PPU, *McB*. www.curia.europa.eu: 'First, according to Article 51(1) of the Charter, its provisions are addressed to the Member States only when they are implementing European Union law. Under Article 51(2), the Charter does not extend the field of application of European Union law beyond the powers of the Union, and it does not establish any new power or task for the Union, or modify powers and tasks as defined in the Treaties'. Accordingly, the Court is called upon to interpret, in the light of the Charter, the law of the European Union within the limits of the powers conferred on it.

the ECHR and EU law) over national law and it also covers the duty to interpret national law in a manner which is consistent with EU law and the ECHR (and the case law of their respective courts). In 1998 the Bulgarian Constitutional Court ruled that 'the Convention constitutes a set of European common values which is of a significant importance for the legal systems of the Member States and consequently the interpretation of the constitutional provisions relating to the protection of human rights has to be made to the extent possible in accordance with the corresponding clauses of the Convention'.[55]

A similar openness seems to be acknowledged to the EU law, at least for structural reasons connected to the ECJ's case law, and in general the Bulgarian Constitutional Court does not hesitate to quote EU law provisions or the case law of the ECJ.[56]

National judges are the first defenders of the priority of EU law and the ECHR. As for the ECHR, both common judges and the Constitutional Court carry out a control *de conventionalité*[57] at least on paper, since scholars[58] have noticed a certain hesitation of the common judges to perform the control of *conventionalité* and the *Simmenthal* mandate.[59]

As pointed out by some scholars, the Bulgarian Constitutional Court has recognized the priority of the Constitution over these two European laws but also admitted how the national constitution shall be interpreted as far as possible in light of the provisions of the ECHR. This solution

It follows that, in the context of this case, the Charter should be taken into consideration solely for the purposes of interpreting Regulation No. 2201/2003, and there should be no assessment of national law as such. More specifically, the question is whether the provisions of the Charter preclude the interpretation of that regulation set out in paragraph 44 of this judgment, taking into account, in particular, the reference to national law which that interpretation involves' (51–52).

55 See Constitutional Court Decision no. 2, of 18 February 1998: Official journal no. 22, 24 February 1998. The cases reported in this section have been taken from M. Fartunova, 'Report on Bulgaria', in Martinico and Pollicino (eds), *The National Judicial Treatment of the ECHR and EU Law*.

56 See Constitutional Decision no. 1, of 13 February 2007: Official journal no. 18, 27 February 2007.

57 See Article 149, Paragraph 2 and 4 of the Constitution.

58 Fartunova, 'Report on Bulgaria', 107.

59 'The national courts prefer to decide that the case pending before them doesn't fall into a field of these two international instruments. Nevertheless, two comments should be made. First, this position does reveal a certain difficulty to solve potential conflicts between the domestic law and European instruments. Second, the national courts do still prefer to apply the relevant domestic law instead of the relevant international clauses. One of the reasons is that the judges' knowledge of these instruments is still insufficient.' Ibid., 107–108.

has been described as the paradoxical consequence[60] of the wording of Article 149 of the Constitution (namely of the combination between paragraphs 2 and 4 of the same provision) which governs both the control of constitutionality (paragraph 2) and of *conventionalité*, interpreting these two controls as different in purpose and scope.[61] That is why the Bulgarian Constitutional Court normally refuses to control the consistency of national law with EU[62] when cases are introduced on the basis of Article 149, paragraph 2, instead of Article 149, paragraph 4.[63] This shows a 'certain reluctance from the Constitutional Court to solve potential conflicts between norms.'[64]

At the same time, over the years some tensions have existed between the ECtHR and the Bulgarian Constitutional Court. The *OMO-Ilinden*[65] case is emblematic in this respect: the Bulgarian Constitutional Court declared the registration of an organization as a political party as contravening Article 13 of the Constitution,[66] and subsequently the ECtHR condemned Bulgaria for the consequences of this judgment, being the violation of Article 11 of the ECHR. This decision was a turning point since: 'Later on, the national jurisdictions were very reluctant to accept the judgment of the European Court of Human Rights and pointed out that its ruling was non binding and thus refused to abide by it when the "Omo-Ilinden" again requested to register as a political party.'[67]

Czech Republic and Slovakia

As for the relationship between EU and national law, the first important judgment was delivered in 2006 (the *Sugar Quota III* case),[68] where the Czech Constitutional Court (CCC) quashed the national act implementing a supranational norms, namely EU regulation of the sugar market. In the

---

[60] Ibid.

[61] Ibid.

[62] See Constitutional decision no. 7, of 23 April 2007 quoted above.

[63] Constitutional decision no. 11, of 18 December 2007: Official journal no. 1, 4 January 2008.

[64] Fartunova, 'Report on Bulgaria', 109. See also Constitutional Decision no. 1, of 27 January 2005: Official Journal no. 13, 8 February 2005.

[65] Constitutional Decision no. 3 of 1999, Official journal no. 3, of 9 March 2000.

[66] Article 13, Paragraph 4, of the Bulgarian Constitution: 'religious communities as well as the religious beliefs cannot serve political purposes'.

[67] Fartunova, 'Report on Bulgaria', 110.

[68] Judgment of 8 March 2006, Pl. ÚS 50/04 ('Sugar Quota III'), no. 154/2006 Coll., available in English at http://www.usoud.cz/file/2274.

same decision, as scholars have pointed out,[69] the Court demonstrated its endorsement of the historical position of the German Constitutional Court.[70]

In the same year, the CCC ruled on the domestic act implementing the European Arrest Warrant.[71] Here the CCC attempted to avoid a clash between national and supranational law by relying on the consistent interpretation doctrine and stressing the equivalence between the European and national standards of fundamental rights protection.[72] We will return to this decision in Part II of this volume.

In 2007, the CCC also indicated that it considers EU law as a source of inspiration for the interpretation of national constitutional provisions.[73]

Finally, the CCC gave two judgments about the Lisbon Treaty. In the first judgment,[74] the CCC took the *Sugar Quota III* argument, pointing out that the transfer of sovereignty – made possible thanks to Article 10a – was conditioned by the respect of some fundamental values like democracy, the rule of law and fundamental rights which represent the untouchable core of the Constitution (Article 9.2). At the same time, it concluded for the compatibility of the Lisbon Treaty with the Constitution.

In 2009, the CCC came back to the Lisbon Treaty in proceedings initiated by a group of senators. If the *Lisbon I* judgment was long and

---

69 M. Bobek and D. Kosař, 'Report on the Czech Republic and Slovakia', in Martinico and Pollicino (eds), *The National Judicial Treatment of the ECHR and EU Laws*, 121.

70 'In the Constitutional Court's view, the conditional nature of the delegation of these powers is manifested on two planes: the formal and the substantive plane. The first of these planes concerns the power attributes of state sovereignty itself: the second plane concerns the substantive component of the exercise of state power. In other words, the delegation of a part of the powers of national organs may persist only so long as these powers are exercised in a manner that is compatible with the preservation of the foundations of state sovereignty of the Czech Republic, and in a manner which does not threaten the very essence of the substantive law-based state.' Judgment of 8 March 2006, Pl. ÚS 50/04 ('Sugar Quota III').

71 Judgment of 3 May 2006, Pl. ÚS 66/04 ('EAW Case'), no. 434/2006 Coll., available in English at http://www.usoud.cz/file/2276.

72 'The contemporary standard for the protection of fundamental rights within the European Union does not, in the Constitutional Court's view, give rise to any presumption that this standard for the protection of fundamental rights, through invoking the principles arising therefrom, is of a lesser quality than the level of protection provided in the Czech Republic.' Ibid.

73 Judgment of 16 January 2007, case no. Pl. ÚS 36/05 no. 57/2007 Coll. All the cases cited in this section have been taken from Bobek and Kosař, 'Report on the Czech Republic and Slovakia'.

74 Pl. ÚS 19/08 ('Lisbon I'), no. 446/2008 Coll., an English translation is available at http://www.usoud.cz/file/2339.

articulated, the *Lisbon II* has been described as 'minimalist'.[75] This judgment has been seen as a response to the Lisbon judgment of the German Constitutional Court given a few months earlier.

The CCC has never raised a preliminary reference to the ECJ and in the *Sugar Quota III* decision it said that 'the Constitutional Court is aware of the delicacy of the question as to whether the Constitutional Court can be considered a court in the sense of Article 234 of the EC Treaty, or in which type of proceedings, and reserves to itself in the future the possibility of adopting an unequivocal answer, in other words, to refer a matter for the adjudication to the ECJ in individual types of proceedings'.[76]

In the Czech Republic it is possible to reopen cases after a judgment of the ECtHR in criminal cases, following a special procedure involving the Constitutional Court.[77] As for the ECHR, the CCC frequently relies on the case law of the Strasbourg Court and also uses the Convention for interpreting national (constitutional and legislative) law. The CCC has also adopted a very broad reading of the Convention and considers it, and other human rights treaties, as different and superior to the other international treaties.[78]

The CCC also considers itself empowered to review the validity of national legislation in light of the ECHR[79] in spite of the text of the Constitution. In fact, the CCC has given a very creative reading to new constitutional provisions, de facto rewriting them. As we saw in the previous chapter, the Euro amendment abandoned the distinction between 'international human rights treaties' and other international treaties. It also

---

75 Bobek and Kosař, 'Report on the Czech Republic and Slovakia', 124. '[T]he Constitutional Court does not consider it possible, in view of the position that it holds in the constitutional system of the Czech Republic, to create such a catalogue of non-transferable powers and authoritatively determine "substantive limits to the transfer of powers", as the petitioners request. It points out that it already stated, in judgment Pl. ÚS 19/08, that "These limits should be left primarily to the legislature to specify, because this is a priori a political question, which provides the legislature wide discretion" [paragraph 109]. Responsibility for these political decisions cannot be transferred to the Constitutional Court; it can review them only at the point when they have actually been made on the political level'. Decision of 3 November 2009, Pl. ÚS 29/09 ('Lisbon II'), no. 387/2009 Coll.; an English translation is available at http://www.usoud.cz/soubor/2506. As reported by Bobek and Kosař, 'Report on the Czech Republic and Slovakia', 124.

76 Judgment of 8 March 2006, Pl. ÚS 50/04 ('Sugar Quota III') no. 154/2006 Coll., available in English at http://www.usoud.cz/file/2274.

77 Articles 119–119b of Act No. 182/1993 Coll.

78 Judgment of 15 April 2003 (I. ÚS 752/02).

79 Judgment of the CCC of 30 November 2004, Pl. ÚS 15/04; Judgment of the CCC of 22 March 2005, Pl. ÚS 45/04.

excluded the ECHR having to be considered as part of the constitutional block, thus decentralizing the control of compatibility between national laws and international treaties.

Nevertheless in 2001 the CCC said that: 'The inadmissibility of changing the substantive requirements of a democratic state based on the rule of law also contains an instruction to the [CCC] that no amendment to the Constitution can be interpreted in such a way that it would result in limiting an already achieved procedural level of protection for fundamental rights and freedoms.'[80]

This way, therefore, the CCC concluded that 'the international human rights treaties have retained their constitutional status'.[81] That is why today the ECHR still enjoys constitutional status in the Czech Republic despite the wording of the Constitution.

More complicated is the issue of the perception of the ECHR by national common judges. As Bobek and Kosař wrote: 'In contrast to the constitutional courts that tend to be perceived as "good guys", the ordinary courts in the Czech Republic and Slovakia have been often portrayed as "bad guys" that apply the ECHR only reluctantly, if at all.'[82]

The ECHR has been also the cause of episodes of jurisdictional clashes between the Supreme Courts and the CCC on the 'constitutionalization' of the ECHR, with judges disapplying national statutes instead of asking for the intervention of the CCC.[83] More generally, judges cite the ECHR extensively, often in an *ad abundantiam* way; sometimes they have also misinterpreted the Convention and the case law of the Strasbourg Court.[84]

Cases dealing with EU law are not numerous in Slovakian jurisprudence and scholars normally recall just two decisions. The first case was in 2005,[85] concerning the implementation of the so-called Race Directive (Council Directive 2000/43/EC of 29 June 2000). Article 8(8) of the Act implementing that Directive (which reproduced another provision of the directive) was challenged by the Slovakian government. The Slovakian Constitutional Court (SCC) annulled the domestic provision, recalling in

---

80 Judgment of the CCC of 25 June 2002 (Pl. ÚS 36/01).

81 Bobek and Kosař, 'Report on the Czech Republic and Slovakia', 135.

82 Ibid., 141.

83 Decision of the CSC of 30 October 2008, no. 1 Skno 10/2008, http://www.nsoud.cz/; Judgment of the SAC of 11 July 2007, no. 6 As 55/2006, available at http://www.nssoud.cz.

84 Bobek and Kosař, 'Report on the Czech Republic and Slovakia', 142 ff.

85 Judgment of the SCC of 18 October 2005, Pl. ÚS 8/04-202, available at http://www.concourt.sk.

an inappropriate way[86] the ECJ's case law for conflicting with the principle of non-discrimination and with the *numerus clausus* of positive actions expressly enumerated in the Constitution.

The other interesting judgment[87] concerned the ratification of the Constitutional Treaty in Slovakia and its subject was the decision of the national parliament approving the Constitutional Treaty. In that case the complainants – 13 Slovak citizens and members of the Slovak Conservative Institute – claimed that the 'basic right to participate in the administration of public affairs within the meaning of Article 30(1) SC would be violated if the Parliament were to decide that no referendum will be held on the Treaty'.[88] The SCC saved the parliament's decision, since a referendum would have been necessary if the European Union had become a '*Staatenbund*'. Moreover, since the Constitutional Treaty incorporated the Charter of Fundamental Rights a referendum was impossible as the Slovakian Constitution[89] expressly excludes referenda on fundamental rights.

As for the ECHR, national legislation admits the possibility to reopen cases after a judgment of the ECtHR, not only in criminal matters (as in the Czech Republic) but also in civil proceedings.[90] The SCC, like its Czech counterpart, regularly uses and cites the ECHR and the case law of the ECtHR. It considers ordinary courts as 'primary defenders of constitutionality'[91] and for 'the observance of the rights and fundamental freedoms guaranteed by [. . .] international treaties'[92] but the ECHR is conceived as a super-primary but also sub-constitutional source.[93]

It is in any case possible for the SCC to strike down a national statute incompatible with the ECHR[94] and the SCC has done so once.[95] The tech-

---

86 Bobek and Kosař, 'Report on the Czech Republic and Slovakia', 125.
87 II. ÚS 171/05, accessible (in Slovak only) at www.concourt.sk.
88 Bobek and Kosař, 'Report on the Czech Republic and Slovakia', 125.
89 Article 93, see *supra* Chapter 2.
90 Bobek and Kosař, 'Report on the Czech Republic and Slovakia', 137.
91 Judgment of the SCC of 21 August 2002, III. ÚS 79/02, available at http://www.concourt.sk.
92 Decision of the SCC of 22 March 2000, I. ÚS 9/00, available at http://www.concourt.sk.
93 See Decision of the SCC of 16 December 1999, II. ÚS 91/99, available at http://www.concourt.sk.
94 Article 125, p. 1. See *supra* Chapter 2.
95 See Judgment of the SCC of 7 November 2002, Pl. ÚS 25/01, where the SCC struck down Article 200i(4) of the Code of Civil Procedure *solely* for inconsistence with Article 6(1) ECHR. See also Judgment of the SCC of 17 May 2006, III. ÚS 84/06, where the SCC quashed the *decision* of the ordinary court solely for violation of the ECHR.

nique of consistent interpretation is frequently used for avoiding collisions between the ECHR and the Constitution or the ECHR and national laws. Even the Supreme Courts tend to apply the ECHR in a regular manner with problems similar to those that have occurred in the Czech Republic.[96] However, recently, the Czech Constitutional Court surprisingly decided to apply the *ultra vires* control (devised by the German Constitutional Court) by declaring a previous decision of the ECJ *ultra vires*. This decision was the outcome of a tension which exploded after the *Landtovà*[97] decision of the ECJ, whereby the Luxembourg Court had challenged the case law of the Czech Constitutional Court.

Cyprus

The Supreme Court of Cyprus constantly refers to the ECHR. For instance, in *Attorney General v Afamis* it did so in order to explain the genesis of Article 11 of the Constitution – 'modelled on paragraph (1) of Article 5 of the European Convention on Human Rights'[98] – but also to show the differences that were, in that case, crucial to declare the unconstitutionality of the legislative act at stake. It should be noticed that at that time the ECHR had not yet been incorporated. In general the case law of the ECtHR is also taken into account by the Supreme Court[99] (especially that on Article 6 of the ECHR) and in case of conflict between the ECHR and national law the issue can be solved in the following ways: either adopting the consistent interpretation technique or recognizing primacy to the ECHR.[100]

As for EU law, tensions with the ECJ have not been lacking, as appears from the case *Attorney General v Kostas Konstantinou* over the unconstitutionality – on the basis of Article 11(2) of the Constitution – of the legislation transposing the Framework Decision101 for the European Arrest Warrant. The Supreme Court in that case attempted to apply the

---

96 Bobek and Kosař, 'Report on the Czech Republic and Slovakia', 140 ff.

97 *Landtová*, C-399/09, www.curia.europa.eu

98 *The Attorney General of the Republic v Andreas Costas Afamis*, 1961. available at www.leginet.eu.

99 For instance, see the following cases: *G. Iosifides v Republic*, 2000; *Loucas Stylianou v Skyra Lima*, 2003; *Andreas Konstantinou v Republic*, 2003, all cited by Nikolas Kyriakou, 'Report on Cyprus' in Martinico and Pollicino (eds), *The National Judicial Treatment of the ECHR and EU Law*, 156 ff.

100 See the case *Andreas Konstantinou v Republic*, 2003, cited by Kyriakou, 'Report on Cyprus', 158.

101 *Attorney General v Kostas Konstantinou*, Civil Appeal No. 294/2005 (Supreme Court of Cyprus November 7, 2005).

consistent interpretation technique to avoid a conflict but in the end went for unconstitutionality; many authors have criticized the domestic judges for this.[102]

France

In France the precedence of international law over national statutes has been accepted by the supreme jurisdictions, namely the *Conseil d'État*[103] and the *Cour de Cassation*.[104] The *Conseil Constitutionnel* does not seem to use international law per se as a parameter for reviewing the constitutionality of national legislation[105] but the issue is still disputed.[106] In any case the ECHR has been de facto taken into account in the constitutional case law.[107] The case law of the ECtHR has acted as an indirect engine for many legislative reforms[108] and this is confirmation of the important impact of the ECHR system on French national law.

As for EU law, in 2004 the *Conseil Constitutionnel* expressly recognized the special nature of EU law.[109] Before 2004 it had always ruled that domestic laws implementing directives were characterized by a sort of presumption of constitutionality (and never used the ad hoc parameter introduced in the light of the ratification of Maastricht Treaty) but in

---

102 See the analysis in Kyriakou, 'Report on Cyprus', 158 ff.

103 *Conseil d'État*, 20 October 1989, Nicolo.

104 Cour de Cassation, *Jacques Fabres* 24 May 1975.

105 Cons. Constit., decision no. 74-54, 15 January 1975.

106 See M. Calamo Specchia, 'Il Conseil constitutionnel e le Corti europee: dall'indifferenza al dialogo?' in G. Franco Ferrari (ed.), *Corti costituzionali e Corti europee* (ESI 2006). The author cited the decision of the Constitutional Council no. 88-1082 DC of 21 October 1988 in order to argue the thesis of the 'incorporation' of the *bloc de conventionnalité* in the *bloc de constitutionnalité.* See also decisions no. 93-325 DC of 13 August 1993 and 98-399 DC of 5 May 1998 of the Constitutional Council.

107 For instance, Cons. Constit., decision no. 88-248 DC, 17 January 1989, CSA; Cons. Constit., decision no. 80-127 DC, 19–20 January 1981; Cons. Constit., decision 89-260 DC, 28 July 1989. 'It could be stressed that the Conseil Constitutionnel takes into account the provisions of the ECHR in its decisions even if it does not refer to the Convention in its judicial review when monitoring the conformity of national laws to the Constitution. The Convention is not part of the constitutional norms of reference for the Conseil Constitutionnel in its judicial review', M. Fartunova, 'Report on France', in Martinico and Pollicino (eds), *The National Judicial Treatment of the ECHR and EU Laws*, 205–222, 212.

108 Among others, see *Bozano v France* [1986]; *Muller v France* [1997]; *Annoni Di Gusola et Debordes et Omer v France* [2000].

109 Cons. Constit., decision 2004-505 DC.

2004[110] it admitted the possibility of monitoring the conformity of these laws with the Constitution, taking into account the *exigence constitutionnelle de transposition*. At the same time the *Conseil Constitutionnel* emphasized the existence of some limitations that cannot be jeopardized by the obligation of transposing directives, namely those principles embodying the constitutional identity of France.[111] It also specified the nature of this form of control: 'however, it considers that such a judicial review is only possible concerning the national laws that transpose a directive concretely. In other words, it expressly refuses to monitor the compatibility of national laws with an EU directive in an abstract sense when they did not transpose it concretely.'[112] Although the primacy of EU law has been acknowledged, the *Conseil d'État* and *Cour de Cassation* have emphasized that the Constitution is the supreme law of the land[113] and tensions have not been lacking, as the reaction to cases like *Poitrimol*[114] or *Borgers*[115] demonstrates.

As for EU law, national judges have agreed to disapply national laws thus recognizing the primacy of EU law.[116] Generally speaking, the preliminary ruling mechanism has been accepted by French judges (even by the highest courts) – but not without some resistance.[117] A turning point in this respect was represented by the *Arcelor* judgment of the *Conseil d'État*.[118]

---

110 Cons. Constit., decision no. 2004-496 DC, 10 June 2004. Cons. Constit; decision no. 2004-497 DC, 1 July 2004.

111 Cons. Constit., decision no. 2006-543 DC.

112 Fartunova, 'Report on France', 213. See Cons. Constit, decision no. 2006-535.

113 See CE, Ass., October 30 1998, CCass., Ass. Plén., 2 June 2000, Mlle Fraisse.

114 ECtHR, Judgment of 23 November 1993, *Poitrimol v France*; See also ECtHR, Judgments of 29 July 1998, *Omar v France* and *Guérin v France*; Judgment of 14 December 1999, *Khalfaoui v France*.

115 ECtHR, Judgment of 30 October 1991, *Borgers v Belgium*.

116 For instance: TA Strasbourg, 19 May 1993 AFRPN du Bas-Rhin, Association Alsace-Nature; CAA Paris, 23 March 1995, Comité interprofessionnel de l'horticulture florale et ornementale et des pepinières; CE, 16 February 2001, APLERMNC et autres; CE, 17 May 2000, Association nationale pour l'épargne retraite des fonctionnaires; CE, 16 June 2000, Société Cegetel; CE, 29 December 2000, *Ministre de l'Intérieur v Olazabal*. Cases mentioned by Fartunova, 'Report on France', 215 ff.

117 D. Marrani, 'Love-Hate Relationship: France and European Law', http://lawlib.wlu.edu/lexopus/works/233-1.pdf.

118 Conseil d'État, *Assemblée Société Arcelor et autres*, 8 February 2007, http://www.conseiletatfr/ce/jurispd/index_ac_ld0706.shtml. On this see: O. Pollicino, 'The Conseil d'Êtat and the Relationship between French Internal Law and European Law after *Arcelor*: Something Has Really Changed?' [2008] CML Rev, 1519.

The case originated from an action brought before the *Conseil d'État* by Arcelor and other plaintiffs on the basis of a presumed violation of the right to property and to trade freely and of the principle of equality guaranteed by the French Constitution, brought about by decree no. 2004-832 of 19 August 2004. The decree had been approved in order to implement Directive 2003/87/EC. Instead of risking a collision with the ECJ, triggered by a declaration of indirect validity of the directive (through the declaration of invalidity of the decree), the *Conseil d'État* acknowledged the primacy of EU law and the 'maturity' of the EU law system in the ambit of fundamental rights protection. In fact, it decided to refer a preliminary question to the ECJ, recalling how the right to property and to trade freely and the principle of non-discrimination were at the same time general principles of EU law.

Recently the preliminary ruling mechanism has been at the heart of the *Melki* case. As we saw in the previous chapter, in its reform of the control of constitutionality, the French legislature has introduced a questionable mechanism granting priority to questions of constitutionality in cases of dual preliminarity. Challenging this provision, the French *Cour de Cassation* referred a preliminary question to the ECJ.[119]

Before the ECJ pronounced on this, the French *Conseil Constitutionnel* (on 12 May 2010) interpreted this provision in a manner consistent with the *Simmenthal* and *Cartesio* doctrines. In June 2010, the ECJ (in C-188/10) decided to take into account the decision of the *Conseil Constitutionnel*,[120] showing great deference to that domestic institution. Moreover the *Cour de Cassation* was strongly criticized by many scholars, who accused it of having exploited the question to challenge the reform of the constitutionality system. The decision of the ECJ in June 2010 in this case was only the last episode of a multilevel saga which involved all the judicial levels in the EU.

---

119 Asking whether 'Article 267 TFEU precludes national legislation which would impose on ordinary courts an obligation to decide first, on submitting a question of constitutionality to the Constitutional Council, which was raised before them, if this question concerns a conflict between the provision of domestic law and the Constitution, because it is contrary to EU law'. ECJ, C-188/10, available at http://curia.europa.eu/jurisp/cgi-bin/form.pl?lang=en&Submit=Rechercher&alldocs=alldocs&docj=docj&docop=docop&docor=docor&docjo=docjo&numaff=C-188/10&datefs=&datefe=&nomusuel=&domaine=&mots=&resmax=100.

120 F. Donnat, 'La Cour de Justice et la QPC: chronique d'un arrêt imprévisible et imprévu' [2010] *Recueil Dalloz*, 1640; F. Fabbrini, 'La Corte di Giustizia si pronuncia sulla "legittimita comunitaria" del nuovo modello di giustizia costituzionale francese' [2010] *Quad. Cost.*, 4; D. Sarmiento, 'L'affaire Melki: esquisse d'un dialogue des juges constitutionnels et européens sur toile de fond française' [2010] *Revue trimestrielle de droit européen*, 588.

It is worth mentioning how the *Melki* case, which might be described as inspired by a generous spirit of the ECJ towards the national courts, actually represents a reaffirmation (although in a 'milder' version) of the *Simmenthal* doctrine,[121] and how the ECJ probably declined to go a step further since the corresponding constitutional interlocutors had already resolved the issue. At the same time, as Millet pointed out, the ECJ took the chance to point out and strengthen the *Foto-Frost* doctrine.[122]

Germany

Originally, Article 24 of the *Grundgesetz* (the Basic Law) was used by the German Constitutional Court in order to explain the authority of EU law.[123] As is well known, the German Constitutional Court has made a fundamental contribution to the evolution of the European legal order. In fact, soon after the ECJ decision in *Internationale Handelsgesellschaft*,[124] national constitutional courts, including that of Germany with the famous *Solange*[125] judgment, started posing some barriers to the primacy of EU law, namely, the fundamental rights aspect, the democratic aspect and the subsidiarity aspect.

Indeed, what was the essence of the German constitutional *diktat* in *Solange*? As everybody knows, in *Solange* – a judgment delivered a few years after the ambivalent judgment in *Internationale Handelsgesellschaft* – the German Constitutional Court said that

> as long as [German: *Solange*] the integration process has not progressed so far that Community law receives a catalogue of fundamental rights decided on by a parliament and of settled validity, which is adequate in comparison with the catalogue of fundamental rights contained in the Basic Law, a reference by a court in the Federal Republic of Germany to the *Bundesverfassungsgericht* in judicial review proceedings . . . is admissible and necessary.[126]

---

121 F. Millet, 'La 'question prioritaire de constitutionnalité' e il dialogo a singhiozzo tra giudici in Europa' [2011] *Giornale di diritto amministrativo* 2:139, 144. ECJ, C-314/85, *Foto-Frost v Hauptzollamt Lubeck-Ost* ECR, 4199.

122 J. Allard and A. Garapon, *Les juges dans la mondialisation* (Seuil 2005).

123 BVerfGE 22, 293 (296).

124 11/70, *Internationale Handelsgesellschaft* [1970] ECR 1125. We are referring to the very famous point in which the ECJ argued that: 'The validity of a Community measure or its effect within a member State cannot be affected by allegations that it runs counter to either fundamental rights as formulated by the constitution of that State or the principles of its constitutional structure'.

125 BVerfGE 37, S. 271 ff

126 BVerfGE 37, 271 2 BvL 52/71 Solange I-Beschluß.

Over the years the German Constitutional Court has mitigated its approach and changed its position by substituting the case by case control (hypothesized in *Solange I*) with an abstract control of the general compatibility of EU law with the demands of the rights guarantee (*Solange II*[127]) announcing that it was 'desisting from its competence to review the compatibility of acts of EU law with domestic fundamental rights "as long as" the Community legal order provides, as it currently does, for a level of protection essentially equivalent to the domestic level of protection'.[128] In other judgments (the *Maastricht* judgment[129]), the Court has repeated its message emphasizing the necessity to respect the democratic principle and the respect for the competences,[130] announcing a check for verifying the *ultra vires* nature of legal acts of the European institutions.

Having recalled this, it is interesting to see how a similar doctrine has been devised with regard to the ECHR's penetration into the domestic legal order. This represented the last link of the chain as we will see, but before proceeding with the analysis of the relationship between EU law and German law it is necessary to step back and recall a judgment formally devoted to the relationship between the ECHR and national law but whose conclusions can be – partly at least – extended to EU law.

In Germany the Second Senate of the Constitutional Court, the *Bundesverfassungsgericht* (BVG), by its order no. 1481/04,[131] clarified the relationship between the German Constitutional Court and the ECHR, which represented a sort of follow up to the Strasbourg Court's decision in *Görgülü v Germany* (no. 74969/01[132]). As explained in the literature,[133] this judgment has to be connected to another case of judicial conflict between the two courts, that is, *Hannover v Germany*.[134] On that occasion the two

127 BVerfGE 73, 339, in http://www.bundesverfassungsgericht.de/en/index.html.

128 Cede, 'Report on Austria and Germany', 59. BVerfGE 73, 339 ('Solange II').

129 BVerfGE 89, 155, in http://www.bundesverfassungsgericht.de/en/index.html.

130 Ibid.

131 2 BvR 1481/04.

132 See A. Di Martino, *Il Tribunale costituzionale tedesco delimita gli effetti nel diritto interno delle sentenze della Corte Europea dei diritti dell'uomo* available at http://www.associazionedeicostituzionalisti.it/cronache/estero/germania_e_diritti_uomo/index.html. *Görgülü v Germania*, n. 74969/, http://www.echr.coe.int/echr/.

133 Francesco Palermo, 'Il Bundesverfassungsgericht e la teoria selettiva dei controlimiti', (2005) *Quad. cost.*, 1, 181, 188.

134 *Hannover v Germany*, no. 59320/00, http://www.echr.coe.int/echr/.

courts had interpreted the right to privacy in different ways. The German BVG thus exploited this in order to clarify the relationship of strength: the ECHR and the case law of the Strasbourg Court bind the Federal Republic of Germany only as a subject of public international law. The ECHR was then ratified as ordinary law[135] and it can be thus derogated by a future ordinary law and it cannot be used as a standard of constitutional evaluation (it is not possible to claim the violation of a conventional right before the BVG). However the case law of the Strasbourg Court may be recalled as a helpful tool to interpret the constitutional clauses if this does not limit another right constitutionally guaranteed.[136] Moreover, the BVG recalled the open character of the German Constitution (Articles 23 and 24), which obliges national judges to take into account the law and the case law of the ECHR system and to interpret the domestic norms in the light of the ECHR, but only if this operation is possible (with reasons for decision in case of avoidance of consistent interpretation).

However, as the Constitutional Court pointed out, in case of unresolvable conflict between the ECHR and domestic law, the latter should prevail. For the first time in its history, the BVG specified the sensitive areas, the off-limits zone, for the primacy of EU law; the areas of family law, immigration law, and the law on protection of personality.[137] The reasoning of the BVG stressed the particularities of the proceedings before the ECtHR, particularities which might lead to a different outcome in the balancing before the two courts.

More recently the German Constitutional Court enriched its view on the ECHR and on the case law of the ECtHR. We are referring a decision handed down in May 2011[138] whereby the German Constitutional Court held preventive detention unconstitutional. An important role in this decision has been played by the Strasbourg Court's decision[139] which offered the basis for a really open interpretation of the *Grundgesetz*.

However, reverting to *Görgülü*, the most interesting element of this decision is that the BVG made use of the selective approach also used in

---

[135] The German Constitutional Court stressed this point again in *B*, 4 May 2011, no. 2365/09.

[136] BVerfGE 74, 358 (370); BVerfGE 82, 106 (115); BVerfGE 111, 307 (317); BVerfGE 120, 180 (200).

[137] On this see: F. Hoffmeister, 'Germany: Status of European Convention on Human Rights in Domestic Law' (2006) 4 Int'l J Constitutional Law 722.

[138] 2 BvR 2365/09.

[139] *Haidn v Germany*, judgment of 13 January 2011 5th Section, App. no. 6587/04.

the Lisbon judgement[140] with respect to EU law.[141] In the Lisbon judgement the BVG listed some 'areas which shape the citizens' circumstances of life'[142] and that may not be touched by the European integration. The BVG thus contributed significantly to define the meaning of Article 4 EUT, namely elucidating the concept of 'national identity' (already used in Article 6.3 EUT, previous version).

In any case, in this decision the German Constitutional Court did not use the counter-limits although it stressed the necessity of a sort of double check on the European enterprise: one exploited by the Parliament and one by the German Constitutional Court itself. In this respect the Lisbon judgement has been considered as a Euro-sceptical judgment: however, the German Court did not understand the Lisbon judgement as inconsistent with its basic norm; on the contrary, it considered the national legislation[143] strengthening the rights of the German chambers as unconstitutional.[144] The judgment is based on a strong criticism addressed to the German Parliament, the real custodians – together with the other national parliaments – of democracy in the EU context. It was criticised for giving up competences too easily, not exploiting the possibility offered by the Lisbon Treaty and not being aware of its fundamental task.[145] For instance, in paragraph 411 of the judgment the German Constitutional Court recalls: '[The] *Bundestag* and *Bundesrat* must take into account that they must exercise their responsibility for integration in numerous cases of dynamic development of the Treaties.'[146] This is an important case since

140 *BVerfG*, cases 2 BvE 2/08 and others, 30 June 2009, available at: http://www.BVerfG.de/entscheidungen/es20090630_2bve000208.html.

141 On this see: E. Lanza, 'Core of State Sovereignty and Boundaries of European Union's Identity in the Lissabon–Urteil', *German Law Journal*, 11, n. 4, 399–418.

142 *BVerfG*, cases 2 BvE 2/08 *supra*, at Paragraph 249.

143 The object of the case was represented by three distinct statutes: first of all, the Act Approving the Treaty of Lisbon, secondly, the Act Amending the Basic Law (Articles 23, 45 and 93) and finally, the Act Extending and Strengthening the Rights of the German Federal Parliament (*Bundestag*) and the German Federal Council of States (*Bundesrat*) in European Union Matters.

144 Paragraph 406 of the Lisbon judgment: 'The Act Extending and Strengthening the Rights of the Bundestag and the Bundesrat in European Union Matters (Extending Act) infringes Article 38.1 in conjunction with Article 23.1 of the Basic Law insofar as rights of participation of the German Bundestag and the Bundesrat have not been elaborated to the extent required'.

145 Similarly, R. Caponi, 'Democrazia, integrazione europea, circuito delle corti costituzionali (dopo il Lissabon-Urteil)', available at: http://www.astrid-online.it/rassegna/12-04-2010/Caponi_LissabonUrteil_Riv-Dir-Pubbl-Com.pdf.

146 Lisbon Case, BVerfG, 2 BvE 2/08 from 30 June 2009, available at:

it shows the risks inherent in relying on national parliaments to act as the watchdogs of the multilevel system.[147]

As noted above, in the *Lisbon* judgment the German Constitutional Court did not apply the counter-limits and avoided triggering the constitutional conflict with the ECJ. In this respect that case was different from the one in which the German Constitutional Court annulled legislation giving effect to the EU third-pillar framework decision on the European Arrest Warrant, by thus using for the first time the menace already invoked in *Solange I*.[148]

Now, these two judgments can be framed within a broader series of exchanges between the Luxembourg Court and the ECJ in recent years.[149] In order to understand the *Lisbon* judgment, in fact, it is necessary to step back to *Mangold*,[150] which shows, in a sense, the dark side of European constitutionalization.

As we saw in the first chapters, constitutionalization has produced a partial convergence which created a situation where EU law and national constitutional law share the same principle and this of course favours the interpretative competition between constitutional courts and the ECJ in order to gain the interpretative monopoly and the last say on the interpretation of these shared principles (see the *Cordero Alonso*[151] case, for

---

http://www.bundesverfassungsgericht.de/entscheidungen/es20090630_2bve000208.html.

147 I. Cooper, 'The Watchdogs of Subsidiarity: National Parliaments and the Logic of Arguing in the EU', (2006) 44 J Common Market Studies 281.

148 That was a real application of the counter-limits doctrine: 'According to the Court, the Act encroaches upon the freedom from extradition (Article 16.2 of the Basic Law (Grundgesetz)) in a disproportionate manner because the legislature has not exhausted the margins afforded to it by the Framework Decision on the European arrest warrant in such a way that the implementation of the Framework Decision for incorporation into national law shows the highest possible consideration in respect of the fundamental right concerned. Moreover, the European Arrest Warrant Act infringes the guarantee of recourse to a court (Article 19.4 of the Basic Law) because there is no possibility of challenging the judicial decision that grants extradition. Hence, the extradition of a German citizen is not possible as long as the legislature does not adopt a new Act implementing Article 16.2 sentence 2 of the Basic Law. As a result, the constitutional complaint lodged by the complainant, who is supposed to be extradited to Spain for criminal prosecution on the basis of a European arrest warrant (Press release no. 20/2005 of 24 February 2005), was successful. The order of the Higher Regional Court (Oberlandesgericht) and the judicial authority's decision that grants extradition were reversed.'

149 More recently the BVG insisted on this tone in cases like BVerfG, 2 BvC 4/10 and BVerfG, 2 BvE 8/11, both available at: http://www.bundesverfassungsgericht.de/.

150 C-144/04, *Mangold* [2005] ECR I-9981.

151 C-81/05, *Cordero Alonso* [2006] ECR I-7569.

instance). This 'partial' appropriation of the fundamental rights discourse by the ECJ emerges in a long series of judgments, and it is most evident in cases such as *Omega*[152] and *Dynamic Medien*[153] (see infra in Part II of this book). As some authors have pointed out, examining those cases one can perceive a certain concern over the '*octroyée* methodology of construing common constitutional traditions'.[154] Now, such a methodology has its own risks, as shown in the *Mangold* case:[155] in fact, some German scholars strongly contest the possibility of inferring such a principle from the constitutional traditions common to the Member States.[156]

More generally the German Constitutional Court has not given up its counter-power mission, as ambivalent decisions like *Honeywell*[157] demonstrate. On the one hand, in that decision, the German Court acknowledged the possibility of margin of error to the ECJ but, at the same time, it has not renounced its role of counter-power to the Luxembourg Court in the process of European integration, even in extraordinary circumstances, and perhaps only after having 'consulted' the ECJ.[158]

---

152 C-36/02, *Omega* [2004] ECR I-9609.

153 C-244/06, *Dynamic Medien*, [2008] ECR I-505.

154 M. Dani, 'Tracking Judicial Dialogue – The Scope for Preliminary Rulings from the Italian Constitutional Court', Jean Monnet Working Paper, 10/2008.

155 'Directive 2000/78 does not itself lay down the principle of equal treatment in the field of employment and occupation. Indeed, in accordance with Article 1 thereof, the sole purpose of the directive is "to lay down a general framework for combating discrimination on the grounds of religion or belief, disability, age or sexual orientation", the source of the actual principle underlying the prohibition of those forms of discrimination being found, as is clear from the third and fourth recitals in the preamble to the directive, in various international instruments and in the constitutional traditions common to the Member States . . . The principle of non-discrimination on grounds of age must thus be regarded as a general principle of Community law.' *Mangold, supra*.

156 For instance, in an Article published in English on the 'EU Observer' website, Herzog and Gerken stressed: 'However, this "general principle of community law" was a fabrication. In only two of the then 25 member states, namely Finland and Portugal, is there any reference to a ban on age discrimination, and in not one international treaty is there any mention at all of there being such a ban, contrary to the terse allegation of the ECJ. Consequently, it is not difficult to see why the ECJ dispensed with any degree of specification or any proof of its allegation. To put it bluntly, with this construction which the ECJ more or less pulled out of a hat, they were acting not as part of the judicial power but as the legislature', R. Herzog and L. Gerken, '[Comment] Stop the European Court of Justice', http://euobserver.com/9/26714, a translated version of 'Stoppt den Europäischen Gerichtshof' *Frankfurter Allgemeine Zeitung*, 8 September 2008.

157 Case 2 BvR 2261/06, Decision of 26 August 2010.

158 'An *ultra vires*-control of European acts by the German Constitutional Court would only occur in extraordinary circumstances and obvious cases, and

As for the preliminary ruling mechanism, the German Constitutional Court has never referred a question for a preliminary ruling. Although in *Solange I*[159] the German Constitutional Court accepted it was in principle bound by Article 234 ECT (now Article 267 TFEU), it is interesting to notice that, in practice, as Mayer points out, the German constitutional judges have never referred a question.[160] Indeed, in order to solve a question of interpretation of EU law in the proceedings that culminated in the 1993 *Maastricht* decision,[161] the German Constitutional Court decided to hear the testimony of the Director General of the European Commission Legal Service. This was done precisely to avoid raising a preliminary reference to the ECJ. Recently the preliminary ruling mechanism has also created a situation of tension between the German and the EU legal orders in the *Winner Wetten* case.[162]

The *Winner Wetten* case originated from a preliminary reference raised by a German court. In 2006 the German Constitutional Court acknowledged that the legislation on the public monopoly on gambling on sporting competitions that was in force in two *Länder* violated Article 12(1) of the *Grundgesetz*. At the same time, it decided not to declare the legislation in question unconstitutional and to maintain it in effect until 31 December 2007, sending a sort of 'message' to the legislature to push it to intervene by that date through the use of its discretionary power to amend the legislation, and thereby save it from being in breach of the *Grundgesetz*.

Despite this judgment, the ECJ decided to push the referring judge to disapply the legal provision that had been 'saved', for a transitional period, by the German Constitutional Court, and concluded that: 'By reason of the primacy of directly-applicable Union law, national legislation concerning a public monopoly on bets on sporting competitions which, according to the findings of a national court, comprises restrictions that are incompatible with the freedom of establishment and the freedom to provide services, because those restrictions do not contribute to limiting betting

---

apparently a preliminary reference to the ECJ would have to take place first'. F. Mayer, 'Rashomon in Karlsruhe – A Reflection on Democracy and Identity in the European Union', Jean Monnet Working Paper, 5/10, available at http://centers.law.nyu.edu/jeanmonnet/papers/10/100501.pdf.

159 BVerfGE 37, S. 271 ff.

160 F. Mayer, 'The European Constitution and the Courts' in A. von Bogdandy and J. Bast (eds), *Principles of European Constitutional Law* (Hart 2006) 281, 287.

161 BVerfGE 89, 155, available at www.bundesverfassungsgericht.de/en/index.html.

162 C-409/06, *Winner Wetten*, available at www.curia.europa.eu.

activities in a consistent and systematic manner, cannot continue to apply during a transitional period.'[163]

This is just one of the many tensions existing between the German and the ECJ, of which the high point is represented by the *Kreil* case,[164] where the ECJ, de facto, affirmed the prevalence of EU law over a national constitutional provision when it held that a general exclusion of women from military posts involving the use of arms (as provided for in Article 12a.4 of the *Grundgesetz*) was in conflict with the content of the Equal Treatment Directive (76/207). Subsequently, the *Grundgesetz* was amended.[165]

However, all these tensions should not lead us to conclude that the German Constitutional Court has a historically hostile attitude towards the ECJ since it has also acknowledged the importance of the ECJ and of the preliminary ruling mechanism, being willing to scrutinize the refusal by common judges to refer preliminary questions as a potential breach of the right to the lawful judge.[166]

Greece

Recently scholars have described the Greek example as a context where 'in spite of the conditions set by a Constitution seeking to retain its primacy, the national judge has no choice but to align her/his practice with the case law of her/his supranational colleague. De facto, supranationalism dominates the municipal order entirely'.[167]

Greek courts tend to apply EU law and to follow the ECJ's case law[168] while there are some cases of non-application of EU law, or tensions created by imperfect knowledge of or lack of familiarity with EU law.[169] Some cases of collisions between the two legal orders in any case exist and in these circumstances EU law has de facto always prevailed: for instance,

---

163 C-409/06, *Winner Wetten*, available at www.curia.europa.eu.

164 C-285/98, *Kreil* [2000] ECR I-69.

165 Article 12a 4: 'If, during a state of defence, the need for civilian services in the civilian health system or in stationary military hospitals cannot be met on a voluntary basis, women between the age of eighteen and fifty-five may be called upon to render such services by or pursuant to a law. Under no circumstances may they be required to render service involving the use of arms.'

166 BVerfGE 82, 159 (195).

167 V. Tzevelekos and S. Vetsika, 'Report on Greece' in Martinico and Pollicino (eds), *The National Judicial Treatment of the ECHR and EU Laws*, 244.

168 See, for instance, StE (4th chamber), 2144/2009, 29-06-2009. The cases reported in this section have been taken from Tzevelekos and Vetsika, 'Report on Greece'.

169 Tzevelekos and Vetsika, 'Report on Greece', 232.

a special law[170] was passed in order to avoid conflict between the Greek Constitution[171] and the ECJ case law[172] on public services.

Another example of the constitutional impact of the ECJ case law on the Greek system is the *Michaniki* case.[173] This case originated from a constitutional reform of 2001, whereby Article 14 of the Greek Constitution was amended. After this reform, Article 14, paragraph 9[174] – in order to promote transparency in the public works sector – provided for a sort of irrebuttable presumption of general incompatibility between the sector of the media and that of public contracts. On the basis of this provision, a company, Michaniki AE, failed to win the contract at the end of the tendering procedure and brought an action before the Greek Council of State, which referred a preliminary question to the ECJ concerning the interpretation of Directive 93/37/EC on public works contracts. The ECJ concluded that 'Community law must be interpreted as precluding a national provision which, whilst pursuing the legitimate objectives of

[170] Article 1 of Law 2431/1996 (FEK 175/A, 19-07-1996) reproduces *verbatim* the ECJ definition of public service.

[171] Article 4 of the Greek Constitution reading: 'only Greek citizens shall be eligible for public service, except as otherwise provided by special laws'. Article 4 is also considered as part of the Greek untouchable core under Article 110, p. 1. Tzevelekos and Vetsika, 'Report on Greece', 232.

[172] For instance, cases like: ECJ, C-290/94, *Commission of the European Communities v Hellenic Republic* [1996] ECR I-3285.

[173] ECJ, *Michaniki AE v Ethniko Simvoulio Radiotileorasis and Ipourgos Epikratias* [2008] ECR I-9999.

[174] Article 14, p. 9: 'The ownership, financial standing and means of financing of the media must be disclosed, as stipulated by law.

The measures and restrictions necessary to ensure full media transparency and pluralism shall be specified by law.

It is prohibited to concentrate control of several media of the same or different form.

In particular, it is prohibited to concentrate control of more than one electronic medium of the same form, as specified by law.

The status of owner, partner, main shareholder or management executive of a media undertaking shall be incompatible with the status of owner, partner, main shareholder or management executive of an undertaking which undertakes with the State or a legal person in the public sector in the broad sense to perform works or provide supplies or services.

The prohibition in the previous subparagraph shall also extend to any form of intermediary, such as spouses, relatives or financially dependent persons or companies.

A law shall set out the specific regulations, the sanctions (which may go as far as revocation of a radio or television station's licence and an order prohibiting the signature of, or cancelling, the contract in question), the system of supervision and the guarantees to prevent circumvention of the foregoing subparagraphs.'

equal treatment of tenderers and of transparency in procedures for the award of public contracts, establishes an irrebuttable presumption that the status of owner, partner, main shareholder or management executive of an undertaking active in the media sector is incompatible with that of owner, partner, main shareholder or management executive of an undertaking which contracts with the State or a legal person in the public sector in the broad sense to perform a works, supply or services contract'.

It also said that the directive does not forbid per se a Member State from providing other exclusionary measures in order to ensure transparency and equal treatment of the tenderers if these measures are consistent with the principle of proportionality.

The history of the relationship between Greek law and the ECHR has been characterized by an intermittent nature, as scholars have pointed out.[175] In any case now the situation shows a frequent use of the Convention, which is seen as a document whose provisions are by nature complementary to the Constitution, and this implies that judges have read national provisions in connection with parts of the Convention[176] or in light of the Convention. Tensions between the ECHR system and the Greek one have not been lacking[177] but the domestic judiciary has had but a minor role in these.[178]

---

[175] 'Greece signed the Convention in 1950 and first introduced it into the domestic order in 1953. However, its effectiveness remained limited for several decades, if not nilpotent. The dictatorship of 1967 derogated from the ECHR on the basis of the clause of Article 15. The famous Greek case allowed the ECtHR to deliver a report on the merits, whereby it rejected the grounds for derogating from the ECHR and found several systematic breaches of the most fundamental human rights. The colonels' regime reacted by denouncing the ECHR and quitting the Council of Europe. Greece did not return to Strasbourg and to the ECHR regime until 1974, when democracy was restored. Although the GC of 1975 granted a supra-legislative (but not supra-constitutional) force to the ECHR, until the early 1990s its effectiveness (in spite of its self-executing nature) was limited. A new era commenced in 1985 when the government recognised the competence of the ECtHR to examine individual applications.' Tzevelekos and Vetsika, 'Report on Greece', 237.

[176] See the examples given by Tzevelekos and Vetsika, 'Report on Greece', 238 ff.

[177] For instance, ECtHR, *Tsalkitzis v Greece*, 16 November 2006; *Syngelidis v Greece*, 11 February 2010; ECtHR, *Kokkinakis v Greece*, merits, 25 May 1993; ECtHR, *Lykourezos v Greece*, merits, 15 June 2006.

[178] 'While scholars suggest that conflicts between the GC and the ECHR do exist, so far the case law of the ECtHR has dealt with only a marginal number of cases of that kind. Interestingly, not all of these cases concerned the practice of the judiciary', Tzevelekos and Vetsika, 'Report on Greece', 240.

Hungary

The analysis of the Hungarian case shows how the courts there are 'rather friendly towards international treaties and this naturally applies to the European Convention of Human Rights as well'.[179] However, despite such a positive attitude, the Constitutional Court has never accepted the ECHR as a source having constitutional status.

From a formal point of view, as we saw in the previous chapter, the Hungarian Constitutional Court is empowered to review national acts in light of international treaties, but the respective sources governing the procedure permit just a few actors – not the courts – to initiate such procedure.[180] Not even the power of the judges to suspend proceedings raising a question of constitutionality to the Constitutional Court can be relied upon for inferring the constitutional status of the ECHR, since Section 38 of the Constitutional Court Act does not offer such a possibility as for international treaties.[181] The only thing common judges can do in order to ensure the prevalence of the ECHR over national law is represented by the consistent interpretation of national law with the Convention (this duty of consistent interpretation has been conceived as part of the constitutional mandate of the judges).[182]

If a basic right codified in the Hungarian Constitution reflects a provision of the ECHR, the ECHR can be taken into account by the Constitutional Court, but generally speaking the Hungarian Court has never gone so far as to infer binding constitutional standards from the Convention. Only once has the Court found that the understanding of the freedom of expression of the ECHR is 'forming and binding the Hungarian jurisprudence', yet this statement had no consequences in later

---

179 P. Sonnevend, 'Report on Hungary', in Martinico and Pollicino (eds), *The National Judicial Treatment of the ECHR and EU Laws*, 258.

180 As Sonnevend (ibid. 259) points out: 'According to Section 21 (3) Constitutional Court Act, review on the basis of Section 1 c) of the Act can be petitioned by:

(a) the Parliament, its standing committees or any MP,
(b) the President of the Republic,
(c) the Government or its members,
(d) the President of the State Audit Office,
(e) the President of the Supreme Court,
(f) the Chief Prosecutor'.

181 Ibid.

182 See decisions 53/1993. (X. 13.) Ab, ABH 1993, 323, 327; 4/1997. (I. 22.) AB, ABH 1997, 41, 51. The decisions reported in this section have been taken from Sonnevend, 'Report on Hungary'.

decisions.[183] The Constitutional Court takes into account the case law of the ECtHR in its jurisprudence but this does not lead to the recognition of a sort of *erga omnes* or binding effect for the judgment of the Court of Strasbourg.[184]

Sometimes the Constitutional Court has seemed to accept the possibility of controlling Hungarian laws implementing EU law[185] but the issue is still disputed. Courts have in general accepted the principle of the primacy of EU law as a concept stemming from the EU law system, however, since the Constitution does not provide for the primacy of EU law, the respect of this principle is not the business of the Constitutional Court.[186]

Generally speaking, EU law is considered to be different from international law[187] and this implies the impossibility to infer from the Constitutional Court's power of review of conformity of Hungarian legislation with international treaties, an analogous power with regard to EU law.[188]

Italy

The Constitutional Court originally established the basis for accepting EU law as a supranational law with primacy and direct effect in Article 11 of the Italian Constitution. This acceptance, however, did not come about immediately. On the contrary, it was the result of a long series of judgments. One of the reasons for this can be attributed to the absence of an explicit European clause in the Italian Constitution. As a matter of fact, Article 11 was originally conceived to deal with Italian membership of organizations like the United Nations rather than to justify the consequence of supranationalism (a phenomenon that was unknown when the Italian Constitution came into force). This changed in 2001 with the constitutional reform of Title V of the second part of the Italian fundamental charter with the introduction of Article 117, paragraph 1.

---

183 Sonnevend, 'Report on Hungary', 259–60. See the decisions 18/2004. AB, ABH 2004, 303, 306, mentioned ibid.

184 'It occurs that the Court did not want to tie its hands for the future, even if it was ready to follow the path of interpretation drawn by the European Court of Human Rights', ibid, 260.

185 See the decisions 17/2004. (V.25) AB, ABH 2004, 291 ff. This decision can be traced back to the 'Sugar saga'. On this see: A. Albi, 'From the Banana Saga to a Sugar Saga and Beyond: Could the Post-Communist Constitutional Courts Teach the EU a Lesson in the Rule of Law?' (2010) CML Rev, 791.

186 Sonnevend, 'Report on Hungary', 261–62.

187 Decision 72/2006.

188 See decisions 72/2006. (XII. 15.) AB, ABH 2006, 819, 861, reinforced by 946/C/2005 AB, ABH 2007, 2744, 2746.

Another feature of the approach of the Italian Constitutional Court to EU law is given by the counter-limits doctrine, devised by the *Consulta* in 1973 soon after the well-known judgment of the ECJ in *Internationale Handesgeselschaft*.[189] In this judgment, the ECJ pointed out the primacy of EU law over the national law, including the national constitutional principles.[190] In this respect the Italian position – along with the German one – is relevant for a complete understanding of the reasons for the 'resistance'. Constitutional courts have claimed to maintain their own role (the role of the guardians of the national constitutional identity) without exceptions. They have denied the acceptance of dangerous monist visions in order to preserve the constitutional identity of their legal orders. On the contrary, they have raised some ultimate barriers against the penetration of EU law in order to define the fundamental principles of the legal orders of which they are the guardians. Hypothetically, if an EU provision conflicted with the fundamental principles of the national legal order, the constitutional court could strike down the national statute executing the EC Treaty, thus causing a 'rupture' between the national and supranational legal orders. Constitutional courts in fact normally have jurisdiction over national legislation (including the legal source of execution of treaties) but not over the EC provisions: the latter are beyond their jurisdiction because, in their argumentation, they belong to another legal order.

Starting from this approach, one can understand why the constitutional courts have refused the possibility of striking down EU law provisions, since the acceptance of this option would have implied adhesion to the monist theory of the ECJ. It is by a legal fiction that it is possible to defend the hard core of constitutional legal orders by preserving the formal autonomy of the national and supranational orders and the jurisdiction of the ECJ. The identification of these barriers to European integration represents the essence of the counter-limits doctrine (*dottrina dei controlimiti*), devised by the Italian Constitutional Court in case 183/73, the *Frontini* judgment[191] (but see also case 170/84, the *Granital* judgment[192]).

---

[189] ECJ Case 11/70 *Internationale Handesgeselschaft* [1970] ECR 1125.

[190] 'Therefore the validity of a Community measure or its effect within a Member State cannot be affected by allegations that it runs counter to either fundamental rights as formulated by the constitution of that State or the principles of its constitutional structure'.

[191] Corte Costituzionale, sentenza 183/1973, *Frontini*: [1974] 2 CMLR 372.

[192] Corte Costituzionale, sentenza 180/1974, *Granital*: [1984] CMLR 756: '*nella sent. n. 183 del 27 dicembre 1973, già avvertito come la legge di esecuzione del Trattato possa andar soggetta al suo sindacato, in riferimento ai principi fondamentali del nostro ordinamento costituzionale e ai diritti inalienabili della persona*

The consequence of a possible declaration of invalidity could spell Italy's withdrawal from the EU: according to Cartabia,[193] in these two cases in fact the counter-limits test was conceived as a way to carry out an exceptional control on the respect of the conditions of constitutionality of the Italian adhesion to the EC.

Following this reconstruction, the counter-limits worked as conditions for evaluating the legitimacy of the limitations of sovereignty accepted by the Italian adhesion to the European venture. Later on (with the decision no. 232/1989, the *Fragd* judgment[194]), the nature of the counter-limits doctrine changed, transforming itself from an exceptional control into a 'simple' control of compatibility of the EU law with the Constitution which could not threaten Italy's membership of the EU.

Because of the 'transformation' of this doctrine, the counter-limits have worked as a limitation to European primacy: that is why, according to the same scholarship, from the *Fragd* judgment, the Italian Constitutional Court has implicitly admitted that the possible conflict with the Constitution would not cause invalidity of the statute of execution of the EC Treaty, but just the non-applicability of the EC rule.[195]

The preliminary ruling mechanism illustrates the imperfect coincidence between the position of the Italian Constitutional Court and the ECJ. The refusal by the constitutional courts to conceive of themselves as judges under Article 234 of the EC Treaty (now Article 267 TFUE) is well known, and the Italian *Consulta* was one of the pioneers in this respect. On 15 April 2008, for the first time in its history, the Italian Constitutional Court agreed to refer a preliminary question to the ECJ.[196]

The Italian Constitutional Court limited its referral decision to direct proceedings, stressing the different structure characterizing the indirect form of constitutional review of legislation. The distinction made by the Court in this case seems to be in accordance with its previous case law. One should not overestimate the value of this revirement: the Court was careful to prevent the revolutionary component of the decision from spreading and causing unexpected consequences. This distinction also seems to be very coherent with the previous case law of the Constitutional Court. Do

umana'. On this, see M. Cartabia, *Principi inviolabili e integrazione europea* (Giuffrè 1995).

193 Cartabia, *Principi inviolabili*, 110.

194 *Corte Costituzionale*, sentenza 232/1989, in www.cortecostituzionale.it. In English: *Fragd* (1990) 27 CML Rev 93.

195 See Marta Cartabia and J.H.H. Weiler Weiler, *L'Italia in Europa* (Bologna 2000), 171–72.

196 ICC, *ordinanza* No. 103/2008, available at www.cortecostituzionale.it.

not think the Italian Constitutional Court will give up this distinction easily, by extending, for instance, the acceptance of the preliminary ruling to *incidenter* proceedings: in the logic of interpretive competition, such an extension could lead to the loss of control over the national common judges, fundamental actors for the activity of the Italian Constitutional Court.

Another factor that should be taken into account is the self-exclusion of the Italian *Consulta* from the preliminary mechanism, which did not produce the automatic denial of any form of dialogue with the ECJ. On the contrary, over the years, the Italian Court has devised some alternative modes of dialogue with the Luxembourg Court in order to combine respect for EU obligations with the preservation of the constitutional core.[197] Our impression is that in the near future the Italian

---

[197] See G. Martinico and F. Fontanelli, 'The Hidden Dialogue: When Judicial Competitors Collaborate' (2008) *Global Jurist* 8.3, available at http://www.bepress.com/gj/vol8/iss3/art7. By the formula 'hidden dialogue' we mean that unexplored side of the relationship between Constitutional Courts and the ECJ which is nourished by the somewhat non-orthodox ways of judicial communication (that is, ways of judicial communication that are different from the preliminary ruling and are not formalized according to the letter of the Treaties i.e. Article 267 TFEU). From the domestic courts' perspective there are two ways of cooperating with the ECJ: the former represents the 'official' route provided by Article 234 ECT (although entirely 'governed' by the interpretative competitor: the ECJ), the latter is the parallel and informal route whose dynamics are mostly discretionary (so that both the procedures and the outcome of such a cooperation can be negotiated). The second way is the one historically preferred by the constitutional courts, which have traditionally opted for levelling the playing field, thus avoiding the preliminary ruling (being the ECJ's domain), which would have implied the loss of interpretative sovereignty, given the fact that the game within the preliminary ruling's field is governed by the Treaties, the fundamental charters of the competitor (i.e. the ECJ). As we know both the Constitutional Courts and the ECJ conceive of their own documents (respectively the national Constitutions and the Treaties) as the highest law and claim the ultimate authority in the interpretation of the legal materials in the multilevel legal system. This context was described as interpretative competition (K. Alter, 'Explaining National Court Acceptance of European Court Jurisprudence: A Critical Evaluation of Theories of Legal Integration', in A. Slaughter, A. Stone Sweet and J.H.H. Weiler (eds) *The European Court and National Courts – Doctrine and Jurisprudence. Legal Change in its Social Context* (Hart 1997)), and it represents the judicial and dynamic side of the struggle for sovereignty. Schematically, we have identified the following techniques of hidden dialogue:

(a) introduction of a new step in the hierarchy of legal sources;
(b) distinction between 'primacy' and 'supremacy';
(c) admissibility of *recurso de amparo* against the domestic judges' refusal to raise the preliminary ruling;

Constitutional Court will rely on this kind of alternative mode of dialogue in the field of indirect proceeding, especially in the dual preliminarity mechanism.[198]

According to the technique of dual preliminarity (*doppia pregiudizialità*), the Constitutional Court could be asked to solve a question of constitutionality regarding an Italian norm in cases where such a question is strongly related to another preliminary ruling question contemporarily raised before the ECJ (either by the same or by another common judge) on the meaning or validity of an EC act. Should these two questions be strongly related, the Italian Constitutional Court can decide either to return the question (declaring it 'inadmissible') to the common judge (decision no. 536/1995) or to 'wait for' the ECJ to pronounce itself before determining it (decision no. 165/2004). This way the Constitutional Court acknowledges an interpretive priority to the questions pending before the ECJ and de facto suspends its own trial by reaching an effect that is equivalent to that requested by Article 267 TFUE (i.e. the stay of trial) without using the preliminary ruling mechanism.

As we can see, dual preliminarity is a technique by which the Italian Constitutional Court acknowledges 'priority' to the ECJ and to Article 234 ECT (now 267 TFEU) questions; at the same time, it can work as a 'safety valve', since it avoids a conflict with the ECJ with regard to the possible violation of counter-limits. In the *Berlusconi* case (decision no. 165/2004), for example, the Italian Constitutional Court waited for the ECJ's answer, preparing itself for a decision that could possibly be incompatible with its fundamental principles. Using dual preliminarity, the Italian Court allows the ECJ to decide whether to challenge the risk of a jurisdictional 'clash' or not. On the other hand, perhaps one can read the *Berlusconi* case as an attempt to avoid such a danger and as a chance to show the maturity of the EC system about fundamental rights. This technique is based upon a judicial triangle and obviously this can only happen in the framework of *incidenter* proceedings. Thanks to dual preliminarity,

---

(d) acknowledgement of *erga omnes* effects for the ECJ's interpretive rulings;
(e) dual preliminarity (*doppia pregiudizialità*);
(f) distinction between disapplication and non-application.

198 On dual preliminarity see: M. Cartabia, 'Il processo costituzionale: l'iniziativa. Considerazioni sulla posizione del giudice comune di fronte a casi di "doppia pregiudizialità", comunitaria e costituzionale', (1997) 5 *Il Foro italiano* 222. For a very similar point of view about dual preliminarity, see M. Cartabia, 'Taking Dialogue Seriously'. The Renewed Need for a Judicial Dialogue at the Time of Constitutional Activism in the European Union', Jean Monnet Working paper, 12/07, 2007, http://www.jeanmonnetprogram.org/papers/07/071201.html.

the Italian Constitutional Court can maintain control over the national common judges and, at the same time, a symmetrical dialogue with the ECJ.

As for the ECHR, in two fundamental decisions given in 2007 the Italian Constitutional Court[199] clarified the position of the ECHR in the domestic legal system. Without going into details,[200] the main contents of these two decisions can be summarized as follows:

1. The ECHR has a super-primary value;
2. In some cases, the ECHR can stand as 'interposed parameter' for assessing the validity of primary laws, since the conflict between them and the ECHR can result in an indirect violation of the Constitution;
3. This does not imply that the ECHR has a constitutional value; on the contrary, the ECHR has to respect the Constitution;
4. The ECHR cannot be compared to the EU law, as we will see below;
5. The constitutional favour accorded to the ECHR implies the necessity to interpret national law in light of the provisions of the ECHR.[201]

In order to understand the reasoning and the final outcome of the two decisions noted here, it is important to set them in the context of previous case law in the light of the meaning attributed by Italian constitutional scholars and by the Constitutional Court to the relevant constitutional provisions. In its case law, the Constitutional Court has not shown any great enthusiasm towards these attempts to give special constitutional protection to the ECHR. In relation to Article 10 of the Constitution, the Constitutional Court has specified that the privileged constitutional status enjoyed by the tenets of international law as generally recognized rules cannot extend to international obligations – as is the case of the ECHR – undertaken by the state under an international treaty.[202]

Regarding Article 11, the Constitutional Court, treating the issue as if it

---

199 Corte Costituzionale, judgments nos. 348 and 349/2007, available at www.cortecostituzionale.it.

200 For a detailed analysis of the judgments, see: F. Biondi Dal Monte and F. Fontanelli, 'The Decisions No. 348 and 349/2007 of the Italian Constitutional Court: The Efficacy of the European Convention in the Italian Legal System' (2008) German L J, 889; O. Pollicino, 'The Italian Constitutional Court at the Crossroads between Constitutional Parochialism and Co-operative Constitutionalism. Judgments Nos. 348 and 349 of 22 and 24 October 2007', 2008 363.

201 The next two pages have been taken from O. Pollicino, 'The Italian Constitutional Court' cit, 363 ff.

202 Corte Costituzionale, judgments No. 48/1979, No. 32/1960, No. 104/1969, No. 14/1964, No. 323/1989.

were beyond dispute,[203] affirmed that no international treaty – irrespective of its subject area – can entail any limitation on sovereignty under the terms provided by Article 11 of the Constitution. In relation to interpreting Article 2 of the Constitution as an open clause suitable to give constitutional protection to new fundamental rights, the Constitutional Court did not assess the issue with specific reference to the ECHR. In more general terms, it clarified that the guarantee provided by Article 2 is intended to refer only to the rights expressly enunciated in the Constitution and to those directly connected to them.[204]

By rejecting any attempt to find a constitutional basis for the ECHR, the Constitutional Court has substantially confirmed the dualistic matrix of the Italian legal system. In particular, it has argued that the ECHR, as well as all ratified international treaties, have the same position in the hierarchy of Italian sources of law as mandated by the national statute through which they have been assigned in the internal legal order.[205]

Given the fact that the ECHR, like other international treaties, has been implemented via an ordinary statute,[206] the Constitutional Court, apart from an isolated decision,[207] has attributed to the ECHR the legal value proper to an ordinary statutory law prior to delivering the judgments analyzed here. To put it simply, according to this jurisprudential orientation, the ECHR could be abrogated by any successive statutory law that conflicts with it. The abrogative effect, in the absence of any constitutional protection for the ECHR, would result in the rule of *lex posterior derogat legi priori* being applied in order to solve the conflict between two statutes placed in the same position on the scale of sources of law.

At the end of the 1990s, the Constitutional Court, without changing its opinion on the place occupied by the ECHR in the hierarchy of Italian sources of law, began looking at the relationship between the Italian constitutional legal system and the ECHR in a different and complementary way. In particular, in decision no. 388/1999 the Court seems to have drawn a distinction, in relation to the sources of international law, between the

---

203 Corte Costituzionale, judgment No. 188/1980.

204 Corte Costituzionale, judgment No. 98/1979.

205 Corte Costituzionale, sentenze n. 188/1980, n. 153/1987, n. 323/1989 and n. 315/1990, available at www.cortecostituzionale.it.

206 Law 4-8-1955 n. 848.

207 Decision no. 10/1993, in which, in relation to the ECHR and its ratification by ordinary law, the Constitutional Court speaks in terms of an 'atypical source of law'. This special status enjoyed by the ECHR, according to this judgment, would place it in a higher position in the hierarchy of sources of law with respect to the ordinary legal order.

content, the material area on which the international treaty is concluded, and its container, the ordinary statute which transforms the international source into a national law. In this regard, it is argued by the Constitutional Court that in cases where the content is characterized by the aim to protect human rights, those rights should enjoy a constitutional guarantee independent of the position of the bearer of these rights. In other words, starting with this decision, the Constitutional Court began to appear more interested in looking not only from a formal(istic) point of view at the static position of the ECHR in the hierarchy of the sources of law, but also from a substantial and axiological point of view, and due to its fundamental rights-based content, at its suitability to complement the recognition of inviolable fundamental rights protected by Article 2 of the Constitution.[208]

The constitutional scenario described above has been integrated by the adoption of the new Article 117, paragraph 1, in 2001, as we saw in the previous chapter. As the literature has already stressed,[209] the Italian common (*comuni*) judges started disapplying domestic norms conflicting with the ECHR.[210] In 2007, the Italian Constitutional Court decided to tackle this practice, which represented an extension of an important 'constitutional exception' to the constitutional supremacy and a derogation from the regime of centralized control of constitutionality. Moreover, in order to challenge such a trend by ensuring, at the same time, the super-primary nature of the ECHR, the Italian Constitutional Court agreed, for the first time in its history, to assess the validity of national provisions using the ECHR as the standard. Thus the Court extended the doctrine of the 'interposed norm' ('*norma interposta*').[211] The message sent by the

---

208 D. Tega, 'La Cedu e l'ordinamento italiano', in M. Cartabia (ed.), *I diritti in azione* (Il Mulino 2007), 67.

209 Biondi Dal Monte and Fontanelli, 'The Decisions No. 348 and 349/2007'; Pollicino, 'The Italian Constitutional Court'.

210 See: Court of Pistoia on 23 March 2007: Court of Genoa, decision of 23 November, 2000; Court of Appeal of Florence decisions No. 570 of 2005 and No. 1403 of 2006, and the State Council (*Consiglio di Stato*), I Section, decision No. 1926 of 2002: 'Some judges had already started applying this method, which comes from the judicial practice of disapplying the internal statutory norm conflicting with Community law. In some recent occasions, even the Supreme Court of Cassation (*Corte di Cassazione*) and the Supreme Administrative Court (*Consiglio di Stato*) had endorsed the use of disapplication in cases of conflict with ECvHR law', Biondi Dal Monte and Fontanelli, 'The Decisions No. 348 and 349/2007', 891.

211 'Scholars have minted the wording "interposed provision" to individualize the cases in which a constitutional standard can be invoked only indirectly in a constitutional judicial proceeding, because different primary provisions are inserted between the constitutional standard and the reported provisions (suspected of

Constitutional Court to the common judges was: 'Don't disapply, rather refer the preliminary question of constitutionality to the Constitutional Court!'

The reasoning of the Italian Constitutional Court was based on the distinction between the ECHR and EU law.[212] This explains the different treatment reserved for the ECHR, as regards the practice disapplication and the necessity that the Convention be consistent with the whole Constitution, not just with the counter-limits (i.e. those fundamental principles forming an untouchable constitutional core).

Quite surprisingly, after the intervention of the Constitutional Court, some ordinary judges kept disapplying national provisions conflicting with the ECHR,[213] for various reasons:

1. Sometimes the judges seemed not to understand the Constitutional Court's diktat, or know the difference between the ECHR and EU law.[214]
2. In other cases, the judges duly recalled the *Corte Costituzionale*'s instructions, yet misunderstood the meaning of the new (post-Lisbon) Article 6 TEU, which paves the way for EU's accession to the ECHR. In other words, they thought that the ECHR has (already) become part of EU law *ipso iure*, after the coming into force of the Lisbon Treaty and, therefore, has now direct effect and primacy. This is perhaps the case of a judgment *Consiglio di Stato* (Supreme Court of Administrative Law), dated March 2010.[215]

---

being unconstitutional)'. Biondi Dal Monte and Fontanelli, 'The Decisions No. 348 and 349/2007', 897. See: C. Lavagna, *Problemi di giustizia costituzionale sotto il profilo della 'manifesta infondatezza'* (Milan 1957), 28; M. Siclari, 'Le norme interposte nel giudizio di costituzionalità', 1992

212 'This is because, according to the constitutional judges, the ECHR legal system has distinct structural and functional legal features as compared to the European legal order. According to the Italian Constitutional Court, the EHCR is a multilateral international public law Treaty which does not entail and cannot entail any limitation on sovereignty in the terms provided by Article 11 of the Constitution', Pollicino, 'The Italian Constitutional Court'.

213 Carlotto, 'I giudici comuni e gli obblighi internazionali dopo le sentenze n. 348 e n. 349 del 2007 della Corte costituzionale: un'analisi sul seguito giurisprudenziale', in www.associazionedeicostituzionalisti.it. E. Lamarque, 'Il vincolo alle leggi statali e regionali derivante dagli obblighi internazionali nella giurisprudenza comune', in www.associazionedeicostituzionalisti.it (2010).

214 Tribunale di Livorno, Sez. Lav., ordinanza del 28 ottobre 2008. See I. Carlotto, 'I giudici comuni' *supra*.

215 Consiglio di Stato, sent. 2 marzo 2010, n. 1220. On this decision see: Colavitti and Pagotto, 'Il Consiglio di Stato applica direttamente le norme CEDU

3. Finally, there are cases of open civil disobedience of common judges who demonstrate that they know, but will not follow, the instructions of the Constitutional Court.[216]

It is possible to see in the Italian case as a demonstration that a problem of application of 'external' law in the multilevel legal system might result in an 'internal' judicial conflict (Constitutional Court versus ordinary judges).[217]

More recently[218] the Italian Constitutional Court confirmed the interpretative favour to be acknowledged to the case law of the ECtHR and indeed the important role of the Strasbourg Court in this context seems to contribute to the special nature of the ECHR itself, which has been conceived as a supra-legislative instrument for the closeness between the wording of its provisions and the language of the Constitution.

Another symptom of the importance of the case law of the ECtHR in the national legal system is the recent judgment no. 113/2011[219] of the Constitutional Court whereby the *Consulta* declared Article 630 c. 1 lett. (a) of the Code of Criminal Procedure unconstitutional in the part in which it does not allow the re-opening or review of a case amounting to *res iudicata*, which it found to be in breach of the Convention.

Luxembourg

In Luxembourg, despite the silence of the Constitution on this issue, courts have normally excluded the application of the chronological criterion to the case of conflicts between national legislation and international treaties, as both the two Supreme Courts (*Cour supérieure de justice* and *Conseil d'État*) have said in their case law.[220] This rule applies to the EU law case as acknowledged by the Council of State in its case-law.[221]

---

grazie al Trattato di Lisbona: l'inizio di un nuovo percorso?', http://www.associazionedeicostituzionalisti.it/rivista/2010/00/Colavitti-Pagotto01.pdf (2010).

216 Tribunale di Ravenna, 16 January 2008. On this see Carlotto, 'I giudici comuni' *supra*.

217 For a wider analysis coming to this conclusion, see Carlotto, 'I giudici comuni' *supra*: Lamarque, 'Il vincolo' *supra*.

218 Among others, 311/2009, 317/2009 80/2011, available at www.corte costituzionale.it.

219 Corte Costituzionale, sentenza 113/2011, available at www.corte costituzional.it.

220 Cour supérieure de justice (cassation criminelle), 14 July 1954, Pas. lux., XVI, 150, *Chambre des Métiers v Pagani*. ÉÉ, 28 July 1951, Pas. lux., XV, 263, *Dieudonné v Administration des Contributions*.

221 'En cas de conflit entre une norme de droit interne et une norme de droit

Over the years the Courts have confirmed 'the directly self-executing character of many of the Convention's provisions.[222] Hence, the ECHR and its Protocols are considered to be directly applicable in the Luxembourg legal order.'[223] Although the Constitutional Court has never referred a preliminary question to the ECJ, it seems that the preliminary ruling mechanism has been regularly used by the common courts.[224]

National judges use the provisions of the ECHR (especially Article 8, 13, 1 of Protocol no. 1) quite often in civil, criminal and administrative cases.[225]

Malta

Malta's accession to the EU occurred on 1 May 2004; however, the country had already incorporated the ECHR pursuant to *Act XIV of 1987*, according to which national laws may not be inconsistent with the rights and freedoms included in the Convention. The annual reports of the ECJ[226] contain very few cases initiated from Maltese judges, hence information on the application of EU law is scarce.[227] As for the ECHR, in 2011 the Council of Europe criticized the country's immigration detention system and this has created tensions with the domestic government[228] but even for this case scant data can be collected. In general it seems that the national government respects the ECHR.[229]

---

international ayant des effets directs dans l'ordre juridique interne, la règle établie par le Traité doit prévaloir. Cette règle s'impose plus particulièrement lorsque le conflit existe entre une norme de droit interne et une norme communautaire puisque les traités qui ont créé le droit communautaire ont institué un nouvel ordre juridique au profit duquel les Etats membres ont limité l'exercice de leurs pouvoirs souverains dans les domaines que ces traités déterminent', Conseil d'État, 21 November 1984, Pas. lux., XXVI, p. 174.

222 For instance: Cour supérieure de justice (chambre des mises en accusation), 2 April 1980, and Cour de cassation, 17 January 1985, No. 2/85.

223 E. Mak, 'Report on the Netherlands and Luxembourg' in Martinico and Pollicino (eds), *The National Judicial Treatment of the ECHR and EU Laws*, 313.

224 Ibid.

225 Ibid. 317.

226 http://curia.europa.eu/jcms/jcms/Jo2_11035/rapports-annuels.

227 As also pointed out in other researches, see: A. Dyevre, 'European Integration and National Courts: Defending Sovereignty under Institutional Constraints', paper presented at the Max Weber Programme Lustrum Conference, EUI, Florence, 8 June 2011.

228 http://www.detention-in-europe.org/index.php?option=com_content&view=Article&id=299%3Amalta-no-change-in-detention-policy&catid=3%3Anewsflash&Itemid=52.

229 Bureau of Democracy, Human Rights, and Labor 2006, Country Report on Malta, http://www.state.gov/g/drl/rls/hrrpt/2006/78827.htm.

The Netherlands

In the Netherlands, the openness of the formal parameter seems to correspond to what results from the analysis of the law in action. International law, including the ECHR, prevails over national law in case of conflicts and some legislative reforms have been introduced following the outcome of the case law of the ECtHR.[230] For instance, Article 457 of the Dutch Criminal Code admits the possibility of reopening criminal proceedings after a judgment of the ECtHR.[231]

As some scholars pointed out, the status of the ECHR (and in general public international law) and EU do not present considerable differences[232] since even the ECHR is considered as self-executing in nature with few exceptions. However, the extent of this self-executing nature may be limited in some cases.[233]

As said, thanks to the constitutional provisions judges are empowered to carry out the control of *conventionalité* by disapplying national law which is incompatible with the ECtHR, thus achieving an effect which is similar to that required by the *Simmenthal* doctrine. The control of *conventionalité* with regard to the ECHR has de facto expanded the mandate of national

---

230 Mak ('Report on the Netherlands and Luxembourg') cites the cases: ECtHR, 28 September 1995, no. 14570/89, Series A, Vol. 326, *Procola v Luxembourg*. and ECtHR, 27 November 2008, no. 36391/02, *Salduz v Turkey*; ECtHR, 26 March 1985, no. 8978/80, Series A, Vol. 91, *X and Y v The Netherlands*; ECtHR, 21 June 1988, no. 10730/84, Series A, Vol. 138, *Berrehab v The Netherlands*. See also E. de Wet, 'The Reception Process in the Netherlands and Belgium', in H. Keller and A. Stone Sweet (eds), *A Europe of Rights: The Impact of the ECHR on National Legal Systems* (Oxford University Press 2008) 229, 260.

231 Article 457 of the Dutch Criminal Code: 'On the basis of a judgment of the European Court of Human Rights in which it has been established that the European Convention on Human Rights or a Protocol to this treaty was violated in the proceedings which have led to the conviction or to a conviction for the same offence on the basis of the same evidence, if revision is necessary with an eye to the just satisfaction as meant in Article 41 of the treaty'.

232 G. Betlem and A. Nollkaemper, 'Giving Effect to Public International Law and European Community Law before Domestic Courts. A Comparative Analysis of the Practice of Consistent Interpretation' (2003) Eur J Intl Law, 569 ff.

233 'However, the extent of this self-executing nature may be limited by the circumstances of the case. Thus, with regard to Article 13 ECHR, the Supreme Court of the Netherlands pointed out that the Article "could not be relied upon to attribute to the court system more powers than had been granted by national legislation". (Supreme Court of the Netherlands [HR], 19 April 1996, NJ 1996,474.) A similar restriction was voiced with regard to Article 6 ECHR'. (Supreme Court of the Netherlands [HR], 18 February 1986, NJ 1987, 62)', Mak, 'Report on the Netherlands and Luxembourg', 313.

judges by opening an exception to Article 120 forbidding any form of control of constitutionality. The Netherlands Supreme Court considers the authoritative interpretations of the Strasbourg Court as 'incorporated into the treaty provisions'.[234]

As recalled in Chapter 2, the Netherlands is often cited as an example of a legal system that does not impose any limitations on the primacy of EU law or on the ECHR.[235] More recently tensions have emerged, however:[236] 'These examples suggest that in the future a judicial limit might be set concerning the acceptance of the European courts' jurisprudence in the domestic legal order.'[237] Dutch judges frequently cite decisions of the two European Courts although sometimes just *ad abundantiam*. Consistent interpretation is frequently used as first weapon in the face of potential conflicts between national and supranational law and only as an *extrema ratio* will Dutch courts agree to set aside national legislation conflicting with the ECHR.

As for EU law, Dutch Courts have acknowledged all the structural principles of EU law for a long time. They also regularly use the preliminary ruling mechanism and the technique of consistent interpretation. Even the *Simmenthal* mandate has been acknowledged and applied by courts and, as with the ECHR, the disapplication power can be seen as an important factor of empowerment for national judges.

The Nordic Countries

As Lebeck put it, 'the EC/EU/EEA law in Scandinavian law and the ECtHR are regarded as *lex superior*, despite [the fact] that the explicit formal basis for that remains limited. The special character of European law within domestic law in Scandinavia (except for the ECHR in Norway and Sweden) tends to be expressed through judicial practice rather than through acknowledgment of their constitutional role'.[238]

---

234 Ibid., 315. Mak mentions the following cases: Supreme Court of the Netherlands [HR], 10 November 1989, NJ 1990, 628; Supreme Court of the Netherlands [HR], 10 May 1996, NJCM-Bulletin 21 (1996), 683–95.

235 'The Dutch courts have not set any limits to either the primacy of EU law as understood by the ECJ or to the impact of the ECtHR's judgments in the domestic legal order. However, recent debates in the Netherlands have focused on the role of the national highest courts under the effect of the increased internationalization of the legal order', Mak, 'Report on the Netherlands and Luxembourg', 315.

236 ECtHR, 11 January 2007, no. 1948/04, *Salah Sheekh v The Netherlands*.

237 Mak, 'Report on the Netherlands and Luxembourg', 316.

238 C. Lebeck, 'Report on Scandinavian Countries', in Martinico and Pollicino (eds), *The National Judicial Treatment of the ECHR and EU Laws*, 407.

These lines confirm the importance of judges in understanding the real impact of EU law and the ECHR on these contexts. In the Nordic countries the respective Supreme Courts have acknowledged the special role of EU law and the ECHR.[239] A sort of interpretative priority has been accorded to these European laws and consistent interpretation and indirect effects have been employed as privileged tools for avoiding constitutional conflicts between national and supranational laws. In these contexts the decisions of the ECJ or the ECtHR cannot be used in order to reopen proceedings, at least in Sweden and Denmark.

Danish and Swedish Courts[240] normally rely on the case law of the European Courts in their activity. The preliminary ruling mechanism has seldom been used as scholars have extensively pointed out and maybe this is one of the most emblematic features of the Scandinavian judicial approach to EU law.[241] Another evident characteristic is the massive use of consistent interpretation which, at the end of the day, has also had an impact on the legal reasoning of Scandinavian courts since, according to scholars,[242] this technique has been used by the ECJ and by Nordic Courts in two slightly different ways and with different limitations. Swedish Courts have accepted the prevalence of EU law over national law for a long time.[243]

As for the ECHR, in decision NJA 1981 s. 1205[244] the Supreme Court of Sweden also established a presumption of consistency between the

---

239 As for Denmark, see the decisions U.1979.117/2H. U.1988.454H. Many of these cases have been taken from Lebeck, 'Report on Scandinavian Countries'. As for Sweden, see the decision NJA 1996 s. 668.

240 For Sweden, see, for instance, the decision RÅ 1997 ref 56. For Denmark see the cases U.2006.3359H, U.2006.2551H, U.2006.639H.

241 More recently, see M. Wind, 'The Nordics, the EU and the Reluctance Towards Supranational Judicial Review' (2010) J Common Market Studies, 1039.

242 'In relation to EU-law, the legal problem of Danish law is whether the duty of consistent interpretation is sufficiently extensive to ensure consistency with the duty of consistent interpretation under EC-law. That has to some extent also been a problem in relation to EC/EU-law, since the approach of the ECJ is slightly different, although the ECJ has accepted limits to consistent interpretation that is detrimental to individuals in criminal law, but less so in the context of criminal procedure. There are certain obvious fields that are problematic, which include the cases where it is used to the detriment of private individuals in Danish law and it [is] irrelevant in implementation of "soft law" measures of EU', Lebeck, 'Report on Scandinavian Countries', 413.

243 For Sweden, see the decisions: NJA 2001 s. 214, NJA 2002 s. 314, NJA 2003 s. 82, RÅ 2005 ref 87, NJA 2006 s 310, NJA 2006 s. 683, NJA 2007 s. 227. RÅ 2007 ref 24, RÅ 2007 ref 83, RÅ 2008 ref 30, RÅ 2009 ref 33.

244 See, for instance, decision NJA 1981 s. 1205.

Instrument of Government (IG) and the ECHR. Nevertheless the use of consistent interpretation does not exclude the possibility of disapplying national law that conflicts with EU law or with the ECHR and this solution has been applied only to cases of irreconcilable conflicts between the ECHR and national law.[245]

In decision NJA 1984 s. 903 the Swedish Supreme Court said that, once ratified the ECHR stands, with the supreme principles recognized in Sweden, as an ultimate barrier that cannot be contradicted by the national law of Sweden.[246]

However, in another case[247] the Swedish Supreme Court said that the ECHR is an important but non-mandatory source of inspiration and the same applies to the case law of the ECtHR: they both can be used for interpreting the meaning of legislative provisions[248] and over the years they have also induced changes in the traditional interpretations given to domestic statutes.[249]

Something similar has happened in Denmark. As for the limits imposed on European laws, Lebeck argued that 'the Scandinavian supreme courts have never considered any clear constitutional limits to the applicability of EC/EU/EEA-law within national law on constitutional grounds'.[250] This is questionable, however, if we think of cases like *Carlsen*[251] where the Danish Supreme Court has clearly raised some ultimate barriers against the ECJ's activism and the penetration of EU law, claiming the last say on potential constitutional conflicts even though it has accepted the preliminary ruling mechanism.[252]

As for the ECHR, since the Convention has played an important function in the last few years in enriching the constitutional parameter, there have been few tensions between national 'constitutional' provisions and the ECHR.[253]

With regards to conflicts or tensions with EU law in Sweden, scholars are used to recalling certain cases[254] but it seems they have been resolved by means of consistent interpretation and by insisting on the ECHR as a sort

---

245 NJA 2005 s. 805.
246 NJA 1984 s. 903, 907.
247 NJA 1989 s. 131.
248 NJA 1989 s. 131, 135.
249 NJA 2005 s. 805.
250 Lebeck, 'Report on Scandinavian Countries', 433.
251 *Højesteret, Carlsen v Rasmussen* [1999] 3 CMLR 854.
252 P. Craig, 'The ECJ, National Courts and The Supremacy of Community Law', available at: http://www.estig.ipbeja.pt/~ac_direito/craig.pdf.
253 Lebeck, 'Report on Scandinavian Countries', 430–431.
254 See the decisions NJA 2001 s 409 and the AD 99/2004.

of minimum '*common denominator*'.[255] Something similar has occurred in Denmark.[256]

Turning to Finland, it has been said that the judiciary has been greatly empowered by European integration and the ECHR.[257] Both EU law and the ECHR are normally applied, on a daily basis, by all Finnish Courts and they have gained a growing importance in the resolution of the cases, especially those concerning the activities of the administrative courts.[258]

Courts have also acquired the power to set aside national legislation conflicting with EU law and this has increased the importance of case law as an autonomous source of law.[259] Courts seem to acknowledge the structural principles of EU law and pay attention to the case law of both courts.[260] The ECHR has been an important source of inspiration for the reform of the Constitution.[261]

As for EU law, however, 'the cases in which Finnish courts have taken advantage of the primacy of EU law and, accordingly, set aside conflicting provisions of Finnish law have remained few in number'.[262] This is due to the traditional importance of the consistent interpretation doctrine in the Nordic constitutional experience. This often implies that EU law and the ECHR play an auxiliary role, ancillary to that of the constitutional provisions to be interpreted, or have been an important engine for the silent update of domestic legislation by means of interpretative judgments[263] given by the highest courts. As in the other Nordic contexts, few preliminary references have been raised by Finland's national courts and almost exclusively they were questions concerning the interpretation of some EU law provisions.[264]

---

255 Lebeck, 'Report on Scandinavian Countries', 433.

256 See decisions HD 2 April 1981, sag II 190/1980, UfR 1982H.109; UfR 2003 H.1331.

257 T. Ojanen, 'The Impact of EU Membership on Finnish Constitutional Law' (2004) Eur Public Law 531, 558.

258 Ibid., 559 ff.

259 Ibid.

260 Ibid.

261 M. Scheinin 'Finland', in M. Scheinin, (ed.), *International Human Rights Norms in the Nordic and Baltic Countries* (Martinus Nijhoff 1996), 257.

262 Ojanen, 'The Impact of EU Membership on Finnish Constitutional Law', 559.

263 Scheinin 'Finland', 276.

264 Ojanen, 'The Impact of EU Membership on Finnish Constitutional Law', 561.

Poland

The ECHR and EU law have had a significant impact on the Polish system. While the former has not induced any constitutional changes, the latter, in a way, was the engine of the 1997 amendment to the Constitution, namely that of its Article 55. Before the amendment this provision did not allow the extradition of a citizen but it was amended in order to allow extradition by stating that 'such a possibility stems from an international treaty ratified by Poland or a statute implementing a legal instrument enacted by an international organisation of which the Republic of Poland is a member (. . .)'.[265]

The ECHR has induced some legislative/primary level changes thanks to the pressure exercised by the Strasbourg Court[266] and the same applies to the EU law.[267] The Polish system allows the reopening of proceedings subsequent to an ECtHR judgment only in the case of criminal proceedings, pursuant to Article 540, paragraph 3, of the Code of Criminal Procedure 1997.

As for the primacy of EU law, the Polish Constitutional Tribunal has dealt with the issue of the primacy principle in at least two decisions: the Accession Treaty case[268] and the European Arrest Warrant case.[269] In the first case, the Constitutional Court verified the constitutionality of the Accession Treaty on the basis of Article 188 of the Constitution, rejecting all the grounds raised by the applicants. However, as Kowalik-Bańczyk stressed, 'the sole fact of accepting the competence to control [the] legality of [the] Accession Treaty might be seen as problematic: it implicitly indicates that the Constitutional Tribunal considers that the national Constitution can be a basis for this type of control. However it is mainly

---

265 Article 55, p. 2.

266 See the examples described by K. Kowalik-Bańczyk, 'Report on Poland', in Martinico and Pollicino (eds), *The National Judicial Treatment of the ECHR and EU Laws*, 330: for instance, Judgment of 26.10.2000, *Kudła v Poland*, app. no. 30210/96; Judgment of 22.06.2004, *Broniowski v Poland*, app. no. 31443 Judgment of 19.06.2006, *Hutten-Czapska v Poland*, app. no. 35014/97; Judgment of 25.03.1998, *Belziuk v Poland*, app. no. 23103/93.

267 Judgment of 18.01.2007 *Brzeziński v Dyrektor Izby Celnej w Warszawie* [2007] ECR I-513; Judgment of 22.05.2008 *Nerkowska v Zakład Ubezpieczeń Społecznych Oddział w Koszalinie* [2008] ECR I-3993; Judgment of 13.11.2008 C-227/07 *Commission v Poland* [2008] ECR I-8403; Judgment of 5.06.2008 C-170/07 *Commission v Poland* [2008] ECR I-87. On these, again, see Kowalik-Bańczyk, 'Report on Poland', 330 ff.

268 Judgment of 11.05.2005, K 18/04.

269 Judgment of 27.04.2005, P 1/05.

the reasoning of the Constitutional Tribunal that seems quite particular and raises the serious question of acceptance (or rather lack of acceptance) of supremacy of European law over [the] Constitution in Poland.'[270]

In the second case, which will be analyzed in greater detail in the second part of this volume, the Tribunal put pressure on the Polish Parliament in order to induce it to change the Constitution but in any case, 'in the opinion of the Tribunal, the Constitution remains the most important source of law, superior over international instruments (including EU law)'.[271] This last decision is paradoxical, since the Constitutional Tribunal seemed very deferential towards the EU law order even though, in the end, it declared the invalidity of a national provision adopted for implementing the Framework Decision on the European Arrest Warrant.[272]

However, the Polish Constitutional Tribunal seems to accept the primacy of EU law over national provisions (more complicated, as we said, is the issue of the relationship with the Constitution), and the disapplication of national law in case of conflict with EU law provisions[273] but, in any case, the primacy of EU law is seen as the product of the self-limitation of the State.[274]

The same idea has been accepted by administrative and common judges who, after some initial tensions – in this respect the *Brzeziński* case[275] could be seen as a landmark decision – started accepting the *Simmenthal* doctrine.[276] Polish judges regularly refer preliminary questions to the ECJ. Even the Supreme Court has accepted the primacy principle[277] and the disapplication doctrine. Although it generally refuses to consider

---

270 Kowalik-Bańczyk, 'Report on Poland', 334.

271 K. Kowalik-Bańczyk, 'Should We Polish It Up? The Polish Constitutional Tribunal and the Idea of Supremacy of EU Law' (2005) German L J 1355, 1356. Kowalik-Bańczyk, 'Report on Poland', 334. Judgment of 11.05.2005, K 18/04.

272 'Paradoxically, the first one – invalidating a provision of Polish Criminal Procedure Code – might be seen as a sign of respect for Polish international obligations stemming from the EU law. The second, confirming the validity of Accession Treaty of 2003, is a clear refusal of supremacy of this Treaty over national Constitution', Kowalik-Bańczyk, 'Should We Polish It Up?', 1358.

273 Order of 19.12.2006, P 37/05.

274 Judgment of 27.04.2005, P 1/05.

275 Judgment of 18.01.2007 *Brzeziński v Dyrektor Izby Celnej w Warszawie* [2007] ECR I-513.

276 Warsaw Administrative Court, judgments of 12.10.2005, III SA/Wa 2219/05, of 4.8.2006, III SA/Wa 1381/06 and 21.6.2006, III SA/Wa 656/6, of 5.4.2007, III SA/Wa 223/07 and 14.6.2006, III SA/Wa 1101/06; Lublin Administrative Court, judgment of 25.5.2005, I SA/Lu 77/; Białystok Administrative Court, judgment of 6.2.2007, I SA/Bk 406/06. All reported in Kowalik-Bańczyk, 'Report on Poland'.

277 Supreme Court judgment of 10.2.2006, II CSK 112/05.

EU law as part of the standard for reviewing national law,[278] the Polish Constitutional Tribunal has agreed to it in one case, by declaring some legislative provisions unconstitutional.[279]

Nevertheless, the Constitutional Tribunal has in many cases agreed to consider the ECHR for evaluating the legislative provisions of Poland[280] with one exception.[281] In all these case, nevertheless, the Court did not rely exclusively on the ECHR. The Convention is rather used for enriching or for inspiring the reading of constitutional provisions.[282]

The Constitutional Tribunal has also paid attention to the case law of the Strasbourg Court and once expressly recognized its importance, saying 'a decision of the ECtHR in an individual case (. . .) must be taken into account by the Constitutional Tribunal in its assessment of legal provisions',[283] clearly indicating that the control of constitutionality of any provision of Polish law must be made taking into account the case law of the Strasbourg Court.[284] The Constitutional Court also cites the ECHR and the case law of the Strasbourg Court[285] or treats them as a source of inspiration for reading constitutional provisions.[286] The ECHR is also used by national judges who have adopted the technique of consistent interpretation for avoiding conflicts between the Convention and national law. Although the Polish Constitutional Tribunal has said that the ECHR can be directly applied by domestic courts,[287] there are few cases where this has happened.[288]

There are also cases of tensions between the Polish and the EU legal orders. The first one is represented by the case of the European Arrest Warrant, where the Polish Constitutional Tribunal declared a provision of

---

278 Judgment of 7.11.2007, K 18/06; Order of 19.12.2006, P 37/05.

279 Judgment of 6.2.2007, P 25/06.

280 Judgment of 8.10.2002, K 36/00; judgment of 12.01.2002 P 11/98; judgment of 10.05.2000, K 21/99; judgment of 10.04.2002, K 26/00; judgment of 7.03.2000, K 26/98.

281 Order of 18.04.2000, SK 2/99.

282 For instance, judgment of 18.05.2004 SK 38.

283 Judgment of 18.10.2004, P 8/04.

284 Judgment of 28.04.2003, K 18/02.

285 Judgment of 20.2.2007, P 1/06; judgment of 28.1.2003, K 2/02; judgment of 29.9.1997, K 15/97; judgment of 28.3.2000, K 27/99; judgment of 20.3.2006 K 17/05.

286 Judgment of 18.10.2004, P 8/04.

287 Judgment of 5.03.2003, K 7/01); judgment of 8.11.2001, P 6/01; judgment of 14.09.1999, K 14/98; judgment of 9.06.1999, K 11/98; judgment of 9.06.1998, K 28/97; judgment of 9.06.2002, P 4/01; judgment of 9.06.2003, SK 12/03; judgment of 2.03.2004, SK 53/03; judgment of 27.10.2004, SK 1/04.

288 Kowalik-Bańczyk, 'Report on Poland', 342 ff.

the national Criminal Procedure Code unconstitutional. At the same time the Constitutional Tribunal gave the Parliament 18 months (during which period the national provisions would have remained valid) in order to give the Parliament the possibility of amending the Constitution and ensuring the implementation of the European Arrest Warrant.

The Constitutional Court has never referred a preliminary question to the ECJ. As we noted in the previous chapter, Article 193 of the Constitution permits judges to raise *incidenter* questions to the Constitutional Court in case of conflict with a ratified international agreement or statute, 'if the answer to such a question is decisive for the determination of an issue pending before such court'. The duty of the judges in these cases has been interpreted in different ways by the Supreme and the Constitutional Courts.[289] In a later judgment the Constitutional Tribunal said that it 'does not require the national courts to raise the *incidenter* question where the conflict between the EU and Polish provisions appears. The courts are expected to either independently disapply the conflicting Polish provision or to ask the preliminary question to the ECJ.'[290]

The *Simmenthal* doctrine has been accepted by the Polish Constitutional Court.[291] Polish Courts take into account the ECJ case law and use the consistent interpretation doctrine when interpreting national law[292] but cases of conflict with the ECJ have still occurred as the *Filipiak* case confirms.[293]

---

289 Judgment of 6.05.2003, I CO 7/03; judgment of 9.07.2003, IV CKN 357/01; judgment of 4.12.2001 TK 18/00.

290 Kowalik-Bańczyk, 'Report on Poland', 339.

291 Order of 19.12.2006, P 37/05.

292 Judgment of 21.9.2004, K 34/03; judgment of 21.4.2004, K 33/03; judgment of 31.5.2004, K 15/04; judgment of 27.05.2005, K 11/03; judgment of 21.04.2004, K 33/03; judgment of 13.09.2005, K 38/04; judgment of 26.01.2005, P 10/04.

293 The *Filipiak* case is emblematic in this respect. It originated from a preliminary question raised by a Polish judge with regard to proceedings on tax issues between Mr Filipiak, a Polish national carrying on an economic activity in the Netherlands (where he regularly paid the social security and health insurance contributions required by Dutch legislation), and the Director of the Poznań Tax Chamber. What is interesting to us is that before the judgment, in the appeal against the refusal, the Polish Constitutional Tribunal ruled that the income tax law in question infringed the principles of equality and social justice codified in the Polish Constitution but, at the same time, by exploiting its powers ad hoc provided, decided to postpone the loss of validity of the legislation until 30 November 2008. The ECJ concluded that 'the primacy of Community law obliges the national court to apply Community law and to refuse to apply conflicting provisions of national law, irrespective of the judgment of the national constitutional court which has deferred the date on which those provisions, held to be unconstitutional, are to lose their binding force', C-314/08, Filipiak [2009] ECR I-11049.

More recently the Polish Constitutional Tribunal joined the club of the Constitutional Courts which have decided on the compatibility between Lisbon Treaty and the constitution. In a decision characterized by long digressions on the concept of sovereignty and by a sort of comparison with the doctrines of the other constitutional courts, it admitted the possibility of carrying out the *ultra vires* control over the EU acts, sending an indirect message to the ECJ in order to preserve the untouchable core of its own Constitution.[294] At the same time the Polish Constitutional Tribunal considered the EU membership as confirmation of Polish sovereignty rather than evidence of its loss.

Portugal

As we saw in the previous chapter, in Portugal, from a theoretical point of view, it might be argued that the combination of Articles 204[295] and 8[296] of the Constitution would permit national judges to disapply national law conflicting with constitutional and international law, but scholars seem to describe such an option as a sort of sleeping giant that has never been applied.[297]

The case law of the two European Courts is normally followed[298] by the Supreme Courts while common judges rarely cite the ECHR. At the same time, the Portuguese Constitutional Court has sometimes used the ECHR as a tool for interpreting human rights provisions included in

---

[294] See the judgment given on 24 November 2010 by the Polish Constitutional Tribunal.

[295] Article 204 of the Portuguese Constitution: 'In matters that are brought to trial, the courts shall not apply rules that contravene the provisions of this Constitution or the principles enshrined therein'.

[296] Devoted to the relation between international and national laws, see *supra* Chapter 2.

[297] 'Although authorized by the Portuguese Constitution, I could not find cases where Portuguese judges had directly invoked the ECHR to put aside conflicting national law', F. Coutinho, 'Report on Portugal', in Martinico and Pollicino (eds), *The National Judicial Treatment of the ECHR and EU Laws*, 364. See Report of the Portuguese Constitutional Court to the XII Congress of the European Constitutional Courts, 14–16 May 2002, at 53, cited by Coutinho, 'Report on Portugal'.

[298] For instance, Supreme Administrative Court, decision no. 24643, judgment of 29 January 2003, *Diário da República*, 2 July, at 21; Supreme Administrative Court, decision no. 25138, judgment of 25 October 2000, *Diário da República*, 31 January 2003, at 3761. For the ECtHR case law, see: Supreme Administrative Court, decision no. 0227/08, judgment of 29 March 2009, available at www.dgsi.pt.

the Constitution.[299] The ECtHR has been the engine of some reforms, as the aftermath to the *Lobo Machado* case[300] on the participation of the public prosecutor in the judgment deliberation shows.

As for EU law, the Constitutional Court has rarely referred to EU laws in its judgments and it has never raised a preliminary reference to the ECJ, although it has admitted such a possibility.[301] In 1989[302] the Constitutional Court seemed to vindicate 'that it is for the constitutional order of each Member State to determine the conditions and the means for implementing EU law',[303] perceiving the primacy of EU law as a self limitation of the constitution. In 1990 the Constitutional Court admitted the possibility of considering itself as a judge but it has never referred a preliminary question to the Luxembourg Court.[304]

Many courts other than the Constitutional Court seem to perceive the primacy of EU law as a self limitation of the Constitution[305] but the issue is still disputed. In any case this reconstruction has given a sort of super-primary but also sub-constitutional strength to EU law within national boundaries. Such a vision has created tensions among judges since some of them have considered a conflict between national law and the EU law as an indirect breach of the Constitution.[306] At the same time, other judges decided to review the constitutionality of EU law,[307] menacing the monopoly of the ECJ (although they have never in the end disapplied EU law).[308]

---

299 Constitutional Court, decision no. 345/99, judgment of 15 June 1999; decision no. 412/2000, judgment of 4 October 2000; decision no. 222/90, judgment of 20 June 1990; and decision no. 547/98, judgment of 23 September 1998, all available at www.tribunalconstitucional.pt. See Coutinho, 'Report on Portugal'.

300 *Lobo Machado* (App. 15764/89) ECHR 1996-6.

301 Constitutional Court, decision no. 163/90, judgment of 23 May 1990, *Acórdãos do Tribunal Constitutional*, 16, 1990, at 301.

302 Constitutional Court of Portugal, decision no. 184/89, judgment of 1 February 1989, *Diário da República*, 9 March 1989, at 1051.

303 Coutinho, 'Report on Portugal', 358.

304 Constitutional Court of Portugal, decision no. 163/90, judgment of 23 May 1990, *Acórdãos do Tribunal Constitutional*, 16, 1990.

305 Supreme Administrative Court, decision no. 26392, judgment of 31 October 2001, *Antologia de acórdãos do Supremo Tribunal Administrativo e Tribunal Central Administrativo*, 1, 2001, at 194, mentioned by Coutinho, 'Report on Portugal'.

306 E.g. Supreme Administrative Court, decision no. 14042, judgment of 17 February 1993, *Diário da República*, 16 January 1996, 594–604.

307 For instance, Supreme Administrative Court, decision no. 23066, judgment of 18 November 1998, *Acórdãos Doutrinais do Supremo Tribunal Administrativo*, 451, 1999, at 914.

308 All the cases mentioned in this section have been taken from Coutinho, 'Report on Portugal'.

Generally speaking EU law is conceived as a sophisticated form of international law. The Portuguese courts have recognized its primacy and direct effect and applied the *Simmenthal* mandate.[309] Finally, even the technique of consistent interpretation has been largely used.[310]

Romania

Despite the content of Article 20 of the Romanian Constitution, the Supreme Courts and the Romanian Constitutional Court appear to struggle somewhat with the case law of the ECtHR and with the ECHR itself as Raducu pointed out.[311]

Moreover among Romanian courts the ECHR has been also used to challenge the case law of other courts.[312] The case law seems to offer a rather contradictory picture where the different courts present a variety of positions, but, according to the scholarship: 'For now, it seems that the judicial practice is consistent with the ECJ jurisprudence except the position of the Constitutional Court in the case of data protection, where it gave precedence to the ECHR standards.'[313] A clearer picture seems to emerge with regard to the ECHR despite the fact that the application of the ECHR also has problematic results for reasons connected to powers

---

309 Supreme Administrative Court, decision no. 22401, judgment of 28 January 1998, *Diário da República*, 6 April 2001, at 30. Supreme Administrative Court, decision no. 22367, judgment of 4 April 2001, *Diário da República*, 10 March 2003, 100–105, Supreme Administrative Court, decision no. 28840, judgment of 1 April 1993, *Boletim do Ministério da Justiça*, 426, 1993.

310 For instance, Supreme Court of Justice, decision no. 02B4591, judgment of 13 February 2003, available in www.dgsi.pt.

311 'Several times the Constitutional Court has either ignored an ECtHR decision against another State given in a similar matter or was contradicted by a subsequent ECHR decision. The problem in these cases is for the national judges to ignore the wrongful decisions of the Constitutional Court or the Supreme Court and apply directly the ECtHR's decisions to the case at hand', I. Raducu, 'Report on Romania', in Martinico and Pollicino (eds), *The National Judicial Treatment of the ECHR and EU Laws*, 374.

312 'For instance, the High Court of Cassation and Justice did not hesitate to consider inapplicable the disposition of the law in the light of Article 20 of the Constitution, Article 6 of the ECHR and Article 47 of the Charter of Fundamental Rights. It thus disregarded the Constitutional Court's decision that considered Law 554/2004 in conformity with the Constitution. The Supreme Court invoked the jurisprudence both of the ECJ and the ECHR. This example shows the influence of the ECHR/EU law on the internal relationship between supreme courts that might result on divergent views.' Ibid., 375.

313 Ibid., 386.

other than the judiciary.[314] In any case Romanian judges normally respect the structural principles of EU law and adopt the consistent interpretation of national provisions.

Slovenia

In Slovenia the Constitutional Court emphasized the special nature of the ECHR in the domestic legal order even before the accession of Slovenia to the ECHR.[315] It has also cited the ECHR and the relevant case law of the Strasbourg Court but, at the same time, the Constitutional Court has pointed out the precedence of the Constitution 'unless the ECHR as expounded in the Strasbourg jurisprudence provides for a higher standard of protection.'[316] This implies that, normally, the Constitutional Court does not use the ECHR as a parameter but it can nevertheless employ it as an argument in support of the decision of unconstitutionality. The exception to this scheme is represented by the case 'in which the Constitution would not explicitly contain a right stemming from the ECHR as expounded by the ECtHR',[317] since in this case the Constitutional Court could rely on the ECHR on the basis of Article 15 of the Constitution.[318]

As for EU law, it is provided with a 'special constitutional status'[319] but there are few cases involving EU law, especially before the Constitutional Court, because of the recent membership of Slovenia. In any case, as we saw in the previous chapter, Article 3a of the Constitution requires the application of EU law and the Constitutional Court has thus acknowledged primacy and direct effect of EU law.[320] As the Constitutional Court pointed out in 2007, 'neither Article 3.a of the Constitution nor Article 249.3 of the TEC determine by which legal act EU law is to be transposed into the Slovene legal system. Thus, the fact that the Rules are an implementing regulation does not exclude or limit the jurisdiction of the Constitutional Court.'[321]

---

314 Ibid., 374 ff.

315 See Constitutional Court Decision No. U-I-98/9, 10.12.1992, U-I-48/92, 11.2.1993, U-I-60/92, 17.6.1993. All the cases mentioned have been taken from M. Avbelj, 'Report on Slovenia', in Martinico and Pollicino (eds), *The National Judicial Treatment of the ECHR and EU Laws*.

316 Avbelj, 'Report on Slovenia', 447.

317 Ibid.

318 See, for instance, the following cases: Constitutional Court Decision Up-555/03 and Up-827/04, 6.7.2006.

319 Avbelj, 'Report on Slovenia', 447.

320 Constitutional Court, Decision Up-328/04, U-I-186/04, 8.7.2004.

321 Constitutional Court, Decision U-113/04, 7.2.2007.

At the same time it declined to be in charge of the control of compliance of national laws with EU directives[322] or to have the competence to control the constitutionality of EU secondary norms.

Normally Slovenian Courts apply the doctrine of consistent interpretation[323] taking into account EU law provisions and the ECJ's case law.

Spain

The ECHR may function as an auxiliary tool to read the Spanish Constitution but, like all the international human rights treaties recalled by Article 10.2 of the Constitution, it cannot be considered as a source having constitutional rank.[324] However, 'the *Tribunal Constitucional* (TC) has admitted that to an extent, as a result of Article 10.2, the ECHR integrates the content of constitutional rights.[325] Hence, formally, the ECHR has not been awarded a different status from other international treaties, but it is clear from the constitutional case law that it has special relevance for the interpretation of constitutional rights.'[326]

Spanish Courts use and cite judgments of the ECtHR but this does not automatically imply their binding nature and the Spanish Constitutional Tribunal once said that ECtHR case law is 'not only an interpretive criterion for applying the constitutional provisions protecting fundamental rights', but also 'of direct application in our legal system'.[327] In any case usually such references are made only *ad abundantiam* although sometimes the Constitutional Tribunal has demonstrated willingness to adopt the interpretative criteria of the Strasbourg Court in the field, for instance, of the unreasonable duration of the due process or in other cases.[328]

The Constitutional Tribunal has also referred to the case law of the ECJ on fundamental rights[329] and also cited the Charter of Nice even before its proclamation,[330] without, however, recognizing EU fundamental rights

---

322 Constitutional Court, Decisions U-I-44/05, 11.9.2007; U-I-32/04, 9.2.2006; U-I-116/07, 25.5.2007.

323 Constitutional Court, Decision U-I-321/02, 27.5.2004.

324 STC 292/2000; SSTC 120/1990, FJ 3; 137/1990, FJ 3; 214/1991, FJ 1; 77/1995, FJ 2; 51/1996, FJ 1.

325 SSTC 20/1995, FJ 4; 36/1991, FJ 5.

326 A. Torres Pérez, 'Report on Spain', in Martinico and Pollicino (eds), *The National Judicial Treatment of the ECHR and EU Laws*, 461.

327 STC 303/1993, FJ 8, cited ibid., 462.

328 STC 124/1999, FJ 2.

329 SSTC 145/1991, 58/1994, 268/1994, 147/1995, 136/1996, 198/1996, 324/2006, 17/2007.

330 STC 28/1991, FJ 5.

provisions or doctrines as part of the standard for assessing the constitutionality of domestic legislation.[331]

Further on the ECHR, it should be noticed that a potential factor to be taken into account in the search for convergence in the national treatment of European laws is given by Article 96 whose effects and scope are debated among scholars: does it empower judges to disapply national legislation in conflict with provisions of the ECHR?

Certainly, according to the Constitutional Tribunal, Spanish judges may disapply national laws conflicting with international treaties.[332] More complicated is the issue of the possible disapplication of national law for conflict with provisions included in human rights treaties like the ECHR. On this specific issue the Constitutional Tribunal has never given a decision. Since the Constitutional Tribunal has demonstrated its willingness to take the ECHR into account – via Article 10.2 of the Constitution – scholars have suggested that common judges should refer to the Constitutional Tribunal in case of these conflicts instead of disapplying national law.[333] This could also be argued keeping in mind the distinction existing between normal international treaties (Article 96) and human rights Treaties (Article 10).

The Constitutional Tribunal conceived of Article 93 of the Spanish Constitution as a basis for the primacy of EU law without giving the EU law a constitutional degree in the legal sources system. Nevertheless, it is possible to note a strong evolution in the case law of the Constitutional Tribunal from the judgment no. 28/1991[334] and *Declaración* no. 1/1992[335] up to the very recent *Declaración* no. 1/2004. In this case the Constitutional Tribunal adopted a more substantial reading of Article 93 of the Constitution, no longer conceiving it only as a procedural clause.

The position of EU law in the domestic ranking is however ambiguous. Once forced to renounce a dualistic strategy, according to which EU laws are sources external to their domestic legal order, constitutional courts have accepted the erosion of the boundary between legal orders by 'devising' a new step (in the legal sources hierarchy) which is 'super-legislative'

---

331 STC 64/1991, FJ 4.

332 SSTC 49/1988, FJ 14; STC 180/1993.

333 V. Ferreres Comella, 'El juez nacional ante los derechos fundamentales europeos. Algunas reflexiones en torno a la idea de diálogo', in Alejandro Saiz Arnaiz and Maite Zelaia Garagarza (eds), *Integración Europea y Poder Judicial* (IVAP 2006), 231.

334 *Tribunal Constitucional*, sentencia n. 28/1991, in www.tribunalconstitucional.es.

335 *Tribunal Constitucional*, declaración, 1/1992, in www.tribunalconstitucional.es. On this, see P. Pérez Tremps, *Constitución española y comunidad europea* (Madrid 1993).

but also 'sub-constitutional': in this way they guarantee the prevalence of EU law over domestic law without infringing constitutional supremacy. The Spanish Constitutional Tribunal does not represent an exception to this trend. Such an attempt has, however, created confusion in the case law of the constitutional courts themselves, as the contradictions found in decisions of the Spanish Constitutional Tribunal demonstrate. In case no. 28/1991, in fact, the Constitutional Tribunal used two formulae to define the normative strength of EU law – 'non-constitutional law' and 'infra-constitutional law' – while in other cases it has used the formula 'constitutionally relevant [law]'.[336] Consequently, according to the Constitutional Tribunal, the contrast between EU law and national law cannot be seen as a figure of the national rule's un-constitutionality: it is a legality issue which has to be resolved by common judges.[337] As a consequence, the reasons of EU law do not touch upon the supremacy of the national Constitution, which according to the perspective of the Constitutional Tribunal remains the highest law.

Moreover, even more clearly, the Spanish Constitutional Tribunal has raised some ultimate barriers (resembling the Italian *controlimiti*) against the penetration of EU law with the famous distinction between primacy and supremacy ('*primacia y supremacia*') conceived by the Constitutional Tribunal.[338]

According to the language used by the Spanish judges:

> in principle, all supremacy implies primacy (which leads to its occasional equivalence, as in our DTC 1/1992, FJ 1), unless the same supreme regulation has set

---

[336] See *Tribunal Constitucional*, sentencia 28/1991, www.tribunalconstitucional.es. Concerning the terminology used by the *Tribunal Constitucional*, see C. Vidal Prado, *El impacto del nuevo derecho europeo en los Tribunales Constitucionales* (Editorial Colex 2004).

[337] Similarly, there is an evident manipulation of the constitutional text by the Belgian *Cour d'Arbitrage* with regard to Article 34 of the Constitution in order to give a partial super-constitutionality to the EU law, without endorsing the competence of its guarantee.

[338] *'Supremacy and primacy are categories which are developed in differentiated orders. The former, in that of the application of valid regulations; the latter, in that of regulatory procedures. Supremacy is sustained in the higher hierarchical character of a regulation and, therefore, is a source of validity of the lower regulations, leading to the consequent invalidity of the latter if they contravene the provisions set forth imperatively in the former. Primacy, however, is not necessarily sustained on hierarchy, but rather on the distinction between the scopes of application of different regulations, principally valid, of which, however, one or more of them have the capacity for displacing others by virtue of their preferential or prevalent application due to various reasons'*, *Tribunal Constitucional*, declaración 1/2004, www.tribunalconstitucional.es.

> forth, in some scope, its own displacement or non-application. The supremacy of the Constitution is therefore compatible with application systems which award applicative preference to regulations of another legislation other than the national legislation as long as the Constitution itself has set forth said provision, which is what happens exactly with the provision set forth in Article 93 . . . In short, the Constitution has accepted, by virtue of Article 93, the primacy of the Union legislation in the scope inherent to said Law, as now recognised expressly in Article I-6 of the Treaty.[339]

Here again the national judges respected the prevalence of EU law by assuming that primacy rests in acceptance and self-limitation by the Spanish Constitution, which is conceived as the highest law.

As we said above, the questions of potential conflicts between EU law and national law are not questions of constitutionality; thus they do not belong to the competence of the Spanish Constitutional Tribunal *stricto sensu* conceived. However, in a very important decision, the Constitutional Tribunal acknowledged[340] the exhaustibility of the *recurso de amparo* when the common judge refuses to refer a preliminary question to the ECJ pursuant to Article 267 TFEU. If this refusal implies the violation of a fundamental right guaranteed by the *recurso de amparo*, it is possible to proceed before the Constitutional Tribunal for a violation of Article 24 of the Spanish Constitution.[341] With this revirement the Constitutional Tribunal has balanced its refusal to accept the mechanism of preliminary rulings by ensuring the loyalty of its national judges.

The Constitutional Tribunal specified that a refusal to refer preliminary questions to the ECJ is relevant for the admission of the *recurso de amparo* whenever the domestic judge is obliged to refer to the ECJ according to Article 267 TFEU and when there is no precedent ruling

---

339 *Tribunal Constitucional*, declaración 1/2004, www.tribunalconstitucional.es, emphasis added.

340 *Tribunal Constitucional,* sentencia 58/2004, www.tribunalconstitucional.es.

341 'En el presente caso la Sentencia impugnada, al inaplicar el recargo autonómico por supuesta incompatibilidad con el Derecho comunitario europeo, viola el derecho al proceso con todas las garantías (art 24.2 CE) y el derecho a una Sentencia que fundamente razonablemente la inaplicación de la ley española (art 24.1 CE). Ello se aprecia en especial cuando, como aquí sucede, se funda la decisión en la Sentencia del Tribunal de Justicia de las Comunidades Europeas de 26 de junio de 1997, que versa sobre unos puntos bien distintos de aquellos otros en que reposa la decisión de inaplicar la ley española en la Sentencia contra la que se pide el amparo, que contiene un razonamiento palmariamente insostenible que no hace sino deformar el sentido propio de los rasgos caracterizadores del impuesto sobre el valor añadido o sobre el volumen del negocio.' *Tribunal Constitucional*, sentencia 58/2004, www.tribunalconstitucional.es.

by the ECJ on analogous or identical cases. A mere refusal to refer a preliminary question does not, on its own, give rise to the possibility of using the *recurso de amparo*; in this sense EU law continues not to have constitutional status.

In any case the issue has been debated among scholars for different reasons, for instance for the parallelism – made by the Spanish Tribunal – between the question of constitutionality and the preliminary ruling mechanism.[342] As for the *Simmenthal* doctrine, it has been accepted, although with some resistance.[343]

Recently, the Spanish Constitutional Tribunal has for the first time in its history referred a preliminary ruling question[344]; even in the recent past it had avoided doing so, and emblematic of this old trend is the decision of the Spanish Constitutional Tribunal in 2009 regarding the European Arrest Warrant.[345]

The preliminary ruling mechanism has also created another interesting case of interpretative competition between the ECJ and the Spanish Constitutional Tribunal: the *Cordero Alonso*[346] case. This case originated from a reference raised by a Spanish judge to the ECJ. The *a quo* judge basically asked about the necessity to disapply a national statute (Article 33 of the Workers' Statute) which had already been acknowledged as

---

342 'This decision was celebrated because the TC [Constitutional Tribunal] gave constitutional relevance to the failure to raise the preliminary question. The reasoning, however, was rather disturbing because the TC seemed to limit its eventual intervention to cases in which a legislative act had been set aside. In addition, the comparison with the constitutional question was quite unfortunate. In a later decision, the TC emphasized that it was necessary for ordinary courts to raise a preliminary reference before setting aside a legislative act. The TC added a caveat parenthetically: "provided that the conditions established by EU law concur, and this is for the ordinary courts to decide." But, if this is for ordinary courts to decide, what is the TC going to examine in order to decide whether the right to due process has been violated? The relevant issue should be whether an obligation exists from the standpoint of EU law, rather than whether a legislative act has been set aside', Torres Perez, 'Report on Spain', 467.

343 STS (Sala Tercera), 30-11-1990. Ruiz-Jarabo Colomer (1993) 673–75.

344 STC, Auto 86/2011, http://www.tribunalconstitucional.es/es/jurisprudencia/Paginas/Auto.aspx?cod=10386.

345 See also the dissenting opinion of Pérez Tremps, Paragraph 1 *Tribunal Constitucional*, sentencia 199/2009, www.tribunalconstitucional.es. For a comment, see F. Fontanelli, 'A Comment on Tribunal Constitucional's Judgment no 199/2009 and Czech Constitutional Court's Judgment no 29/2009: How Interpretation Techniques can Shape the Relationship between Constitutional Courts', STALS Research Paper No. 1/2010, http://stals.sssup.it/files/stals_Fontanelli_012010.pdf.

346 C-81/05, *Cordero Alonso* [2006] ECR I-7569.

inconsistent with the EC principle of non-discrimination by the ECJ in a previous judgment[347] but which, after the first ECJ judgment on this matter, had also been interpreted in a way consistent with the constitutional principle of non-discrimination by the Spanish Constitutional Tribunal.[348] Even in this second case the ECJ concluded for the inconsistency of the national provision with EC law.[349]

In this case the national judge was not able to decide which court he should follow (either the ECJ or the domestic constitutional judge) and, in order to avoid a decision which would have been seen as challenging the case law of the Spanish Constitutional Tribunal, decided to refer an interpretive question to the ECJ about the meaning and the scope of the non-discrimination principle in EU law. The ECJ confirmed its previous interpretation, recalling how the *Simmenthal* doctrine and the principle of autonomy of EU law required the disapplication of national law contrasting with European legislation. This way the ECJ offered an interpretation of the same principle (principle of non-discrimination) very different from that provided by the Spanish Constitutional Tribunal: although a provision is consistent with the national Constitution it has to be disapplied if it contrasts with the EU law as interpreted by the ECJ.

The United Kingdom and Ireland

The history of the judicial application of the ECHR in the UK is that of the Human Rights Act, which has been accused of 'continuing futility'[350] by scholars. This is because of the questionable effects achievable through the declaration of incompatibility, since, as we saw in the previous chapter, such a declaration touches neither the validity nor the efficacy of the domestic provision. In Britain judges have used such a declaration and it is interesting to notice that once handed down it has always been followed by an amendment of the legislation thanks to the intervention of the

---

347 C-442/00 *Rodríguez Caballero* [2002] ECR I-11915.

348 Tribunal Constitucional, judgment no. 306/1993 of 25 October 1993, available at www.tribunalconstitucional.es.

349 'Since the general principle of equality and non-discrimination is a principle of Community law, Member States are bound by the Court's interpretation of that principle. That applies even when the national rules at issue are, according to the constitutional case law of the Member State concerned, consistent with an equivalent fundamental right recognised by the national legal system', *Cordero Alonso*, Paragraph 41.

350 K. Ewing and J.-Cheong Tham 'The Continuing Futility of the Human Rights Act' (2008) Public Law 668.

government and Parliament.[351] Does this imply the birth of a new constitutional Convention? Scholars[352] are sceptical but it is probably too early to conclude on this.

As we will see in the second part of this book, even recently, the case law of the ECtHR has had a certain impact on the UK in fields like counter-terrorism legislation and the saga of prisoners' right to vote,[353] with the famous judgment in *Hirst v The United Kingdom*[354] and with the more recent *Greens and MT v The United Kingdom*[355] decision, cases that have triggered a deep debate about the voting rights of convicted prisoners in the UK[356] and which, in a way, fostered a certain discontent.

As for EU law, whereas the most famous image representing the English perspective on European integration was given by Lord Denning's definition of EU law as an 'incoming tide', another significant 'picture' of the EU law's impact over the English legal order is framed in the famous *Thoburn* judgment where Judge Laws (*nomen et omen . . .*) attempted to combine

---

351 C. Murphy, 'Report on the UK and Ireland', in Martinico and Pollicino (eds), *The National Judicial Treatment of the ECHR and EU Laws*, 496.

352 'Even though the offending legislation has usually been changed, in some instances the factual situation of those affected by the law has not improved. For example, after the much-heralded Belmarsh detainees case led to the repeal of Part IV of the Anti-Terrorism, Crime and Security Act, the Government replaced it with the Prevention of Terrorism Act 2005. The effect was to replace internment with house (effective) arrest for those concerned. While the legal status of the individuals concerned has changed, their personal liberty has been seriously infringed upon by the state for almost a decade', Ibid.

353 G.F. Ferrari and O. Pollicino, 'The Impact of Supranational Laws on the National Sovereignty of Member States, with Particular Regard to the Judicial Reaction of UK and Italy to the New Aggressive Approach of the European Court of Human Rights', paper presented at the Hart Legal Workshop, Institute of Advanced Legal Studies, London, June 2011.

354 *Hirst v The United Kingdom* (No. 2) (Application no. 74025/01) [2005] ECHR 681: http://www.unlock.org.uk/userfiles/file/Votes/Hirst%20v%20UK%20Grand%20Chamber%20Judgment%206%20Oct%202005.pdf.

355 ECtHR, *Greens and MT v The United Kingdom* [2010] ECHR 1826, 23 November 2010.

356 'Voting rights of convicted prisoners detained within the United Kingdom – the UK Government's response to the Grand Chamber of the European Court of Human Rights judgment in the case of Hirst *v the United Kingdom*', consultation paper. Department for Constitutional Affairs, 14 December 2006, available at http://www.dca.gov.uk/consult/voting-rights/cp2906.pdf. 'Voting rights of convicted prisoners detained within the United Kingdom: second stage consultation. Consultation Paper CP6/09, Ministry of Justice', 8 April 2009. Available at http://www.justice.gov.uk/consultations/docs/prisonervoting-rights.pdf.

the need for guaranteeing EU law primacy with the untouchability of the sovereignty of the English Parliament.[357]

It is quite impossible to summarize all the judgments (coming both from ECJ and English judges) that could be relevant to our topic. Focusing attention on the latest years only, we can recall the strongest impact of judgments like *K.B.*,[358] *Richards*[359], and *P. v S.*,[360] under pressure of which important reforms and debates have risen. In the last year the UK was involved in at least three famous cases (*Singh*,[361] *Zhu and Chen*[362] and *Akrich*[363]) concerning the right to family reunion and citizenship.

Schematically we can distinguish three seasons in the (judicial) relationship between the internal and the European legal order. In the earliest years of EU membership the English judges tried to restrict the application of EU law to the uttermost limit by avoiding having to deal with 'legal positions' (*Rechtsstellung*) acknowledged by EU provisions. In case of legal conflicts the judge was bound to interpret the national law in conformity with the EU law; where this was not possible, the hypothesized solution was the application of the chronological criterion according to which *lex posterior derogat priori*. According to this approach, the European Community Act 1972 was conceived as an ordinary statute which was not empowered to limit parliamentary sovereignty.[364] The hidden premise of such an argument is the pure vision of the prevalence of the Westminster parliament's undiminished sovereignty: looking at the dicta in the *Felixstowe* and *Dock*[365] cases, for example, we could appreciate the reasoning according to which 'if there were to be any conflict between UK law and Community law then it would have to be the latter which would fall'.[366]

---

357 On this issue, see: W. Wade, 'Sovereignty and the European Communities' [1972] LQR 1; F. Trindade, 'Parliamentary Sovereignty and the Primacy of European Community Law' [1972] MLR 375 ff.; G. Winterton, 'The British Grundnorm: Parliamentary Supremacy Re-Examined', [1976] LQR 591 ff.; J. Warner, 'The Relationship between European Community Law and the National Laws of Member States', [1977] LQR 349 ff.; J. Mitchell, 'What Happened to the Constitution on 1st January 1973?' [1980] Cambrian L Rev 69ff.; See also: M. Elliott, 'Parliamentary Sovereignty and the New Constitutional Order: Legislative Freedom, Political Reality and Convention' [2002] Legal Studies 340.

358 C-117/01 *K.B.* [2004] ECR I-541.

359 C-423/04 *Richards* [2006] ECR I-3585.

360 C-13/94 *P v S* [1996] ECR I-2143.

361 C-370/90 *Singh* [1992] ECR I-4265.

362 C-200/02 *Zhu and Chen* [2004] ECR I-9925.

363 C-109/01 *Akrich* [2003] ECR I-9607.

364 *Felixstowe Dock v British Transport Docks Board* [1976] CMLR 655.

365 Ibid.

366 Craig, Report, 198.

The classic ('pure') concept of sovereignty adopted here was expressed in Dicey's works[367] and it implied the impossibility for successors of a certain parliament to be bound by its decisions; in other words: 'There is one, and only one, limit to Parliament's legal power: it cannot detract from its own continuing sovereignty.'[368]

In a second moment, this conception was overcome because of the increasing body of ECJ case law and the awareness that the EC Act had been adopted when the structural principles of EU law (direct effect and primacy) were already well known.[369] In those years, Lord Denning described the Treaty 'like an incoming tide. It flows into the estuaries and up the rivers. It cannot be held back. Parliament has decreed that the Treaty is henceforward to be part of our law . . . The governing provision is section 2 (1) of the European Communities Act 1972 . . . The statute is expressed in forthright terms which are absolute and all-embracing.'[370]

For the UK, the 'main event' of the troubled European experience is represented by the *Factortame* saga,[371] the contents of which are very famous and extensively analyzed by the literature. In 1990 the ECJ[372] ruled that national courts were granted the authority of striking down laws which contravened EU law. Consequently, the House of Lords held in favour of *Factortame*, acknowledging that: 'If the supremacy within the European Community of Community law over the national law of member states was not always inherent in the EEC Treaty it was certainly well established in the jurisprudence of the Court of Justice long before the United Kingdom joined the Community. Thus, whatever limitation of its sovereignty Parliament accepted when it enacted the European Communities Act 1972 was entirely voluntary.'[373]

Paul Craig wrote that the *Factortame* doctrine represented 'a refusal to continue to shelter behind a traditional constitutional doctrine which,

---

367 A. Dicey, *An Introduction to the Study of the Law of the Constitution* (Macmillan 1959) 10.

368 Craig, Report, 197.

369 'The relevant Common Market law should be applied in this country, and should, where there is a conflict override English law', *Aero Zipp Fasteners Ltd and Lightning Fasteners Ltd v YKK Fasteners (UK) Ltd* (1973) CMLR 819, 820.

370 *Bulmer Ltd v Bollinger SA* [1974] 2 All ER 1226.

371 K. Magliveras, 'Fishing in Troubled Waters: The Merchant Shipping Act 1988 and the European Community' (1990) 39 Intl Comparative L Q 899 ff.; W. Wade, 'What Has Happened to the Sovereignty of Parliament?' (1991) 107 LQR 1, 3.

372 C-213/89, [1990] ECR I-2433.

373 *R v Secretary of State for Transport ex parte Factortame (No. 2)* [1991] AC 603, 658.

taken literally, coheres so badly both with the political fact of membership and the nature of the Community legal order. When viewed from this perspective the House of Lords' decision can be seen as a form of "constitutional catch-up": a modification of constitutional doctrine in order that it might better reflect the existing political reality of our membership of the EC.'[374]

The UK Independence Party, the most euro-sceptical among UK's political parties,[375] labelled the *Factortame* decision as a symbol of erosion of the UK's sovereignty and a breach in parliamentary sovereignty.

Having assumed the primacy of EU law, the English judges' resistance insisted either on the identification of the limits to such primacy, repeating what Lord Denning had already stated,[376] or on the separation of competences between internal and supranational law.[377]

It is possible to argue that the notion of sovereignty brought forward in cases like *Thoburn*[378] or *Mc Wirther*[379] introduces a new phase in the English constitutional debate. This is precisely what happened in *Thoburn.*[380] In this judgment, Laws LJ recognized the existence of a constitutional group of statutes and acts which included the European Communities Act 1972: the Magna Charta, the Bill of Rights of 1689, the Acts of Union of 1707, the Reform Acts, the HRA of 1998, the Scotland Act of 1998, the Government of Wales Act of 1998 and the European Communities Act of 1972 all belong to the category of 'constitutional' statutes. Looking at the judges' reasoning, it is possible to appreciate a further effort to reconcile

---

374 Craig, 'Report', 211.

375 See the very interesting piece by G. Drewry, 'The Jurisprudence of British Euroscepticism: A Strange Banquet of Fish and Vegetables', 3 Utrecht Law Review 2, 101. See the UKIP's website: http://www.ukip.org/ukip/index.php.

376 'If the time should come when our Parliament deliberately passes an Act – with the intention of repudiating the EEC Treaty or any provision in it – or intentionally of acting inconsistently with it – and says so in express terms – I should have thought that it would be the duty of our courts to follow the statute of our Parliament', *Macarthys Ltd v Smith* [1979] 3 All ER 325.

377 'The Treaty does not touch any of the matters which concern solely the mainland of England and the people in it. These are still governed by English law. They are not affected by the Treaty', *Bulmer Ltd v Bollinger SA* [1974] 2 All ER 1226.

378 *Thoburn v Sunderland City Council* [2002] 1 CMLR 50.

379 *Mc Whirter and Gouriet v Secretary of State for Foreign Affairs* [2003], EWCA civ 384. On these two cases, see: A. Biondi, 'Principio di supremazia e "Costituzione" inglese. I due casi "Martiri del sistema metrico" e "Mc Whirter and Gouriet"', at www.forumcostituzionale.it/site/index3.php?option=com_content&task=view&id=101&Itemid=82.

380 *Thoburn v Sunderland City Council* [2002] 1 CMLR 50.

the primacy of EU law (now vested with constitutional status) with parliamentary sovereignty. According to this judgment, in fact, the EU law's primacy is based on the Parliament's self-limitation; in other words, the legal basis of the UK's relationship with the EU rests on national provisions, not on EU law:

> There is nothing in the [European Communities Act] which allows the Court of Justice, or any other institutions of the EU, to touch or qualify the conditions of Parliament's legislative supremacy in the United Kingdom. Not because the legislature chose not to allow it; because by our law it could not allow it.

If the EU law were to violate a constitutional right guaranteed by the UK's (unwritten) Constitution, the former could not prevail over the latter. This idea of the existence of some counter-limits to EU law (i.e. those national fundamental principles which have been raised by the national Courts – like impenetrable barriers – against the penetration of EU law) was again brought forward in *Mc Whirter and Gouriet*[381] where the Court of Appeal conceived the possibility of denying the primacy of EU law whenever it challenged the English legal order's constitutional principles.

In any case, according to other scholars,[382] one should not overestimate the importance of *Thoburn*, since the statements of Laws LJ have not been confirmed by the House of Lords, from this one could infer that *Factortame* still remains the reference judgment in the UK context.

The UK was also characterized by a relatively low number of preliminary references[383] sent to the ECJ; however, over the years, national judges have overcome this reluctance and today the preliminary ruling mechanism.[384]

---

[381] *McWhirter and Gouriet v Secretary of State for Foreign Affairs* [2003] EWCA civ 384. On this point, see Biondi, 'Principio di supremazia e "Costituzione" inglese'.

[382] For instance, Murphy, 'Report on the UK and Ireland': 'However, it must be noted that Laws' statement in *Thoburn* came in the Court of Appeal and has not been approved by the House of Lords. As such, the more deferential approach in *Factortame* remains the binding precedent in the UK'.

[383] *Bulmer Ltd v Bollinger SA* [1974] 2 All ER 1226. As noticed by M. Patrono, 'I giudici inglesi e le Corti europee: "alti" e "bassi" di un rapporto "difficile"', in G. F. Ferrari (ed.), *Corti costituzionali e Corti europee* (ESI 2006) 35 ff. there were three main reasons for the low number of preliminary rulings in the UK (specifically English) context: (1) the English judges were not accustomed to something like the proceeding described in Article 234 ECT; (2) the lack of pragmatism and the initiative shown by the ECJ in the Marshall and Van Duyn case; (3) the notion of parliamentary sovereignty.

[384] Murphy, 'Report on the UK and Ireland', 492. In *Customs and Excise Commissioners v ApS Samex* [1983] 1 All ER 1042; *R v International Stock*

The importance of judicial interactions could still be confirmed after the Reform Treaty of Lisbon. Recently scholars have stressed the absurdity of the famous Polish and UK 'opt out'[385] (although it does not represent an 'opt out' properly speaking[386]). It has been said, rightly, that the goal of this protocol consisted in limiting the effect of the Charter without saying – and it would have been impossible under Article 6 of the EUT[387] – that it is not binding on the UK and Poland. How is it possible to limit the ECJ and the national judges – the most efficient allies of the Luxembourg Court, thanks to the preliminary ruling mechanism? The ECJ is the master of the principle of direct effect (a precondition of the disapplication of national acts inconsistent with EU law). Contesting the possibility to

---

Exchange ex parte Else [1993] QB 534, Bingham J. said that '[i]f the national court has any real doubt, it should obviously refer'. This case can be seen as an evidence of the new trend.

[385] In order to escape the risk of being subject to such provisions, the UK and Poland insisted on signing a specific protocol (no. 30) stating that: '1. The charter does not extend the ability of the Court of Justice of the European Union, or any court or tribunal of Poland or of the United Kingdom, to find that the laws, regulations or administrative provisions, practices or action of Poland or of the United Kingdom are inconsistent with the fundamental rights, freedoms and principles that it reaffirms.

2. In particular, and for the avoidance of doubt, nothing in Title IV of the charter creates justifiable rights applicable to Poland or the United Kingdom except in so far as Poland or the United Kingdom has provided for such rights in its national law.'

Article 2 of the Protocol: 'To the extent that a provision of the charter refers to national laws and practices, it shall only apply to Poland or the United Kingdom to the extent that the rights or principles that it contains are recognised in the law or practices of Poland or of the United Kingdom'.

[386] 'The opt-out is not an opt-out at all': Catherine Barnard, 'The "Opt-out" for the UK and Poland from the Charter of Fundamental Rights: Triumph of Rhetoric over Reality?', paper presented at the Conference 'The Lisbon Treaty and the Future of European Constitutionalism', 11–12 April 2008, EUI, Fiesole. Confirmation of this hypothesis could be found in the words of the House of Lords EU Select Committee: 'The Protocol is not an opt-out from the Charter. The Charter will apply in the UK, even if its interpretation may be affected by the terms of the Protocol. The Preamble itself of the document does not use the qualification in terms of opt-out, its goal consists of the clarification of certain aspects of the application of the Charter', House of Lords EU Select Committee, 'The Treaty of Lisbon: an impact assessment', available at: http://www.publications.parliament.uk/pa/ld200708/ldselect/ldeucom/62/62.pdf.

[387] As we know, in fact, Article 6 EUT states:

'The Union recognises the rights, freedoms and principles set out in the Charter of Fundamental Rights of the European Union of 7 December 2000, as adapted at Strasbourg, on 12 December 2007, which shall have the same legal value as the Treaties'.

derogate from the interpretive monopoly of the ECJ (codified by Article 344[388] of the TFEU) would imply contesting the autonomy of EU law. Moreover, since in many parts the Charter is repetitive of preexisting principles, the ECJ or the national judges could refer to such principles obtaining the same result without need to recall the formal text of the Charter. Despite the letter of such a text, probably the last say will be that of the (national and supranational) judges in the actual application of EU law and the game for sovereignty will be played at the level of the cultural sources of law following the tradition of the path of European integration. Indeed, recently, the ECJ endorsed this view in its *NS* judgment by saying that:

> In those circumstances, Article 1(1) of Protocol (No 30) explains Article 51 of the Charter with regard to the scope thereof and does not intend to exempt the Republic of Poland or the United Kingdom from the obligation to comply with the provisions of the Charter or to prevent a court of one of those Member States from ensuring compliance with those provisions.[389]

As we saw in the previous chapter, in Ireland the primacy of EU law finds its confirmation in the constitutional text in Article 29, which seems to acknowledge a priority of EU law over all the domestic sources of law (including the Constitution).[390]

Case law has tried to interpret the meaning of the formula 'the State necessitated by the obligations of membership of the Communities' against this background. In *Crotty*[391], for example, the Supreme Court ruled that Title III of the Single Act was not a measure necessitated by EU membership and therefore another referendum was needed for its ratification. Similarly in *Maher v Minister for Agriculture*[392] the judge gave a strict

---

388 Article 344 TFEU: 'Member States undertake not to submit a dispute concerning the interpretation or application of the Treaties to any method of settlement other than those provided for therein'.

389 C-411/10 NS & Others v SSHD and C-493/10 M.E. and Others v Refugee Applications Commissioner, Minister for Justice, Equality and Law Reform, http://curia.europa.eu/juris/document/document.jsf?text=&docid=117187&pageIndex=0&doclang=en&mode=req&dir=&occ=first&part=1&cid=211472, Paragraph 120.

390 'No provision of this Constitution invalidates law enacted, acts done or measures adopted by the State necessitated by the obligations of membership of the Communities, or prevents laws enacted or acts done or measures adopted by the Communities or the institutions thereof, from having the force of law in the State.'

391 *Crotty v An Taoiseach* [1987] IR 173.

392 *Maher v Minister for Agriculture* [2001] 2 IR 139.

definition to the word 'necessitated' emphasizing that the term could not simply be equated to what was 'desirable' or 'convenient'.[393]

Irish Courts regularly apply EU law taking its primacy into account,[394] as stated in *Pigs and Bacon Commission v McCarren*,[395] for instance. Moreover, in 1997, Henchy, a Judge of the Supreme Court of Ireland, clearly explained:

> Because Community law is part of domestic law, it is the duty of the courts set up under the Constitution to implement it; but it is the exclusive function of the European Court to interpret and determine conclusively the validity of the Treaties and of acts put forward as Community law; and where a conflict is found between national law and Community law, it is an absolute imperative that the Community law shall prevail.[396]

However, dangerous risks of collision between orders could not be avoided in these years thus making the *Grogan* judgment a point of reference in the Irish case law. In this case the Irish Supreme Court sent a message to the Luxembourg Court saying that: 'If and when a decision of the Court of Justice of the European Communities rules that some aspect of European Community law affects the activities of the defendants impugned in this case, the consequence of that decision on these constitutionally guaranteed rights and their protection by the courts will then fall to be considered by these courts.'[397]

---

[393] J. Tomkin, 'Implementing Community Legislation into National Law: The Demands of a New Legal Order' [2004] Judicial Studies Institute J, 130.

[394] W. Phelan, 'Can Ireland Legislate Contrary to European Community Law?' wtphelan.googlepages.com/PhelanIrelandLegislateECLawShort21Fe.pdf.

[395] 'The effect of [Section 2 of the European Communities Act 1972] is that Community law takes legal effect in the Irish legal system in the manner in which Community law itself provides. Thus, if according to Community law a provision of the Treaty is directly enforceable so that rights are conferred on individuals which national courts must enforce, an Irish court must give effect to such a rule. And if, according to Community law, the provisions of Community law take precedence over a provision of national law in conflict with it an Irish court must give effect to this rule. That Community law enjoys precedence over a conflicting national law has been made clear in a number of decisions of the European Court and most recently in Case 106/77, *Amministrazione delle Finanze dello Stato v Simmenthal*'. *Pigs and Bacon Commission v McCarren* [1978] JISEL 87.

[396] S. Henchy, 'The Irish Constitution and the E.E.C.' [1977] Dublin University L J 20, 23.

[397] *S.P.U.C. v Grogan* [1989] IR 753. In a similar case the Irish Court preferred not to take EU law in account (in order to avoid the collision with the ECJ) arguing that: 'Apart from the practical time scale difficulties of obtaining a ruling by way of preliminary ruling from the Court of Justice of the European

Despite (the avoided collision of) the *Grogan* and *X* cases, it is possible to say that the Irish judges have generally accepted the structural principles of EU law and a strong confirmation of this Irish Court can be found in the *Campus Oil* case,[398] where the Supreme Court held that the High Court judge's decision to refer to the ECJ could not be subject to appeal. This decision was strongly criticized, as it was seen as a sort of judicial submission,[399] but it confirms the positive approach of the Irish judges to EU law and the ECJ.

The Irish judges conceive the preliminary ruling mechanism as a physiological tool for guaranteeing the uniform application of EU law, although this conviction is subject to change when they deal with issues involving religious or nationalistic ethos (see the *Grogan* or *X* cases).

Another and perhaps the most important difference from the UK case consists of the tool used to overcome real conflicts between supranational and national law: looking at the Irish case following the *Crotty*[400] doctrine, the possibility of a contrast between these laws has caused a never-ending process of formal constitutional updating[401] while in the British case the last say seems de facto granted to the judges.

Community, pursuant to Article 177 of the Treaty, in time for the due resolution of the problems arising in this case, it is consistent with the jurisprudence of the Court that there being a ground on which the case can be decided without reference to European law, but under Irish law only, that method should be employed', *The Attorney General (Plaintiff) v X. and Others* [1992] 1 IR 1.

398 *Campus Oil Limited v Minister for Industry and Energy* [1983] IR 82.

399 D. O'Keefe, 'Appeals Against an Order to Refer under Article 177' (1984) 9 E L Rev 87.

400 *Crotty v An Taoiseach*: 'It is the opinion of the Court that the first sentence in Article 29, s. 4, sub-s. 3 of the Constitution must be construed as an authorisation given to the State not only to join the Communities as they stood in 1973, but also to join in amendments of the Treaties so long as such amendments do not alter the essential scope or objectives of the Communities. To hold that the first sentence of Article 29, s. 4, sub-s. 3 does not authorise any form of amendment to the Treaties after 1973 without a further amendment of the Constitution would be too narrow a construction; to construe it as an open-ended authority to agree, without further amendment of the Constitution, to any amendment of the Treaties would be too broad.'

401 T. Groppi, 'La primauté del diritto europeo sul diritto costituzionale nazionale: un punto di vista comparato', Astrid-Rassegna, 13/2005, www.astrid-online.it/rassegna/Rassegna-2/29-07-2005/Groppi_primaut-DirittoUE_ScrittiPizz.pdf. See, for example, the amendment of Article 40, paragraph 3.3 of the Irish Constitution after the *Grogan* and *AG v X cases*: '3° The State acknowledges the right to life of the unborn and, with due regard to the equal right to life of the mother, guarantees in its laws to respect, and, as far as practicable, by its laws to defend and vindicate that right.

This context does not exclude risks of collision when the fundamental principles of the Irish Constitution are challenged. In these cases the Supreme Court's behaviour (not only but mainly) changes because the Irish judges perceive their function of constitutional protection as contested. Thus, despite the above mentioned 'formal openness' as per Article 29 of the Constitution, this ambivalent judicial attitude of the Irish Courts shows the existence of some substantial 'counter-limits' that have to be conceived as untouchable by the rationale of supranational integration and confirms the importance of the judicial side of the relationship between legal orders even in a context characterized by a written Constitution.

Lastly, when looking at the Irish and UK experiences it is possible to notice some shared judicial trends: in both jurisdictions the judges have played a crucial role in combining the primacy of EU law with constitutional supremacy (or, in English terms, with parliamentary sovereignty), by changing both their starting case law and the very way of interpreting domestic law.

Less rich is the story of the application of the ECHR within the Republic of Ireland because of the fresh incorporation of the Convention by means of the Human Rights Act 2003. Here again, like in Britain, many doubts have been raised about the real effectiveness of the declaration of incompatibility. Moreover, the Irish Constitution offers constitutional remedies much more efficient than the declaration of incompatibility, which gives 'rise only to political obligations'[402] and that is why even in the case law it is very easy to find evidence of a sort of scepticism towards this instrument.[403]

Although it is probably too early to assess the impact of the ECHR system in the Irish context, even in the recent past tensions have not been

---

This subsection shall not limit freedom to travel between the State and another state.

This subsection shall not limit freedom to obtain or make available, in the State, subject to such conditions as may be laid down by law, information relating to services lawfully available in another state'.

[402] 'Not only does [the declaration] give rise only to political obligations and leave the offending law intact, but it is likely to provide little more than a symbolic victory to the applicant. In some circumstances – such as social movements litigation for example – such a symbolic victory can be extremely valuable. However, in cases where someone is in urgent and immediate need of counsel, or housing (for example) the victory is phyrric', F. de Londras, 'De Londras on Carmody' (Blog entry to http://humanrightsinireland.wordpress.com /2009/11/27/ de-londras-on-carmody/#more-1990).

[403] *Carmody v Minister for Justice, Equality and Law Reform* [2009] IESC 71.

missing – the case of *A, B and C v Ireland*, on the always burning issue of abortion, is a signal of that.[404]

3. AN APPRAISAL

As we have seen, despite the variety of constitutional provisions, EU law is treated in the same manner in all the Member States or, better, the structural principles of EU law are respected elsewhere although phenomena of national resistance are not missing.[405]

Something similar can be said with regard to the ECHR, as Keller and Stone Sweet pointed out.[406] In order to realize this, it was necessary to go beyond the wording of formal provisions and examine how national judges treat these European laws.

The first element these two European laws share is thus the crucial role of national judges, who are the real 'natural judges' of European laws, for different reasons: they are the first guardians of the *Simmenthal* doctrine for EU law,[407] while they are the first adjudicators of the ECHR in national systems like the French and the Dutch, and because of the principle of judicial subsidiarity.[408]

The emphasis on the case law explains why we have devoted so much attention to the case law of national courts. Having recalled both the wording of the constitutional provisions and the doctrines of the respective courts, we are now ready to give an answer to our first research question: Are national judges extending the structural EU law principles (primacy and direct effect) to the European Convention on Human Rights?

From the analysis of the case law a clear convergence does not seem to emerge, EU law is often treated in a very particular manner and this for different reasons. First of all is the fabric of principles that is the preliminary ruling mechanism, which in a constant way contributes to transforming EU law and which has given the ECJ over the years a great interpretative power. The ECJ exercises this interpretative power not only on the EU law

---

404 *A, B and C v Ireland* [2010] ECHR 2032 (Application no. 25579/05), available at: http://cmiskp.echr.coe.int/tkp197/view.asp?action=html&documentId=878721&portal=hbkm&source=externalbydocnumber&table=F69A27FD8FB86142BF01C1166DEA398649.

405 See the reaction to the *Mangold* case, for instance.

406 Keller and Stone Sweet, *A Europe of Rights*, 685–86.

407 Claes, *The National Courts' Mandate*.

408 P. Carrozza, 'Subsidiarity as a Structural Principle of International Human Rights Law' (2003) 97 *American Journal of International Law* 38ff.

provisions properly understood but also, in an indirect manner, on those national legislations of implementation of EU acts, influencing, at the end of day, the meaning of national law.

This has also been perceived by those national constitutional courts that have recently started accepting the preliminary ruling mechanism governed by Article 267 of the TFUE.[409] Another explanation for this growing use of the preliminary reference is given by what we called 'the dark side' of the constitutionalization of the EU we discussed when mentioning the *Mangold* case.

Given that the ECJ has expressly begun to use national constitutional materials to shape the common constitutional traditions and the principles of EC/EU law, it could be very dangerous for the guardians of those very national principles to wait and witness such an interpretation passively. One can imagine the setting of a common 'currency' in judicial transactions[410] as the real motive of a strategy change from the perspective of the constitutional courts. Our suspicion (but we will see what the future holds) is that the communitarization of counter-limits has partially frustrated the constitutional courts' trigger strategy.[411]

However, if the preliminary ruling mechanism and the existence of the secondary EU law (including that requiring national implementation) are the main reasons behind the strong penetration of EU law within the national boundaries, our position does not abandon, totally at least, the convergence hypothesis.

At a closer look, in fact, in our view there is a basis for describing at least a 'minimal convergence' in the national judicial treatments of these two European laws.

In order to explain the essence of this minimal convergence we are going to recall the following national judicial practices that an external observer encounters when dealing with the ECHR and EU law:

(1) consistent interpretation;
(2) judicial disapplication of domestic law;
(3) counter-limits doctrine.

---

[409] G. Martinico, 'Preliminary Reference and Constitutional Courts. Are You in the Mood for Dialogue?' TICOM Working Paper, 10/2009.

[410] Which is represented by the language of fundamental rights and by the will to participate in determining it.

[411] F. Fontanelli and G. Martinico, 'Between Procedural Impermeability and Constitutional Openness: The 102 and Decision of the Italian Constitutional Court', European L J, 345.

(3.1) Consistent Interpretation

A first analogy in the national judicial treatment of these two European laws may be found in the interpretive favour accorded to the EU/ECHR by the national judges independently from what the national constitutions provide about their status in the domestic legal order.

Consistent interpretation is a very well-known doctrine in EU law (see the *Von Colson*[412] and *Marleasing*[413] judgments). More generally, consistent interpretation is a widespread doctrine in multilevel systems (even in the USA[414]) since it guarantees great flexibility in the relationship between laws and gives the role of gatekeeper to judges (see the *Hermès*[415] and *Dior*[416] judgments concerning the relationship between EU and WTO laws). Traditionally the literature conceives of consistent interpretation as an indirect effect since it confirms the primacy of EU law, giving a sort of interpretive priority to EU law norms, especially when the conflict between norms cannot be solved by using the *Simmenthal* doctrine because of the absence of the direct effect for the EU law provisions.

It is a well-known story which does not need repeating. The only thing we would like to point out is the increasing importance of consistent interpretation in EU law, as recently stressed by Rodin:[417] the *Simmenthal* doctrine is a rigid one which requires a unilateral conclusion in case of constitutional conflict (i.e. conflict between constitutional supremacy and the primacy of EU law) while the consistent interpretation makes it possible to neutralize or soften constitutional conflicts, where this is possible, of course.

As for the ECHR, an identical effect is achieved on the basis of three different factors: (1) constitutional provisions (e.g. Spain, Romania among others); (2) legislative provisions (United Kingdom); (3) constitutional courts' case law (e.g. Italy and Germany, among others).

This is a first impact of the constitutional variety described in Chapter 2. When describing this practice we have selected just some emblematic experiences but, as we saw in the first part of this chapter, the technique

412 ECJ, C-14/83, *Von Colson* [1985] ECR 1891ff.

413 ECJ, C-106/89, *Marleasing* [1990] ECR I 4345 ff.

414 'Charming Betsy' canon, 6 U.S. (2 Cranch) 64 (1804).

415 ECJ, C-53/96, *Hermès International (a partnership limited by shares) v FHT Marketing Choice BV* [1998] ECR I-3603.

416 ECJ, C-300/98 and C-302/98, *Dior and others* [2000] ECR 11307.

417 S. Rodin, 'Back to Square One. The Past, the Present and the Future of the Simmenthal Mandate', paper presented at the 8th ECLN, Madrid, 6–8 October 2010.

of consistent interpretation is common to all the European national experiences; there is no doubt about that. Starting with the first group, as we saw in the previous chapter, the most important confirmation of the special ranking reserved to human rights treaties in Spain is given by Article 10.2, about the so-called role of interpretive guide for reading the constitutional clauses devoted to fundamental rights, although the Spanish Constitutional Tribunal has specified that such a technique does not give a constitutional status to the human rights treaties. Similar provisions are present in Portugal and in Romania, for instance. As we can see, according to all these provisions, national law shall be interpreted in light of the contents of the ECHR (and other treaties devoted to human rights); this way a sort of interpretive priority is acknowledged to the ECHR.

The duty to interpret national law in a manner which is consistent with the ECHR provisions is sometimes based on legislative provisions, as is the case of the UK, pursuant to Section 3 of the Human Rights Act, which provides the necessity to interpret domestic law 'so far as is possible' in a consistent way to the Convention rights.

Finally, there are cases where in the absence of an expressed written provision (either constitutional or legislative norm) the duty to interpret national law in light of the ECHR can be found in the case law of the Constitutional Court. This is exactly the German and Italian case as we saw above.

In conclusion, as we have seen, the consistent interpretation technique has been extended from EU law to the ECHR by different routes: constitutional, legislative and judicial. This does not mean that the convergence between legal orders in the national treatment is perfect: for instance, it is not always clear whether the duty to interpret national law in light of the ECHR implies the necessity to take into account the case law of the ECtHR. In this respect there are different answers. From a formal point of view the mentioned Constitutions do not say anything about that, while the Human Rights Act UK expressly provides at Section 2 that: 'A court or tribunal determining a question which has arisen in connection with a Convention right must take into account any – (a) judgment, decision, declaration or advisory opinion of the European Court of Human Rights.' As we saw, in Italy and Germany the Constitutional Courts expressly acknowledge the necessity to take into account the case law of the Strasbourg Court.

As a final remark to this sub-section devoted to consistent interpretation: while in the cases of consistent interpretation based on constitutional provisions the constitutions do not distinguish between the ECHR and other international treaties devoted to human rights, in the other two cases (consistent interpretation based on legislation and judicial decisions) such an interpretive favour was conceived ad hoc for the ECHR.

(3.2) Judicial Disapplication of Domestic Law: *Simmenthal* Reloaded?

As already noted, the national judge is considered the first guarantor of the principle of EU law primacy, thanks to the very well-known *Simmenthal* judgment of the ECJ.[418] When looking at *Simmenthal* one can infer: (a) the connection between primacy/precedence of EC (now EU) law and the duty to disapply national law conflicting with it; (b) the crucial role of domestic judges in the protection of the primacy principle.

We want to point out how a second similitude in the national judicial treatment of European laws rests in the solution devised in cases of conflict between domestic norms and EU/ECHR norms: the well-known *Simmenthal* doctrine, as applicable by analogy to ECHR law. Here again, we can find different reasons for this (here again the variety of constitutional provisions analyzed in the first part of the book demonstrates its importance): (1) In some cases the extension of the disapplication practice can be explained on constitutional bases (France, the Netherlands). (2) In other cases, instead, such an extension has been devised by the genius of domestic (common) judges (e.g. in Italy).

A first set of cases is given by countries characterized by specific constitutional provisions empowering national judges to disapply national law that conflicts with international treaties. Beginning with the case of France the super-primary place of international treaties in the domestic system can be inferred from Article 55 which provides the superiority of the ratified treaties over domestic legislation. The superiority of treaties over the national law (control of '*conventionnalité*') is instead entrusted to the national judges.

As we saw, unlike the French case, many Eastern European countries have entrusted the control of the compatibility between international treaties and national legislation to the constitutional courts with a convergence between control of constitutionality and control of '*conventionnalité*'.[419] A similar mechanism – with the important variable represented by the lack of a Constitutional Court properly so-called in the Netherlands – is given by the Dutch case. The Dutch model is based on Articles 91 and 93 of the *Grondwet* (the Basic Law). As we can see, in both France and the Netherlands the convergence between EU law and the ECHR is actually due to a constitutional set of norms which seem not to distinguish between public international law

418 ECJ, C-106/77, *Simmenthal* [1978] ECR 629. On the recent developments of the Simmenthal doctrine, see: Rodin, 'Back to Square One'.

419 About the jurisdiction of the national constitutional courts in this field, see: Bulgaria Article 149.4; Poland Article 188; Czech Republic Article 87; Slovenia Article 160. See Montanari, *I diritti* 99.

and EU law. That is why a few years ago two scholars concluded their comparative piece arguing that in those contexts 'there is no fundamental divide between the application of public international law and EU law'.[420]

The second case of extension of the *Simmenthal* doctrine to the ECHR is completely different as to scope and reasons: it is the Italian case. As the literature has already stressed,[421] the Italian common (*comuni*) judges started disapplying domestic norms conflicting with the ECHR.[422] As we saw, even after the judgment of the intervention of the Italian Constitutional Court,[423] some domestic common judges continued to disapply national provisions conflicting with the ECHR. There are other interesting (yet less clear-cut) cases: in Bulgaria, Portugal, Spain scholars and judges are still debating the issue.

Of course there are also contexts where disapplication is not permitted or non practised, either on the basis of the case law of the respective Constitutional Courts (also in the presence of constitutional provisions which would authorize this, Spain and Portugal as we saw) or because expressly forbidden by the wording of national legislation (see the UK Human Rights Act which expressly excludes the possibility of setting aside the national legislation the subject of the declaration of incompatibility).

(3.3) The Limits to Primacy: the Counter-limits Doctrine

As Maduro pointed out, 'the acceptance of the supremacy of EU rules over national constitutional rules has not been unconditional, if not even, at times, resisted by national constitutional courts. This confers to EU law a kind of contested or negotiated normative authority.'[424] It also reveals

---

[420] Betlem and Nollkaemper, 'Giving Effect to Public International Law and European Community Law before Domestic Courts'.

[421] Biondi Dal Monte and Fontanelli, 'The Decisions No. 348 and 349/2007'; Pollicino, 'The Italian Constitutional Court'.

[422] See: Court of Pistoia on 23 March 2007: Court of Genoa, decision of 23 November, 2000; Court of Appeal of Florence decisions No. 570 of 2005 and No. 1403 of 2006, and the State Council (*Consiglio di Stato*), I Section, decision No. 1926 of 2002: 'Some judges had already started applying this method, which comes from the judicial practice of disapplying the internal statutory norm conflicting with Community law. In some recent occasions, even the Supreme Court of Cassation (*Corte di Cassazione*) and the Supreme Administrative Court (*Consiglio di Stato*) had endorsed the use of disapplication in cases of conflict with ECtHR law', Biondi Dal Monte and Fontanelli, 'The Decisions No. 348 and 349/2007', 891.

[423] Carlotto, 'I giudici comuni'; Lamarque, 'Il vincolo'.

[424] M. Poiares Maduro, 'Interpreting European Law: Judicial Adjudication in a Context of Constitutional Pluralism' (2007) European J Legal Studies, 2, http://ejls.eu/index.php?mode=htmlarticle&filename=./issues/2007-12/MaduroUK.htm.

the existence of a never-ending process of judicial bargaining between domestic courts (especially Constitutional and Supreme Courts) and the ECJ. The conditions posed by the Constitutional Courts and mentioned by Maduro are represented by doctrines such as the 'counter-limits' (*controlimiti*[425]) and *Solange* doctrines.

According to Panunzio,[426] the counter-limits (even in the *Solange* doctrine) represent an instrument to force the courts to communicate; they are like a 'gun on the table' which induces the jurisdictional actors to interact and compare their visions.

It is interesting to see how a similar doctrine has been devised also with regard to the ECHR's penetration into the domestic legal order. The most evident confirmation of such a trend is present in the German case law and in the already mentioned order no. 1481/04.[427] A similar conclusion was made by the Italian Constitutional Court in the decisions of 2007 (nos. 348 and 349), where the Italian *Consulta* pointed out how the favour accorded to the ECHR does not give the ECHR constitutional immunity; on the contrary, the ECHR has to respect the Italian Constitution.

In those decisions, the Italian Constitutional Court specified how the ECHR is considered a particular form of public international law and from this it inferred that the 'constitutional tolerance' shown by the Italian legal order towards the ECHR is inferior to that shown towards EU law. While the 'counter-limits' represent, in the Italian Constitutional Court's case law, a selected version of the domestic constitutional materials (this implies the possibility to decide constitutional conflicts in favour of the EU law provisions in some cases), in the case of the ECHR the Italian Court seems to be less generous, since it seems to ask the ECHR to respect the whole Constitution as such: 'the need for a constitutionality test on the Convention norm excludes the possibility of having a limited set of fundamental rights that could serve as a counter-limit; indeed, every norm of the Constitution shall be respected by the international norm challenged'.[428]

Görgülü is not an isolated case – we mentioned analogous tensions in other contexts. For instance, Krisch[429] compared this case with the *Miltner*

---

425 This formula was introduced in the Italian scholarly debate by P. Barile, 'Ancora su diritto comunitario e diritto interno', in *Studi per il XX anniversario dell'Assemblea costituente*, VI, Florence, 1969, 49.

426 S. Panunzio, 'I diritti fondamentali e le Corti in Europa', in S.P. Panunzio (ed.), *I diritti fondamentali e le Corti in Europa* (Naples 2005), 1, 104.

427 2 BvR 1481/04.

428 Biondi Dal Monte and Fontanelli, 'The Decisions No. 348 and 349/2007', 915.

429 Krisch, 'The Open Architecture'.

case[430] in Austria, with the reactions in the French contexts[431] related to the *Poitrimol* case[432] or the *Borgers* case.[433]

Again, besides these examples it is possible to recognize everywhere the emergence of a set of limits aimed at preserving the national constitutional identity even for the ECHR and EU law. Estonia, Belgium (but this is disputed, as we saw), Luxembourg and the Netherlands appear to be the only exceptions to this trend.

In any case, convergence does not mean perfect coincidence but describes a process of mutual rapprochement between legal entities; it is a work in progress. We will come back to this point in the conclusion of this volume.

However, comparing the current scenario with that studied by Neville and McBride[434] in the 1970s–1980s, it is immediately clear that, today, the issue of ECHR's primacy and direct effect does not depend only on what is written in the constitutions, it is something that seems to go beyond the full control of national constitutions.

In this scenario, EU law has also provided national judges (the Italian case is very clear on this) with arguments for reconsidering ECHR's force, as Keller and Stone Sweet, for instance, noticed.[435]

---

430 Austrian Constitutional Court, Judgment of 14 October 1987, Miltner, VfSlg 11500/1987, available via http://www.ris.bka.gv.at/vfgh/.

431 R. de Gouttes, 'Le juge judiciaire français et la Convention européenne des droits de l'homme: avancées et reticences', in P. Tavernier (ed.), *Quelle Europe pour les droits de l'homme?* (Bruylant 1996), 217.

432 ECtHR, Judgment of 23 November 1993, *Poitrimol v France*; See also ECtHR, Judgments of 29 July 1998, *Omar v France* and *Guérin v France*; Judgment of 14 December 1999, *Khalfaoui v France*.

433 ECtHR, Judgment of 30 October 1991, *Borgers v Belgium*.

434 L. Neville Brown, J. McBride, 'Observations on the Proposed Accession by the European Community to the European Convention on Human Rights', 4 *American Journal of Comparative Law*, (1981) 691, at 695.

435 'European integration – the evolution of the EU's legal system, in particular – has shaped reception in a number of crucial ways. First, the ECJ's commitment to the doctrines of the supremacy and direct effect of Community law provoked processes that, ultimately, transformed national law and practice. Supremacy required national courts to review the legality of statutes with respect to EC law, and to give primacy to EC norms in any conflict with national norms. For judges in many EU States, the reception of supremacy meant overcoming a host of constitutional orthodoxies, including the prohibition of judicial review of statute, the *lex posteriori derogat legi priori*, and separation of powers notions. These same structural issues arose anew under the Convention', Keller-Stone Sweet, 'Assessing', *supra*, at 681.

PART II

4. External convergence: towards a rapprochement of the EU and ECHR regimes after the enlargement of Europe to the East

1. LOOKING AT THE 'ORIGINS': CLOSER THAN THEY SEEM

The aim of this volume, as pointed out in the introduction, is to provide a comparative study devoted to investigating the evolving nature of the European Union legal order and the European Convention of Human Rights (ECHR), with particular regard to their impact on the domestic legal principal objection by analyzing the two supranational organizations from their foundations cannot escape one. That is, it could be easily objected that up until the mid-1970s, when the ECJ finally decided to take the protection of fundamental rights in the European Community 'seriously'[1] and started to make express reference to the case law of ECtHR,[2] the similarities between the two legal orders under investigation were so few as to make an in-depth comparison between them almost pointless.

However, on a closer examination, this objection does not seem so well grounded. On the one hand, in fact, it does not take into due account several structural aspects of the two European integration processes which,

1 See J.H.H. Weiler and N. Lockhart, '"Taking Rights Seriously": The European Court and Its Fundamental Rights Jurisprudence' (1995) CML Rev 51 and 579.

2 See A. Von Bogdandy, 'The European Union as a Human Rights Organization? Human Rights and the Core of the European Union'(2000) CML Rev 1307; S Douglas-Scott, 'A Tale of Two Courts: Luxembourg, Strasbourg and the Growing European Human Rights *Acquis*' (2006) CML Rev 629; T. Ahmed and I. De Jesus Butler, 'The European Union and Human Rights: An International Law Perspective' (2006) Eur J Intl L 771; P. Alston and J.H.H. Weiler, 'An "Ever Closer Union", in Need of a Human Rights Policy', in P. Alston (ed.), *The EU and Human Rights* (Oxford University Press 1999); J.H.H. Weiler, 'Does Europe Need a Constitution? Reflections on Demos, Telos and the German Maastricht Decision' (1995) Eur L J, 219.

already *ab origine*, brought the two supranational organizations closer.[3] On the other hand, this view does not seem to pay enough attention to the original nature of the two European Courts.

The aim of this chapter is, by taking into account the above mentioned, undervalued components, to demonstrate that, in spite of considerable points of divergence, the two European systems seem to share common roots with regard to their establishment, their mission and, especially, their impact on the Members States legal orders.

In the general crisis following World War II, amidst the dust and ashes of what remained of Europe, it was surely a need, felt by government leaders and those governed alike, to adopt a 'new order capable of placating the insatiable hunger of the Nation-States and warding off a third, final world war.'[4]

The driving idea behind this was the need for greater solidarity among European nations that would have led to a more highly integrated collaboration than that proposed by the League of Nations, whose greatest failure, among others, was that of not having been able to avoid the bloodshed of a fratricidal world war.

This collaboration should have led to the creation of a supranational legal system in which the Member States renounced their absolute sovereignty, as Luigi Einaudi strongly recommended, almost prophetically, in 1918[5] and Altiero Spinelli reasserted in 1941, giving shape and soul to that project.[6]

On the basis of these assumptions, in 1948[7], during the international conference on the European Federalist Movement[8] held in the Hague and attended by 173 delegates representing 16 European countries, Winston Churchill, the Honorary President, expressly emphasized:

> We desire a united Europe, throughout whose area the free movement of persons, ideas, ideas and goods is restored. We desire a Charter of Human

---

[3] See G. de Búrca, 'The Road Not Taken: The EU as a Global Human Rights Actor', http://papers.ssrn.com/sol3/papers.cfm?abstract_id=1705690.

[4] See Altiero Spinelli and Ernesto Rossi, *The Ventotene Manifesto* (1941).

[5] See L. Einaudi, 'Il dogma della sovranità e l'idea della Società delle Nazioni', *Corriere della Sera*, December 1918. See also F Perfetti, 'Luigi Einaudi, Il Presidente che ha insegnato ad amare la libertà', (2008) *La Comunità internazionale*, 411.

[6] See Spinelli and Rossi, *The Ventotene Manifesto*.

[7] See C. Russo and P.M. Quaini, *La Convenzione europea dei diritti dell'uomo e la giurisprudenza della Corte di Strasburgo* (Giuffrè 2006).

[8] See *The European Movement and the Council of Europe*, published on behalf of the European Movement, London (Hutchinson 1949), 35.

> Rights guaranteeing liberty of thought, assembly and expression as well as the right to form a political opposition. We desire a Court of Justice with adequate sanctions for implementation of the Charter.

There could not have been a more authoritative summary of the ties closely binding European nations to the objectives of creating a European common market with no obstacles to the free circulation of goods on one hand, and, on the other, safeguarding human rights through a Charter that stressed their inviolability and a Court that guaranteed compliance. In brief, Churchill advocated a virtuous synthesis between the common market and the protection of human rights in Europe: in other words, a combination between what is considered to be the basis, respectively, of the European Economic Community and the European Convention of Human Rights.[9]

After several years, and failed attempts to give the fledgling construction of the European Community a wider scope than it would have had under the provisions of the Treaty of Rome,[10] gradually the two institutions began to follow diverging paths. This trend towards a progressive divergence, however, was not as drastic as many authors have argued. As will be discussed later, in fact, in each of the two supranational organizations there inevitably remained at least a germ of the core on which the other was founded.[11]

The two most significant factors that led to divergence were the

---

[9] Harpaz seems to support this view when he underlines that 'formally, the EU was founded as an economic regime, while the ECHR was established as a human rights regime. Yet, they do share a common historical background [. . .] it is precisely because Europe was not born with the Council of Europe or the European Economic Communities just after the War, but very much earlier, at the convergence of great currents of thought which crossed the continents since Roman law, that it is possible now – literally – to extract the contents of a shared "democratic necessity". More concretely, both regimes were established in the aftermath of the same "constitutional moment" in European history, namely the end of the Second World War and the resultant collective revulsion to its horrific consequences. Hence both regimes shared a similar *raison d'être*, namely the replacement of the old world order with an order that would guarantee peace, stability and a high degree of protection of human rights'. See Guy Harpaz, 'The European Court of Justice and its Relation with the European Court of Human Rights: The Quest for Enhanced Reliance, Coherence and Legitimacy' (2009) CML Rev 105.

[10] The reference is clearly to the failed projects to create a European Defence Community and European Political Community.

[11] See, for the same view, G. Quinn, 'The European Union and the Council of Europe on the Issue of Human Rights: Twins Separated at Birth?' (2001) McGill L J, 849.

progressive deterioration in the immediate post-war years of the relationship between the Soviet Union and the Western powers on the one hand, and, on the other hand, the failure to create a much more ambitious integration at the Community level[12] after France's rejection of the European Defence Community. More specifically, as regards the Soviet Union, Stalin's unscrupulous policies, coupled with worries over German rearmament, caused great alarm in the Western democracies, particularly in England, over a possible Communist encroachment from the East and the possible re-birth of neo-Nazi ideology in Germany.

For these reasons, notwithstanding Churchill's auspices, Britain's post-war Labour government preferred to combine the formation of military-type alliances of a patently anti-Soviet matrix[13] to the creation of an international organization, the Council of Europe.[14] Among other things, this would have united, even symbolically, the Western democracies of the day in order to provide a common front against any temptation to allow a totalitarian ideology to re-emerge. At the same time, the institution of the Council of Europe would have affirmed both the superiority of the rule of law and the liberal gains made in protecting fundamental rights with respect to the ideology of the Communist model, its antagonist.

Having been devised on the wave of enthusiasm that saw the emergence of the European Coal and Steel Community (ECSC), the idea of a European organization with a highly integrationist vocation was thwarted by the failure of the European Defence Community, into which De Gasperi and Spinelli had only partially managed to 'inject' that federalist spirit typical of the Ventotene Manifesto.[15]

For this reason, it was decided to return to the more pragmatic logic that had led to the success of the ECSC. Jean Monnet's gradualist strategy became the guiding theme of the Community process of integration, thus

---

[12] See A. Padoa-Schioppa, *Italia ed Europa nella storia del diritto* (Il Mulino 2003), 581–85.

[13] The reference is, obviously, to the Western European Union and to the North Atlantic Treaty Organization.

[14] The Statute of the Council of European was signed on 5 May 1948, at St James's Palace Hotel, in London, by its ten Founding Members (the United Kingdom, Belgium, Denmark, France, Ireland, Italy, Luxembourg, Norway, the Netherlands and Sweden). See S. Bertozzi, *Crocevia della grande Europa: il Consiglio d'Europa, l'Unione Europea, l'Osce* (Clueb 2001), 17; A.H Robertson, *The Council of Europe. Its Structure, Functions and Achievements* (Stevens 1956); F. Benoît-Rohmer and H. Klebes, *Council of Europe Law, Towards a Pan-European Legal Area* (Council of Europe Publishing 2005).

[15] See A.H. Robertson, 'The European Political Community', (1952) *British Yearbook of International Law* 383.

laying the foundation for a common market culminating in 1957 with the Treaty of Rome which instituted the European Economic Community (EEC).

The EEC was characterized by an economic vocation that, in the opinion of many, did not exclude but merely postponed the project of a supranational integration of Europe with a more generalized vocation including both social and political aspects.[16]

With specific regard to the genesis of ECHR, seminal studies[17] which focused on the rationale behind the institution of the Council of Europe, and more specifically, the adoption of the ECHR, have argued that the almost exclusive intention of the founding members was, by using a symbolic language full of ideological implications, to give pre-eminence to the creation of a system of fundamental values characteristic of Western democracies. Only when it was so firmly established that neither the authoritarian advancement of a single Communist doctrine in Eastern Europe nor the possible re-emergence of neo-Nazi ideology could threaten it, was it possible, according to this opinion, to create a European system for the protection of fundamental rights.

This interpretation, which is clearly a retrospective attempt to preserve the *status quo* of the rationale at the basis of the international treaties drawn up to establish the Council of Europe and the ECHR, could be acceptable for the Council of Europe,[18] but it is without doubt questionable as far as the ECHR is concerned.

Recently,[19] a critical reading of the eight volumes of the Convention's *travaux préparatoires* has been carried out which confirmed what could have already been suspected from looking at both the different degrees of democratic stability characterizing the Founding Nations[20] at the time the text was being negotiated and the unequal level of openness towards international law of the constitutions of the founding Member States. There was by no means a unanimous consensus on the degree of integration to which the Convention should aspire, so the final result was a compromise

16 See M.R. Alaricòn Caracuel, 'La necessità di un capitolo sociale nella futura costituzione europea' (2000) Lavoro e diritto 607, 608–609.

17 Cf. Robertson, *The Council of Europe*, 4.

18 See A. Simpson, 'Britain and European Convention' (2001) Cornell Intl L J 523; S. Greer, *The European Convention, Achievements, Problems and Prospects* (Cambridge University Press 2006).

19 D. Nicol, 'Original Intent and the European Convention on Human Rights' (2005) Public Law 152.

20 See A. Moravcsik, 'The Origins of the Human Rights Regime: Democratic Delegation in Post-War Europe' (2000) International Organization 217.

of the founding members' different positions. As in fact evidenced from the preparatory works, nine out of 15 members of the Consultative Assembly looked upon the institutions of Strasbourg 'as a nucleus [. . .] which may develop into a future federal organisation of Europe.'[21] A rather more intergovernmental approach acted as a counterweight to the spirit of integration within the Assembly and guided the work of the Committee of Ministers.[22]

Similarly, alongside those nations that were striving for closer integration at the international level, others, first among them Great Britain, claimed that the role of the Convention should be to create a purely symbolic effect to reassure Europe that no further totalitarian regimes would re-emerge there in the future.[23] Not only did such a conviction surface continuously even in the comments made by some of the English judges when criticizing the ECtHR's[24] evolutionary approach in later years, but also it was most clearly expressed in the British government's opposition to the wish of some original signatory States to provide for a court that would ascertain whether or not rights protected by the Convention had been violated. Bearing in mind the fact that most of the founding Nations, beginning with Great Britain, were convinced that the level of protection their respective national legal systems afforded fundamental rights was much greater than the minimum standard guaranteed by the Convention, this attitude comes as no surprise.

In the end, the founder States agreed about the creation of a court empowered to monitor violations of the Convention by Member States. The British government, in exchange, however, obtained an undertaking that the States would have the option and not the obligation to accept the right of the individual to petition before the European Commission on Human Rights. Furthermore it succeeded in ensuring that the competence

---

21 Cf. *Travaux préparatoires*, I, 32, cited by Nicol, 'Original Intent', 156, n. 14.

22 At it was stated, 'the Committee of Ministers tried to exclude "human rights" from the agenda of the Consultative Assembly. The Assembly promptly reinstated the item, and ended up proposing the Convention'. Nicol, 'Original Intent', 155.

23 Or, as literally emerges from *Travaux préparatoires*, 'to reassure the ordinary man that never again can the terrors of those totalitarian regimes overwhelm him'. Nicol, 'Original Intent', 157.

24 Lord Hoffmann polemically underlined this when he wrote: '[W]hen we joined, indeed, took the lead in the negotiation of the European Convention, it was not because we thought it would affect our own law, but because we thought it right to set an example for others and to help to ensure that all the Member States respected those basic human rights which were not culturally determined but reflected our common humanity'. See Lord Hoffmann, 'Human Rights and the House of Lords' (1999) MLR 159, 166.

of the Court to accept said recourse would be optional, and would require specific approval of the Member States.

In light of the above observations, it would be rather simplistic to consider the ECHR mechanism merely and exclusively as an ideological one, aimed 'only' at maintaining the *status quo*.

3. DISTINCTIVE FEATURES OF THE TWO SYSTEMS WITH REGARD TO THEIR IMPACT ON THE MEMBER STATES' LEGAL ORDERS

As has emerged above, the EC and the ECHR systems, as far as the objectives and original spirit envisioned by the respective founding Fathers are concerned, were not so far distant from one another as people might think. Indeed, a closer look at them shows that even in reference to their original characteristics or their their respective impacts on the domestic legal order, they were still less different. In both cases, their 'genesis' comes from international law and in both cases it is characterized by distinctive features which, *ab initio*, enhanced their potential to be more intrusive than the 'classic' international law towards the sovereignty of Member States.

3.1 The ECHR System

As for the ECHR, the *sui generis* nature of its content[25] finds immediate implications in the favoured position it attributes individuals with respect to the regime that characterizes international law *tout court*, where the 'main actors' are generally the States.

Even the ECtHR, in a judgment from the 1970s, reflected the *sui generis* characteristics of the ECHR when it emphasized that 'unlike international treaties of the classic kind, the Convention comprises more than mere reciprocal engagements between contracting States. It creates, over and above a network of mutual, bilateral undertakings, objective obligations which, in the words of the Preamble, benefit from a "collective enforcement."'[26]

Certainly the possibility of individual petition and the provision for an international court entitled to be the authentic interpreter of the

---

[25] That is an international instrument that concerns itself with a field of law traditionally reserved to constitutional law, namely the protection of individuals *vis à vis* the State.

[26] ECtHR, 18 January 1978, *Ireland v Regno Unito*, 5310/1971, paragraph 239.

Convention and in a position to deliver binding judgments against States that violate it, is enhanced since the beginning of the potential intrusiveness towards the contracting members of the ECHR legal system.

However, the original potentialities of inter-State petitions should not be underestimated. Such a mechanism is distinctive because it recognizes by law that a Member State has the right to ascertain before a court whether or not a contracting State is responsible for violating Convention provisions. The decision to introduce an inter-State petition was extremely daring. It provided that each contracting State is entitled – and politically even called upon – to act as a guardian of legality in instances where another State party is seen as breaching the provisions of the ECHR.

In effect, this is an exception to the rule of *consensus* that generally governs procedures for resolving controversies in international law as provided for in Article 33, Chapter VI, of the Charter of the United Nations, whereby States have the right to choose the means they use to settle a dispute with another State.[27]

3.2. The EEC Legal Order

As Weiler and Haltern[28] put it, 'the European legal order was begotten from public international law in the normal way that these things happen: there was a communion among some Member States – the high contracting parties – which negotiated, signed and subsequently ratified the constituent Treaties that brought into being, first the nascent European Coal and Steel Community and then its twin sibling, the European Economic Community and the Euratom'.

Nonetheless, there are particular characteristics of the original genetic code that already existed at the foundation of the Community legal order but are not found in 'ordinary' international treaties. These characteristics are common to those found in the 'institutional' international law typical of international organizations, but not in the so-called 'relational' international law.[29]

Among the powers attributed to these organizations, there may be on

---

[27] See L. Wildhaber, 'The European Convention on Human Rights and International Law' (2007) ICLQ 217.

[28] See J.H.H. Weiler and U.R. Haltern, 'The Autonomy of the Community Legal Order – Through the Looking Glass' (1996) Harvard Intl L J, 411, 417. See also, for an opposite view, O. Spiermann, 'The Other Side of the Story: An Unpopular Essay on the Making of the European Community Legal Order' (1999) Eur J Intl L 763.

[29] See for this classification R.J. Dupuy, *Le droit international* (PUF 1966) and

occasion a true attribution of the competence to enact regulations. The said 'regulations' or 'decisions' can be defined, as it has stated,[30] by three concurrent characteristics. In the first place, these are laws with external relevance and are not for the internal functioning of the organization by which they have been enacted. Secondly, they are measures that have been unilaterally adopted by institutional bodies belonging to the same organization. Thirdly, they are obligatory and binding, in contrast to recommendations or other examples of soft law adopted in international law.

Article 189 (now 288 TFEU, ex Article 249 TEC) of the Treaty of Rome attributed, since the beginning, many of the above mentioned characteristics to EC directives and regulations alike. Both kinds of legislation enhanced, *ab origine*, the power of Community law to impinge on Member State legal orders. This does not mean, however, that the founding moment of the European integration process had a supranational or even constitutional nature, as has been claimed.[31] The genesis was and remains in international law.[32]

In the overall institutional scene, three elements contributed to making the intergovernmental component less pronounced than the supranational one, and less developed than in international law *tout court*. First, the genetic characteristics of the Community legal order; secondly, the possibility the Council of Ministers had of adopting decisions with a qualified majority vote in specific instances; lastly, the mechanism of preliminary reference provided by Article 177 (now Article 267 TFEU, ex Article 234 TEC).

The ECJ identified the distinctive characteristics particular to the EC legal order in its judgment in *Costa v Enel*, i.e. the Founding Fathers' will to institute a Community 'of unlimited duration, having its own institutions,

---

idem, *Communauté international et disparité de développement – Cours général de droit international public*, *Recueil des Cours*, vol. 165, 9 ff.

30 B. De Witte, 'Retour à "Costa". La primauté du droit communautaire à la lumière du droit international' (1981) *Cahiers de droit européenne* 425, 447.

31 See T. Oppermann, *Europarecht* (Beck 1991) 196; J. Bengoetxea, 'Institutions, Legal Theory and EC Law' (1991) *Archiv fur Recht und Social Philosophie* 195; F.E. Dowrick, 'A Model of the European Communities' Legal Systems' (1983) Ybk Eur L 224.

32 This thesis is supported by Joseph Weiler who, in 1982, observed that 'the Constituent instruments of the Communities were traditional multi-partite International Treaties. Although including certain novel institutional features they were, in line with precedent, expected to be interpreted in accordance with the normal canons of treaty interpretation, one of which is a presumption against loss of sovereignty by States'. See J.H.H. Weiler, 'The Community System: The Dual Character of Supranationalism'(1982) Ybk Eur L 267, 270.

its own personality, its own legal capacity and capacity of representation on the international plane and, more particularly, real powers stemming from a limitation of sovereignty or a transfer of powers from the States to the Community' (paragraph 3). On a more critical reading, however, as has been argued above, those features do not appear sufficient to render it *ab origine* autonomous, new and supranational *sui generis*.

The EC legal order was conceived, at its genesis, as a sub-system of international law with a marked potential for impinging on the sovereignty of the Member States at its genesis. It would only acquire a supranational character *in itinere*, as a result of the ECJ's much more creative jurisprudence.

4. THE ORIGINAL INTERNATIONAL NATURE OF THE TWO EUROPEAN COURTS

The ECJ, like the ECtHR, was conceived as an international court with exclusive power to interpret the respective founding Treaties. Neither Court was attributed *ab origine* power to void national legislation that contrasted provisions of the respective founding Treaties. In addition, the founding States rejected part of the original project proposed by the French delegation to attribute power to the ECtHR to nullify national laws contrasting with ECHR provisions.

Although the text of the ECHR is not completely telling to this regard, it has always been maintained that ECtHR judgments were intended to have only a declaratory effect and not a constitutive one. Article 46 of the ECHR provides that judgments can only verify whether or not a contracting State has violated provisions of the Convention. If it has, the contracting State is obliged to restore when possible the claimant's situation as it was prior to the violation, using the ways and means of its choice.

If, during negotiations for drafting the ECHR, the powers attributed the ECtHR were scaled down with respect to those initially proposed, because, in particular, of the English fear concerning a possible 'government of judges', it would be certainly inappropriate to conclude the Community founding Fathers' original idea was to attribute considerably more incisive powers to the ECJ than those classically attributed to international courts. Quite to the contrary: the ECSC Treaty provided that the prime objective of the ECJ was to prevent the High Authority from abusing its broad powers.

Within the EEC institutional framework, the ECJ had the power to make only declaratory rulings verifying a Member State's lack of compliance with Community law and to nullify judicial rulings but *solely* as regards Community law (ex Article 263 FTEU, formerly Article 230 TEC). Proceedings were to be filed by 'institutional' privileged actors, and by individuals under certain conditions that were (and still are) rather difficult to satisfy.

With regard to the preliminary ruling procedure, if the mechanism had been a truly innovative instrument with respect to the status quo of international law even of an institutional nature, the original aim of the said mechanism was to favour the dialogue between national and ECJ judges only with respect to the interpretation of Community law and the validity of secondary Community law.

It is well known that, despite those original aims, the ECJ[33] has been able, over the years, to interlace, through the preliminary reference procedure, a relationship of cooperation and at times of complicity with national judges. In other words, the ECJ was able to change de facto the content of the dialogue. It persuaded national judges to request ECJ judges to rule on compliance of national laws with Community law.

This acceleration process characterized the first decades of ECJ law.[34] Its fundamental stages saw the transformation of Europe[35] through the masterpiece of a judicial body capable of conveying Community law from its genesis in international law to a supranational dimension.

To sum up, at a closer look, by comparing the original characteristics the founding Fathers wanted to attribute to the ECHR and the ECtHR, the impression emerges that in both cases they had intended instituting an international court with the same powers and limits as those attributed to an international judge. Furthermore it is arguable that the ECtHR had a

---

33 See A. Tizzano, *La Corte di giustizia delle Comunità europee* (Jovene 1967).

34 See H. Rasmussen, 'Between Self Restraint and Activism: A Judicial Policy for the European Court' (1988) Eur L Rev, 28; Idem, *On Law and Policy in the European Court of Justice* (Martinus Nijhoff 1986); P. Neill, *The European Court of Justice: A Case Study in Judicial Activism*, Intergovernmental Conference, Minutes of Evidence, House of Lords, 1996, 218 ff.; J.H.H. Weiler, 'The Court of Justice on Trial' (1987) CML Rev 555; M. Cappelletti, 'Is the European Court of Justice Running Wild?' (1987) Eur L Rev 3; idem, 'The Law-Making Power of the Judges and its Limits', (1981) Munchen University L Rev 15; D. Keeling, 'In Praise of Judicial Activism, but What Does It Mean? And Has the European Court of Justice Ever Practiced it?', in C. Curti Gialdino (ed.), *Scritti in onore di G.F. Mancini* (Giuffrè 1998) 505; T. Tridimas, 'The European Court of Justice and Judicial Activism' (1996) Eur L Rev 199; Lord Slynn of Hadley, 'What Is a European Community Judge?' (1993) Cambridge L J 234; J. Bengoextea, *The Legal Reasoning of the Court of Justice* (Oxford University Press 1993); J.H.H. Weiler, 'A Quiet Revolution: The European Court of Justice and its Interlocutors' (1994) Comparative Political Studies 510.

35 See J.H.H. Weiler, 'The Transformation of Europe' (1991) Yale L J, 2403.

greater potential for intrusiveness towards Member State sovereignty than the ECJ did, at least *ab origine*. This is especially true with regard to the possibility of individual petition, even though it had to be accepted by the Member States.

If the reality of the European Courts in the following years was quite different than that planned at their genesis, this was fundamentally due to two factors; one, the 'acceleration' of the ECJ mentioned above, and the other, the concomitant 'slow-motion' start up of the ECtHR.

5. THE EEC LEGAL ORDER: THE FIRST STAGE AND THE ACCELERATION OF THE ECJ

At the beginning of the 1960s, the ECJ was known to be the driving force in the process of European integration.[36] It utilized the apparently harmless provision according to which it shall ensure that in the interpretation and application of the Treaties the law is observed[37] as an interpretative lever to give a constitutional or at least 'supranational' framework to the genetic code of the Community law order that, as has been said, in origin was international by nature.

The Member States remained silent, leaving the next move up to the Court. With a great deal of creativity and a considerable dose of argumentative audacity it proposed what was defined as 'constitutional doctrine by a common law method'[38], not hesitating to re-write the Treaties if necessary. Combing through the original documents of the Treaty of Rome line-by-line shows that it would never have been possible to read into or infer from the structure of the institutions it provided for that 'The European Economic Community constitutes a new legal order of international law for the benefit of which the states have limited their sovereign right, albeit within limited fields, and the subjects of which comprise not only the member states, but also their nationals.'[39]

---

[36] In the famous description by Eric Stein: 'tucked away in the fairyland Duchy of Luxemburg and blessed, until recently, with benign neglect by the powers that be and the mass media, the Court of Justice of the European Communities has fashioned a constitutional framework for a federal-type structure in Europe'. See E. Stein, 'Lawyers, Judges and the Making of a Transnational Constitution' (1981) Am J Intl L 1, 1.

[37] Originally provided by Article 164 EEC and today, substantially, reproduced at Article 19 TUE.

[38] R. Posner, *Law and Legal Theory in the UK and USA* (Oxford University Press 1996) 14.

[39] ECJ C-26/62, *Van Gend en Loos* [1963] ECR I-3, 5 February 1963.

Least of all it could never be inferred from reading the Treaty that under certain conditions primary and derived sources of Community law have a direct effect and that both sources occupy a position of primacy over Member States' national and constitutional law.[40] This primacy has to find immediate application if it is to preserve the useful effectiveness of Community law.[41] The text of Article 28 TEC (now Article 34 TFEU) gave no indication that individual Member States could violate its provisions if they were to adopt measures that hinder access and distribution of products in the importing State even though no discrimination is made between national and imported products.[42] The Treaty of Rome never indicated the possibility of individual petition to verify State responsibility before a national court if the legislator violates Community law.[43] Furthermore, it never mentioned that national judges are prohibited from ascertaining the invalidity of Community law[44] because the said prerogative rests solely in the hands of the ECJ judges.

5.1. The Emergence of Fundamental Rights Protection in the EEC Legal Order

If there is a factor which interconnects the two supranational organizations and justifies making a comparative analysis of the impact of EU and ECHR laws on the Member States' legal orders it is the emergence of the issue of the protection of fundamental rights even in the Community dimension.

Given the extensive studies already published on this topic, a detailed explanation is not required; just a few salient points necessary to the analysis will be described. The Treaty of Rome's silence on the protection of fundamental rights is at odds with the wording of the Founding Treaties of both the European Defence Community (5 May 1952), and the European Political Community (26 February 1953). References to human rights protection are evident in both documents.[45]

---

40 ECJ C-11/70, *Internationale Handelsgesellschaft Gmbh v Einfuhr-und Vorratsstelle für Getreide und Futtermittel,* (1970) ECR I-1125, 17 December 1970.

41 ECJ C-106/77 *Amministrazione delle Finanze v Simmenthal* (1978) ECR I-629, 9 March 1978.

42 ECJ C-8/74, *Dassonville* (1974) ECR I-1129, 11 July 1974.

43 ECJ Joined Cases C-6/90 and C-9/90, *Andrea Francovich and Others v Italian Republic* (1991) ECR I-5357, 19 September 1991.

44 ECJ C-314/85, *Foto-Frost v Hauptzollamt di Lubecca-Est* (1987) ECR I-4199, 22 October 1987.

45 It is enough to mention that in the EDF Treaty was specifically provided the

It may be naive[46] to think so, but the idea that this absence could be attributed to the founding Fathers cannot be ignored. Given their failure to endow the Community with an ultra-economic vocation, they thought it would be better to follow Jean Monnet's pragmatic approach and first reach their objective of a common market, by handing over the 'exclusive' protection of human rights to the ECHR.

The silence may also have hidden, as has been pointed out,[47] the Founding Fathers' intent to leave protection of fundamental rights in the Community in the hands of Member States whose Constitutions and Constitutional Courts could guarantee compliance. However at the very beginning this intent was certainly not shared by the ECJ. The application of Community law would have differed from nation to nation had Community law been subjugated to the national legal orders of the Member States. This would have irreversibly damaged the Court's own objective of safeguarding the uniform application of Community law in Member States.

In 1958 the ECJ was invested of a question of this nature in reference to the ECSC Treaty.[48] The Court excluded the possibility of verifying and taking into any consideration whatsoever Community law that violated the founding principles of the German *Grundgesetz*. The fact that 'an early almost primitive form of constitutional assertion was the denial of fundamental constitutional values'[49] has an almost paradoxical implication.

This all transpired before the ECJ 'pulled out of its top hat' the doctrines primacy and direct effect. At that point interest in the ECJ was destined to be reversed. Prior to that moment, any reference to obligations prohibiting Community institutions from adopting laws that impinged on the human rights protection in national Constitutions was extremely risky and to be avoided. Once the principle of primacy of Community law over Member State constitutions was affirmed, however, the Community was obliged to commit itself to protecting fundamental rights.

---

obligation for the Community to le libertés publiques et le droits fondamentaux des individus (Article 3), while, in the EPC Treaty it was provided, beside the same obligation, also the possibility of a preliminary ruling of the ECJ to the ECtHR. For further details see G.F. Mancini, *Democrazia e costituzionalismo nell'Unione europea*, Bologna, il Mulino, 2004, 143, nt. 6.

[46] According to the evaluation of M. Cartabia, 'L'ora dei diritti fondamentali in Europa', in M Cartabia (ed.), *I diritti in azione*), 13, 16.

[47] Ibid.

[48] ECJ C-1/58, *Stork v Alta Autorità* [1959] ECR I-27, 4 February 1959.

[49] Takis Tridimas, *The General Principles* of EU Law, (Oxford University Press 2007), 301.

The *Stauder* judgment[50] was the first time recourse was made to the *passepartout* of general principles of EC law.[51]

The same was true for the *Internationale Handelsgesellschaft*[52] judgment where the one-to-one correspondence between Community primacy and human rights protection is evident. In *Internationale* the ECJ stated that, to judge the validity of Community law, it was irrelevant whether or not Community law impinged on the provisions of Member States' constitutions, even those regarding human rights protection. The reasoning of the above judgment emphasized a passage whose relevance was just as fundamental because, issued right after the judges made this 'shocking statement', it attempted to attenuate the 'subversive' nature of this principle. The reference is, in particular, to the passage where the ECJ stressed that human rights protection was to be considered an integral part of the general principles of Community law, and affirmed for the first time that the protection of fundamental rights was inspired by constitutional traditions common to Community Member States.

This last passage, despite its reassurance intentions, did not convince the German constitutional judges.[53] It was only at this point that Community law regarding human rights took on a 'reactive' connotation, a connotation usually instead attributed to the entire history of ECJ law-making in the field of the protection of fundamental rights.

5.2. End of the ECJ's Golden Age and Post-Maastricht Prudence

The equilibrium among EU institutions in the so-called 'Golden Age' of ECJ jurisprudence had made it possible for the Court to issue its more audacious judgments. This equilibrium was violently jerked off balance at the end of the 1980s and the beginning of the 1990s.

The Single European Act, which in 1987 introduced the rule of majority vote, and the Treaty of Maastricht that, six years later, instituted the European Union, can be considered a clear expression of will of Member States to regain their legitimate position as Community legislators, by taking away the anomalous role of law maker the ECJ had adopted for itself in the inertia of the Council of Ministers.

---

50 ECJ C-29/69, *Stauder v Città di Ulm* [1969] ECR I-419, 12 November 1969.

51 In the words of Tridimas, 'children of national law, but as brought in front of the Court, they became *enfants terribles*'. T. Tridimas, *The General Principles*, 4.

52 *Internationale Handelsgesellschaft*, paragraph 1.

53 German Constitutional Tribunal, 29 May 1974, *Solange I*, 2 BvL 52/71.

While the case law of ECJ related to human rights protection[54] in Community law was being codified, the Member States strongly reasserted that they wanted no excessive intrusion in the few symbolic areas of national sovereignty that were left to them. In fact, the introduction of the principles of proportionality and subsidiarity would have done just that. Several constitutional Courts sent out the same message that, *ex ante*, the Treaty of Maastricht was unconstitutional and that it needed constitutional review to ratify it.[55] Alternatively they evaluated the constitutional adequacy of the Treaty of Maastricht with considerable reserve.[56] There is no doubt that the 'favourable winds' accompanying the origins of the European integration process had changed direction.

Indeed, it is curious to note that after 1991 the Court limited itself to operations of 'decisions enforcement' of its previous judicial acquisitions (primacy,[57] direct effect,[58] and *Francovich*[59] doctrines), probably because the Member States had finally started paying greater attention to its work. Member States, aware of the supranational danger posed by the ECJ, attempted to 'block' its legal route (see the conclusions of the Edinburgh summit in 1992,[60] for example). Curiously, it was from 1992 that the semi-permanent process of Treaty revisions described by de Witte[61] began, giving new energy to the political side of integration and consequently to the political sources of law[62] and political actors. The new importance of such actors and of the political formulas is testified by the strategy of

---

54 See former Article 6, paragraphs 1 and 2 of the Treaty on European Union.

55 See the French *Conseil Constitutionnel*, 9 April 1992, no. 92-308 DC, and the Spanish *Tribunal constitutional* (dec. 1 July 1992, no. 1236/92).

56 See German Constitutional Tribunal, 12 October 1993, *Maastricht*, 2 BvR 2134/92 and 2 BvR 2159/92.

57 *Costa v ENEL* [1964] ECR 1141.

58 *Van Gend en Loos* [1963] ECR I-3.

59 [1991] ECR I-5357.

60 J.H.H. Weiler, 'Journey to an Unknown Destination: A Retrospective and Prospective of the European Court of Justice in the Arena of Political Integration' (1993) 31 J Common Market Studies 417.

61 B. de Witte, 'The Semi-Permanent Treaty Revision Process', in P. Beaumont, C. Lyons and N. Walker (eds), *Convergence and Divergence in European Public Law* (Hart 2002) 39.

62 Political sources of law are the result of an activity purposely aimed at the creation of law, and their acceptance is based on the idea that the law is only the pursuance of the sovereign's will (the king, the people or the parliament) while the idea of cultural sources of law 'responds to the need for rationally determined justice'. A Pizzorusso, *Sistemi giuridici comparati* (Giuffrè 1998), 263–4. See also A. Pizzorusso, 'Fonti politiche e fonti culturali del diritto' in *Studi in onore di T Liebman*, I (Giuffrè 1979), 32 ff.

Conventions introduced with the experience of the Charter of Nice and by the fundamental rule of their work: the vote for consensus.[63] As a consequence, the ECJ's ever attentive attitude to the political context in which it operated, could not help but change as well.

The 'constitutional tolerance'[64] that Member States had so enthusiastically 'exhibited' at the beginning of the process of Community integration began to vacillate. It was now up to the Luxembourg Court to find a way to rekindle the flame of 'voluntary obedience' that was worrisomely growing dimmer. The Maastricht Treaty represented, indeed, an attempt at reacting against the activism shown by the EJC in the previous years and evidence of this is represented by the set of Protocols (the so called 'Grogan', 'Barber' and 'Second Danish Home' Protocols) which represented, according to Curtin, an effort to 'hijack' European integration.[65]

In the 1990s the Court had no alternative but to choose the path of self-

---

63 The Maastricht Treaty has been described as a turning point in the narrative of European integration: 'However political and legal, especially judicial, developments surrounding the adoption of the Treaty of Maastricht . . ., caused a significant blow to the vision of integration espoused by the classical constitutional narrative. In 1993 the Treaty of Maastricht introduced the (in)famous three-pillared temple structure of the European Union, consisting of the pre-existing Community pillar and of two, so called, intergovernmental pillars of the EU, namely the Common Foreign and Security Policy (CFSP) and the Justice and Home Affairs (JHA). Moreover, it introduced a set of protocols and declarations that granted some Member States exemption from the *acquis communautaire* of the Community pillar', M. Avbelj, 'Questioning EU Constitutionalism' (2008) German L J, 1, 8. D. Curtin, 'The Constitutional Structure of the Union: A Europe of Bits and Pieces' (1993) 30 CML Rev, 17–69. See also G. Martinico, 'Chasing The European Court of Justice: On Some (Political) Attempts to Hijack the European Integration Process', International and Community law Review, forthcoming.

64 According to which, in Joseph Weiler's words, the constitutional actors in the Member State accept the European constitutional discipline 'not because as a matter of legal doctrine, as is the case in the federal State, they are subordinate to a higher sovereignty and authority attaching to norms validated by the federal peoples, the constitutional demos. They accept it as an autonomous voluntary act endlessly renewed by each instance of subordination [. . .] The Quebecois are told: in the name *of the people* of Canada, you are obliged to obey. The French or the Italians or the Germans are told: in the name *of the peoples* of Europe, you are invited to obey [. . .]. When acceptance and subordination is voluntary, it constitutes an act of true liberty and emancipation from collective self-arrogance and constitutional fetishism: a high expression of Constitutional Tolerance'. J.H.H. Weiler, 'Federalism and Constitutionalism, Europe's Sonderweg', in K. Nicolaidis and R. Howse (eds), *The Federal Version: Legitimacy and Levels of Governance in the US and the EU* (Oxford University Press 2001), 54, 69.

65 D. Curtin, 'The Constitutional Structure of the Union: A Europe of Bits and Pieces' (1993) 30 CML Rev 17, 21.

restraint. *Grogan*[66] [1991], *Meng*[67] [1993], *Keck*[68] [1993], *Kalanke*[69] [1995], *Opinion* C 2/94 regarding the possibility for the EU to join the ECHR[70] (1996) and *Grant*[71] [1998] are all classic examples of deference to legislative power.

The evolution of the case law of the ECJ in the field of sex discrimination and preferential treatment was used as a model in an attempt made elsewhere[72] to demonstrate that it had used the strategy of the so-called *majoritarian activism approach* in order to place the impact of its judgments on a graduated scale according to the degree to which the majority of Member States were willing to accept them.

6. THE ECHR DIMENSION: THE ECtHR AND ITS 'SLOW MOTION' START

At the precise moment, when, in the 1960s, with judgments *Van Gend en Loos* and *Costa*, the ECJ was laying down the foundations for the departure of EC law from its original roots of international law, a judge of the ECtHR pointedly asked whether the Strasbourg Court still had a future or whether its brief existence[73] was drawing to an end.[74]

At the time Judge Rolin expressed this preoccupation, the ECtHR had ruled on only two cases in six years. In its first case, a judgment was adopted in 1960[75] whereas, in 1961, it ruled on the merits of a controversy.

---

[66] ECJ C-159/90, *The Society for the Protection of Unborn Children Ireland v Stephan Grogan* [1991] ECR I-4695, 4 October 1991.

[67] ECJ C-2/91, *Meng* [1993] ECR I-5751, 17 October 1993.

[68] ECJ C-267/91 and C-268/91, *Keck and Mithouard* [1993] ECR I-6097, 24 November 1993.

[69] ECJ C-450/93, *Kalanke* [1995] ECR I-3051, 17 October 1995.

[70] ECJ C-2/94, Opinion [1996] ECR I-1759, 28 March 1996.

[71] ECJ C-249/96, *Grant v South West Trains Ltd* [1998] ECR I-2143, 13 October 1998.

[72] See O. Pollicino, *Discriminazione sulla base del sesso e trattamento preferenziale nell'ordinamento comunitario* (Giuffrè 2005) and idem, 'Legal Reasoning of the Court of Justice in the Context of Principle of Equality between Judicial Activism and Self-Restraint' (2004) German L J 283.

[73] The ECtHR has been operative 'only' since 1959.

[74] H. Rolin, 'Has the European Court of Human Rights a Future?' (1965) Howard L. J. 442. It is, in particular, quite telling that Rolin remarks here: 'I hesitate as to whether I deserve the name or the title of judge. I never have been called so much Mr Judge, Judge Rolin and so on. I find it quite nice, I love titles, but I'm afraid that will be the end of it'.

[75] ECtHR, 14 November 1960, *Lawless v Irlanda*, 332/57.

In 1962, in the second of the cases assigned them, ECtHR judges could only ascertain its irrelevance because, in the meantime, the Belgian government had adopted measures to restore the claimant's position. Another two years were to pass before the Court was assigned a third case, the judgment for which was only delivered in 1967.

With only three cases in eight years, there was reason to be worried.

There are several explanations for the ECtHR's 'slow motion' start. The main one is, perhaps, that most founding Member States felt that the level of human rights protection afforded by the legal orders of the Western democracies signatory to the Convention needed no external control. This conviction, one of the reasons the ECtHR started its activity only in 1959, was shared by such countries as France, which had rather drastically decided not to ratify the Convention, and by the majority of the other signatory States that, instead, did ratify it so that it could come into force in 1953.[76]

In light of what has been said above, it is not difficult to wonder that the atmosphere surrounding Strasbourg was not the most encouraging when the European Commission for Human Rights entered into effect in 1954.

Neither of the two mechanisms that would have represented the added value of the ECHR over international law *tout court* had entered into force by that date because the required minimum number of countries to make a declaration of acceptance was lacking. At that time only Denmark, Ireland and Sweden had accepted the right to individual petition. Of these three, only Denmark and Ireland had accepted the mandatory jurisdiction of the ECtHR. The Parliamentary Assembly of the Council of Europe stepped in to take the initiative. From the outset it had always been firmly convinced of the need to keep alive the integration spirit characterizing the ECHR's initial work.

In a recommendation adopted in September 1953,[77] the Parliamentary Assembly 'invited' all the governments of Member States to accept the right to individual petition 'in order to avoid transforming the complaint of an individual into a dispute between States' and to accept the jurisdiction of the ECHR 'in order that any complaint which the Commission considers legitimate and which it is not able to settle by conciliation, should be referred to a judicial rather than a political institution'. This invitation bore fruit but once again not all Member States accepted it. Individual petition finally entered into effect but only for residents of Belgium, Denmark, Ireland, Sweden, Iceland and the Federal Republic of Germany.

---

[76] Only in 1958 was the minimum number of eight declarations of the acceptance of the obligatory jurisdiction of the ECHR reached.

[77] Recommendation 24-9-1953, no. 52.

It required more time for jurisdiction of the Court to be accepted. In 1955 Belgium, Holland and the Federal Republic of Germany were added to the three States that had originally accepted it in 1953. In 1958, exactly five years after the Convention entered into effect, the remaining three Member States accepted the jurisdiction of the Court.

The ECHR legal order took its first steps against this difficult background. It gives an idea of the priorities it, and from 1959, the ECtHR had at the beginning of its activity. It also shows how their priorities differed from those of the ECJ and its bolder orientation.

While the ECJ, 'tucked away in the fairyland Duchy of Luxemburg and blessed, until recently, with benign neglect by the powers that be and the mass media'[78] could afford to 're-write' the EEC Treaty, shifting Community law from an international dimension to a supranational one, both the European Human Rights Commission and the ECtHR were struggling to guarantee they could survive in the future, something even the Strasbourg judges doubted.

It is evident that the interlocutors of the Luxembourg and Strasbourg Courts did not agree given the different objectives the two had. In the first case the interlocutors were and still are the national judges. The ECJ has, since the beginning, successfully attempted to install a relationship of complicity with them. By so doing it managed to convince the national judges to infringe in some cases, especially in Germany and Italy, the constitutional mandate[79] to which they were and still are subject.

By contrast, the Member States political powers were the prime interlocutors of both the European Commission of Human Rights and the ECtHR. On the one hand, in fact, they had to send reassuring messages to the political powers to persuade them to accept the innovative mechanism of individual petition and the Court's mandatory jurisdiction. On the other hand, they had to reassure them that this did not inevitably mean that their internal standard of human rights protection would be challenged in a impartial and external (not domestic) forum. On the contrary, the political powers of the contracting States needed to be reassured that the competent forum for resolving such questions would remain a more political and less neutral one, like the Council of Ministers.

This background of highly charged political tension explains why so few cases were directly dealt with by the ECtHR up to the beginning of the 1970s. When individual petition finally came into effect in 1955, the new

---

[78] Stein, 'Lawyers, Judges and the Making of a Transnational Constitution', 1.

[79] See M. Claes, *The National Courts' Mandate in the European Constitution* (Hart, 2008).

mechanism did not live up to the expectations the citizens of contracting States had for its success. They did not understand its added value, perhaps because it had just been introduced. In 1955 only 138 individual petitions were filed with the Commission. In 1956 this number dropped to 104 and in 1957 to 101. Only 96 petitions, the lowest number yet, were filed in 1958, the year before the Court was inaugurated. Predictably the Commission's attitude in the first years of its operation was prudent. This attitude was due in part to its reticence to involve the ECtHR.

More so it was reflected in the vast use the Commission made of the competence it had to declare petitions inadmissible. Up until 1973 the ECtHR had only made ten decisions on the merits, and in only three of these ten cases was a breach of the Convention ascertained.

With so little case law to go on the ECtHR could not extrapolate a doctrine on the predictability and spatial effectiveness of its own precedents. The ECJ had managed to do this, as we have seen, in a completely opposite context right from the start.

6.1. From the Beginning of the 1970s to the Reform of Protocol 11

In 1973 things began to stir in Strasbourg. The strategy of reassuring the governments previously mentioned seemed to have borne its first fruits. In that year Italy accepted mandatory jurisdiction, and a year later France finally ratified the Convention. The minimum objective to ensure the system's survival seemed to have been reached. Although the attitude of the Commission and the ECtHR remained extremely prudent, they began to plan for the medium to long term.

On the one hand, the Commission further limited its decisions regarding the merit of petitions. On the other hand, it took a less unfavourable stance when choosing the jurisdictional forum of the Court over the political forum of the Committee of Ministers as a seat for controversy resolution. This led to greater activity for the judges of Strasbourg. More cases meant their future was less uncertain. The ECtHR case law started to take on certain identifiable features. From a content viewpoint, in particular, the ECtHR begun to emphasize the need for effective protection of the rights the Convention provided for.

In spite of this evolution, the ECtHR still tended to interpret its powers in a restrictive sense for cases of breach of Convention.[80] It also preferred

---

[80] It has been remarked that until the end of the 1980s the ECtHR 'did not even consider itself competent to make recommendations to the condemned State about which steps it should take to remedy the consequences of the Treaty violation'.

a strategy of reassuring Member State political bodies over that of fostering dialogue with national judges. The jurisprudence of the Strasbourg Court was very attentive to the impact its judgments had on the legal orders of Member States. This attitude was 'endorsed'[81] from its very first judgments[82] through its margin of appreciation[83] doctrine.

The judges of Strasbourg were committed to safeguarding the principle

---

T. Barkuysen and M.L. Van Emmerik, 'A Comparative View on the Execution of Judgments of the European Court of Human Rights', in T. Christou and J.P. Raymond (eds), *European Court of Human Rights: Remedies and Execution of Judgments* (British Institute of International and Comparative Law 2005), 1, 3.

[81] ECtHR, 7 December 1976, *Handyside v Regno Unito*, ric. 5493/72.

[82] European Commission of Human Rights, *Greece v Regno Unito*, 1956, and ECtHR, *Lawless v Irlanda*, 1-7-1961 ric. 332/57.

[83] See G. Letsas, 'Two Concepts of Margin of Appreciation' (2006) Oxford J Legal Studies 705; F. Hoffmann and J. Ringelheim, 'Par-delà l'universalisme et le relativism: la Cour européenne des droits de l'homme et les dilemmas de la diversité culturelle' (2004) *Revue interdisciplinaire d'études juridiques* 109; G. Letzas, *A Theory of Interpretation of the European Convention on Human Rights* (Oxford University Press 2007); P. Mahoney, 'Judicial Activism and Judicial Self-Restraint in the European Court of Human Rights: Two Sides of the Same Coin' (1990) Human Rights L J 57; L.R. Helfer, 'Consensus, Coherence and the European Convention on Human Rights' (1993) Cornell Intl L J 26; Y. Shany, 'Toward a General Margin of Appreciation Doctrine in International Law?' (2006) 16 Eur J Intl L 907; E. Benvenisti, 'Margin of Appreciation, Consensus, and Universal Standards' (1998/9) New York University J Intl Law and Politics 843; M.R. Hutchinson, 'The Margin of Appreciation Doctrine in the European Court of Human Rights' (1999) ICLQ 638; S.C. Prebensen, 'The Margin of Appreciation and Articles 9, 10 and 11 of the Convention' (1998) Human Rights L J 13; I de la Rasilla del Moral, 'The Increasingly Marginal Appreciation of the Margin-of-Appreciation Doctrine', (2006) 7 German L J 611.

According to Shany, the doctrine of margin of appreciation is based on two core elements:

(a) Judicial deference. The courts should grant each other a certain degree of deference and respect each other's discretion.

(b) Normative flexibility. International norms subject to this doctrine can be characterized as being open-ended or unsettled. Such norms provide the States with limited guidance and establish a broad zone of legality within which they are free to operate: 'Application of margin of appreciation doctrine depends on a variety of factors: (a) the comparative advantage of local authorities – broader margins are afforded to local authorities with respect to questions they are better situated to assess (e.g. Local moral sensitivities); (b) the indeterminacy of the applicable standard – broader margins are granted over issues lacking a European consensus; and (c) the nature of the contested interests – broader margins are granted when more important national interests are at stake and the alleged violation appears less fundamental', Y. Shany, *Regulating Jurisdictional Relations between National and International Courts* (Oxford University Press 2007) 187. On this see: G. Martinico, 'Preliminary Reference and Constitutional Courts. Are You in the

of constitutional tolerance[84] in these Member States in the same way that ECJ jurisprudence was after Maastricht. The ECtHR judges, however, continued to neglect to work on the predictability and diachronic coherence of their own jurisprudence.

Meanwhile, thanks to the didactic approach the Luxembourg judges adopted with national judges, they were able both to extend the *res interpretata* effectiveness of their decisions, and turn internal judges into decentralized judges of Community law. On the contrary, 'the Strasbourg Court restricted itself to developing the "horizontal" rather than "vertical" aspects of the precedent'. Because only 'horizontal' aspects were developed, national judges were unable to derive anything useful from the evolution of Strasbourg case law to help them overcome the exclusively *inter partes* effectiveness of ECtHR judgments.

There are at least two further reasons why the Strasbourg Court failed to develop this sensitivity, beside the one just mentioned related to its strategy of reassuring Member State political powers. In particular, in comparison to the ECJ position, the ECtHR had two disadvantages at the 'starting gate'. First of all the EC Treaty did not specify whether ECJ judgments should be accorded *erga omnes* or *inter partes* effectiveness. Instead, Article 53 of the ECHR (corresponding to Article 46 in the current text) clarified that ECtHR judgments are only binding on the Member States for which they are delivered.

Secondly, a judgment of the ECtHR is 'genetically' destined to focus on the individual case. By contrast, thanks to the instrument of preliminary reference, the ECJ is in a position to deliver judgments of a general and systematic significance. It leaves the burden of deciding on specific questions to the national judges who have no channel of institutional dialogue with Strasbourg.

This briefly describes the course of evolution within the ECHR. Over the years the 'new' mechanism of the individual petition started to be fully metabolized. At the beginning of the 1990s, the Council of Europe started its eastward expansion. In just a few years the number of Member States of the ECHR more than doubled, making any reform of the system a task that could no longer be postponed.

The renowned Protocol no. 11[85] increased both the number of petitions

---

Mood for Dialogue?', in F Fontanelli, G. Martinico and P. Carrozza, *Shaping Rule of Law Through Dialogue* (Europa Law 2010), 219, 237–38.

[84] Which is, then, a further component shared by both the ECHR and the European legal order.

[85] See, among others, G. Cohen-Jonathan, *La réforme de la Cour européenne des droits de l'homme: actes de la table ronde du 28 mars 2003* (Bruylant 2004);

and the potential for supranationality inherent in the original ECHR system. Adopted in 1994, it entered into force in 1998. This brought the paradox that, from an original scenario characterized by a lack of case law, there gradually emerged a different situation in which it started to be difficult for the ECtHR to support its ever-increasing caseload. The scenario was the opposite of that present at beginning of its activity.

One year before the entry into force of Protocol no. 11, in 1997, the Commission received 14166 petitions, of which 703 were declared admissible. Up to 1997 the Court had delivered 107 judgments. It would have been difficult to expect more of a Court which was made up of 'part-time' judges who received no regular pay but only a *per diem* for their stay in Strasbourg.

In the first section of the next chapter we will analyze how the new, post-Protocol no. 11 Court of Strasbourg has elaborated its own doctrine in relation to the impact of the ECHR on the Member States' legal orders.

C. Pinelli, 'Judicial Protection of Human Rights in Europe and the Limits of a Judgment Made System', (1996) Diritto dell'Unione europea 987; A. Bultrini, 'Corte europea dei diritti dell'uomo', in *Dig. IV (discipline pubblicistiche)* (UTET 2000) 148.

5. The enlargement of Europe to the East and the reaction of the European Court of Human Rights

INTRODUCTION

Chapter 4 highlighted the differences as well as the common traits characterizing the genesis and first three decades of the EC and ECHR integration processes. At this point, it is necessary to enter more directly *in medias res* and focus on the enlargement to the east that has re-defined the Council of Europe and the European Union's boundaries in recent years.

The process of enlargement to the east, as we will see, presented different challenges for the two supranational organizations in question, provoking different, if not conflicting, reactions in the two European Courts. The questions addressed in the next two chapters are whether, and, if so, to what extent, because of the mentioned different challenges, and the consequent varied, if not opposite, judicial reactions in Luxembourg and in Strasbourg, the two European Courts may, in a quite paradoxical way, have involuntarily started to converge in terms of their 'idea' of the domestic effects of EU law and the ECHR in the legal orders of the Member States of the two supranational organizations.

This chapter will concentrate on the new challenges the ECtHR had to face following the enlargement to the east of the Council of Europe. Successively it will deal with the ECtHR's reactions to the enlargement, which seem to indicate that its case law has taken a new direction and affects Member State sovereignty to a much greater extent than in the past.

Chapter 6 is an in-depth study of the new scenario that the enlargement to the east between 2004 and 2007 created in the European Union. The purpose above all is to determine whether and to what extent the ECJ has re-thought its traditional definition of the relationship between EU law and the constitutional law of the Member States. It will also consider whether the absolute and unconditional primacy of the former over the latter has been attenuated.

1. THE COUNCIL OF EUROPE'S ENLARGEMENT MECHANISMS AND NEW CHALLENGES FOR THE EUROPEAN COURT OF HUMAN RIGHTS

1.1. New Problems Following the Council of Europe's Enlargement to the East

With the accession of Lichtenstein in 1978, there were 20 Member States of the Council of Europe. After the entry of the first 13 States between 1949 and 1950, there were only seven new entries in 27 years. Lichtenstein's entry was the last for the ten-year period from 1978 to 1988. However, in the following 18 years there were 27 'new entries'. After the upheavals of 1989, the Council of Europe generously opened its doors, particularly to the countries of Central and Eastern Europe and those resulting from the break-up of the USSR. The number of its members thus more than doubled, growing from 20 to 47.

If the cause of this expansion is due to what scholars of international relations have called the international legal order's 'idiosyncratic shock'[1] following the fall of the Berlin Wall, the objectives of the 'campaign' to extend the Council of Europe eastward are rather evident. The first objective was to sanction the definitive victory of the Western democratic liberal model over the rival Communist model, by absorbing into the international organization that has 'always' been the symbol of the first model, that is the Council of Europe, all those nations that up to 1989 had represented the living proof of an alternative that failed. Secondly it was to prevent the re-emergence of fascism, the cause of the fratricidal Second World War.

The pursuit of these objectives certainly came at a cost. The highest one was the accession to the Council of Europe of those countries that had and still have an unsatisfactory standard of human rights protection, and, in any case, are not in line with a coherent application of the requirements

---

1 See R.E. Baldwin, *A Domino Theory of Regionalism*, paper available at hei.unige.ch/~baldwin/PapersBooks/dom_old.pdf; P. Harvey, 'The Future of the European Court of Human Rights', PhD thesis, European University Institute, 22. Against this background Croft has remarked, 'the dominant theme has been the enlargement of western institutions, and the dominance of western institutions formed during the Cold War over new, post-Cold War creations. There is, in other words, a unidirectional nature of the enlargement process: central and eastern Europe has looked west, while the west has not looked east for its institutional homes.' S. Croft et al., *The Enlargement of Europe* (Manchester University Press 1999), 17.

provided for by Article 3 of the Statute of the Council of Europe.[2] It is difficult to deny that the Council of Europe applied these requirements with less severity in its accelerated expansion to the east than it had done for previous members. This meant that, in the last enlargement of the Council of Europe to the east, countries whose prerequisites for entry were problematic were still allowed to join. As far as pluralist democracy was concerned, there were problems with organizing free elections and safeguarding local autonomies. As for the requisites of the pre-eminence of law, there were the problems with bringing national constitutions into line with the principle of the rule of law, with the functioning of the constitutional justice system and with the independence of the legislative body.

The massive and accelerated enlargement to the east and in particular the over-indulgent evaluation of the requisite conditions in these countries have been criticized by many scholars. A sort of *ex post* application[3] of the criterion of conditionality was implemented. For many candidate countries from Eastern Europe this meant that accession to the Council of Europe was the point of departure[4] for attaining

2 According to Article 3 of the Statute: 'Every member of the Council of Europe must accept the principles of the rule of law and of the enjoyment by all persons within its jurisdiction of human rights and fundamental freedoms, and collaborate sincerely and effectively in the realisation of the aim of the Council as specified in Chapter I'. It should be added, to the above named conditions, the requirement related to the presence, in the candidate country. As in fact has been declared in the Vienna Declaration of the heads of the governments of the Contracting States, 'accession presupposes that the applicant country has brought its institutions and the legal system into line with the basic principles of democracy, the rule of law and respect for human rights. The People's representatives must have been chosen by means of free and fair elections based on universal suffrage. Guaranteed freedom of expression and notably of the media, protection of minorities, and observance of the principles or international law must remain, in our view, decisive criteria for assessing any application for the membership. An undertaking to sign the European Convention on Human Rights and accept the Convention's supervisory machinery in its entirely within a short period is also fundamental.'

3 Cf. Harvey, *The Future*, 77–78: 'yet, in terms of post accession monitoring procedures, it can hardly be said that they provide any serious compensation for the lack of a rigorous, ex ante application of the Council of Europe's original membership criteria'.

4 As Robert Harmsen remarked, 'Given that perhaps the most attractive prize in the gift of the Council of Europe is membership itself, conceding it at an early stage in a process of democratic transition risks legitimating an inherently unsatisfactory state of affairs'. R. Harmsen, *The European Convention on Human Rights after the Enlargement*, 22.

these standards.[5] In other words, 'l'admission n'est pas que le debut du processus.'[6]

Once the entry of these states was accepted, the Committee of Ministers and the Parliamentary Assembly realized that they did not have instruments or effective means to compel recalcitrant states to carry out the necessary reforms. In this respect, Romania's accession to the Council of Europe in October 1993 produced, in a certain sense, a 'domino effect'. After the entry of State X, in effect, it was maintained that although State Z had not fully met the conditions for membership of the Council, its situation was not that different from that in State X which had been admitted, and so on. The Council even opted to admit the many candidate countries from Central and Eastern Europe that were not ready for accession in order to avoid being accused of discriminating against them.

After the Council's enlargement to the east, in light of the above considerations and due to the forced inertia of the political powers, the ECtHR was requested to maintain at a high level the qualitative standard of human rights protection within Europe's enlarged area of jurisdiction. Besides the inevitable quantitative increase in petitions due to the greater number of Member States, the new situation also affected the 'mission' of the ECHR system and its court. More precisely, alongside its original role as guarantor of the Convention, the ECtHR was obliged to become a 'school of democracy' for those countries that were just starting down the road to democracy.

On top of this, it was essential for the ECtHR to maintain the high standard of human rights protection because, at the same time, the European Union was progressing in that direction first with the Treaty of Maastricht, then with the Treaty of Amsterdam. As Sudre, one of the most well known scholars of the ECHR system pointed out, danger lay ahead for the ECHR. Sudre foresaw in the short term that the centre of gravity would gradually shift away from the ECHR towards the European Union with regard to its privileged position as last guarantor of fundamental

---

5 As Djeric noticed, 'The lack of ability of the state to comply has not been seen to be of a crucial importance as membership has been perceived as a way to promote human rights, the rule of law and democracy in the new member states from Eastern Europe. The argument has been that the admission would result in a continuing and indeed much stronger influence of the CoED than would be in the case if a country were not a member'. See V. Djeric, *Admissions*, 610.

6 L.A. Sicilianos, 'Les mécanismes de suivi au sein du Conseil de l'Europe', in H. Ruis Fabri, L.A. Sicilianos, J.M. Sorel (eds), *L'effectivité des organisations internationales: mécanismes de suivi et de contrôle* (Editions A. Pedone 2000), 247, 250.

rights in Europe. Additionally he emphasized that 'fondé sur les mêmes valeurs, le system communautaire est nécessairement appelé à concurrencer le system propre de la Convention EDH, dont la pérennité, nous semble désormais, paradoxalement, dépendre de la Cour de Justice des Communautés européennes'.[7]

Briefly, following the Council of Europe's enlargement to the east, there was a danger that the guarantees the Convention provided for protection of fundamental rights could be transformed from a 'standard minimum exigeant' to a 'lointaine ligne d'horizon'.[8] The Council of Europe's political bodies also had difficulty promoting human rights protection *ex post* after the entry of new Member States. At the same time they were pressured to encourage institutional reforms in these states before their entry to the Council. Lastly there was a growing competition with the ECJ over which institution provided the 'best' human rights protection. These were all factors that propelled the ECtHR to review its own ideas related to the impact of its case law on the Member States' own legal orders.

It should be added that in 1998 there was a concomitant and, in many ways, correlated reform that led to the entry into force of Protocol no. 11, as remarked in the previous chapter. The reform eliminated any filter on the part of the Commission and any margin for contracting States to avoid individual petitions to Strasbourg. In fact this reform and the Council of Europe's enlargement to the east multiplied the Court's petition caseload; from 1993 to 2000 individual petitions increased by 500 per cent.

The Strasbourg Court was also greatly worried that the Council's enlargement to the east and the absorption into the ECHR of countries with different and often inadequate procedures for fundamental rights protection could lead to a dangerous asymmetry when applying the ECHR in Member States. This would have undermined one of the principal objectives the ECtHR had always pursued, that is, the idea that *ius publicum europæum* in the area of fundamental rights was the basis for the ECHR's[9] effectiveness.

---

[7] F. Sudre, 'La Communauté européenne et les droits fondamentaux après le traité d'Amsterdam: vers un nouveau système européen de protection des droits de l'homme' (1998) 1 JCP, 100, 9.

[8] Ibid.

[9] In this regard Seymour has remarked: 'the main reason for the effectiveness of the European Convention and the Court is the considerable measure of homogeneity among European States [. . .]. There is a feeling among the member states that there exists a common European standard and that standard should be developed.' See D. Seymour, 'The Extension of the European Convention on Human Rights to Central and Eastern Europe: Prospects and Risks' (1993) Connecticut J Intl L, 243, 244.

Finally, it should also be remarked that, with the accession of new countries from Central and Eastern Europe, the ECtHR had to deal with systemic and repeated breaches of essential human rights protection for the first time. In the first 40 years of its history, the judges of Strasbourg had never had to deal with such violations.

1.2. The 'Post-Enlargement' Reaction of the European Court of Human Rights

How did the European Court of Human Rights react to these new challenges, which could be attributed directly or indirectly to the Council of Europe's enlargement to the east and the entry into force of Protocol no. 11?

Here, our assumption is that the ECtHR has reacted with a more explicit understanding of itself as a pan-European Constitutional Court, as a result of both the exponential growth of its case load and the realistic possibility of encountering systemic human rights violations in Central and Eastern European (CEE) countries. This has implied a shifting away from an exclusively subsidiary role as secondary guarantor of human rights to a more central and crucial position as a constitutional adjudicator.[10]

It is arguable that this change in the judicial attitude of the ECtHR emerged for the first time in 1993, in Judge Martens' concurring opinion in the *Branningan* case.[11] On that occasion, the majority of the Court, recalling a judgment from 1978,[12] stated that the determination of whether the life of the nation may be threatened by a 'public emergency' has to be left to the wider margin of appreciation of the Member States. By reason of their direct and constant contact with the current, pressing needs of the moment, in fact, it was observed, the national authorities are in a better position than international judges to decide both on the actual occurrence of such an emergency, and on the nature and scope of the necessary derogations to avert it. Conversely, in his concurring opinion, Judge Martens argued that 'since 1978 present day conditions' have considerably changed. Apart from the developments to which the arguments of Amnesty refer,

---

[10] It was probably not an accident that the ECtHR chose a highly controversial case against Turkey (*Loizidou v Turkey*, judgment of 23 March 1995) to affirm, for the first time in its jurisprudence, the central place of the ECHR as 'an instrument of the European public order'.

[11] ECtHR, *Branningan and McBride v the United Kingdom*, app no 5/1992, 26-5-1993, paragraph 43.

[12] ECtHR, *Ireland v the United Kingdom*, app no 5310/71, 18-01-1978, paragraph 207.

the situation within the Council of Europe has changed dramatically. It is therefore by no means self-evident that standards which may have been acceptable in 1978 are still so. The 1978 view of the Court as to the margin of appreciation under Article 15 was, presumably, influenced by the view that the majority of the then Member States of the Council of Europe might be assumed to be societies which had been democracies for a long time and, as such, were fully aware both of the importance of the individual right to liberty and of the inherent danger of giving too wide a power of detention to the executive. Since the accession of eastern and central European States that assumption has lost its pertinence.

Another call for a more proactive role for the ECtHR as a reaction to the Council of Europe's enlargement came from the same Judge Martens' separate opinion in the Court's 1995 decision in *Fisher v Austria*.[13] To the then typical self-restraint of the Strasbourg Court, according to which 'the European Court should confine itself as far as possible to examining the question raised by the Court before it',[14] Judge Martens objected that 'no provision of the Convention compels the Court to decide in this way on a strict case by case basis. This self-imposed restriction may have been a wise policy when the Court began its career, but it is no longer appropriate. A case law that is developed on a strict case by case basis necessarily leads to uncertainty as to both the exact purport of the Court's judgment and the precise content of the Court's doctrine.'[15]

The message was indeed quite clear: an explicit invitation addressed to the Court to assume a more general constitutional and centralized role, by drawing the necessary conclusions from its then recent proclamation that the Convention was a 'constitutional instrument of European public order'[16] and by, consequently, going beyond the original aim of ensuring (only) individual justice. The Strasbourg Court gradually got the message by applying a more innovative and intrusive judicial approach with respect to its consolidated case law, and more precisely by moving in two distinct directions.[17] The first tendency was to amplify the 'direct effect'[18] of its

---

[13] ECtHR, *Fisher v Austria*, app no 52/1993, 26-4-1995.

[14] Ibid., paragraph 44.

[15] Ibid., separate opinion of Judge Martens, paragraph 16.

[16] Ibid., paragraph 75.

[17] See, for the above mentioned distinction, O. De Shutter, 'La coopération entre la Cour européenne des droits de l'homme et le juge national' (1997) Revue belge du droit international 21.

[18] The notion of direct effect is indeed polysemous. As for the direct effect of the judgment of the ECtHR: 'Regarding the effects of the judgements, it is commonly accepted that they can be classified into different categories: direct effects and indirect or interpretative effects. As I have just mentioned the existence of these categories

judgments, that is, their effectiveness vis-à-vis the state that was party to the case. The second, known as indirect effect, seems to lead to an interpretative primacy of ECtHR jurisprudence with regard to other contracting States not involved in the case in which the particular judgment is delivered.

---

of effects is generally accepted, however the scope of such effects is not clear or, at least, there is no unanimous agreement on their contents. After having studied the question for several years, I have reached the conclusion that the direct effects may be identified with those affecting directly to the victim of the Convention's rights breach; the paradigmatic example of direct effect is the payment of the just satisfaction. And as well, if provided, the domestic execution of the judgement. Such a possibility is foreseen by the German or the Austrian legal orders in criminal matters. Is not foreseen neither in Spain nor in Italy, as far as I am concerned (except for the Pinto's Law). As I said before, the European Court is an international Court, not a supranational one, and for this reason the execution *stricto sensu* of its judgements is so restricted. Regarding the interpretative effects, they could be identified with those that go beyond the execution *stricto sensu* of the European judgements and could be categorized under the French expression *chose interpretée*, used for the first time by J. Velú, a well-known French expert on the European system.

In contrast to what happens with the *chose jugée*, the authority of *chose interpretée* of the European judgements is not established on the Convention', A. Queralt Jiménez, 'The Interpretative Effects of the Judgements of The European Court of Human Rights', paper presented at the University of Trent, Trent, 15 June 2007, available at http://www.eplo.eu/alfaII/docs/The%20Interpretative%20Effects%20Of%20The%20Judgements.pdf.

In EU Law the formula 'direct effect' refers to at least two different things: 'On the one hand, some scholars argue that it should be identified with the possibility for a legislative provision to grant a right to an individual. This is the more restrictive definition of direct effect: only where a private citizen can obtain a personal right from a piece of Community legislation, can it be said that there is direct effect. On the other hand, others have proposed a wider scope for this concept. It should coincide with the capacity of a provision to be relied upon before a court of law. Often it is a French word which is utilised to express this view: "invocabilité". This second acceptation of direct effect includes in itself the first one, but also other occurrences. For instance, it covers cases when a European Union law provision is employed by a judge in order to challenge a domestic statute and declare it inapplicable. Or when, in the absence of relevant national law, the same judge makes use of a European Union measure to rule on the concrete case he has before himself, without however an individual right being granted to the private party', G. Bianco, 'The EU and the Lack of Direct Effect of WTO Law: Behind the Façade of Consistent Interpretation', working paper. On direct effect, see B. De Witte, 'The Continuous Significance of *Van Gend en Loos*' in M. P. Maduro, and L. Azoulai (eds) *The Past and Future of EU Law* (Hart, 2009) 9; S. Prechal, *Directives in EC Law* (Oxford University Press 2005), 231; B. De Witte, 'Direct Effect, Supremacy, and the Nature of the Legal Order' in P. Craig, and G. de Búrca (eds) *The Evolution of EU Law* (Oxford University Press 1999), 207; P. Pescatore, 'The Doctrine of "Direct Effect": An Infant Disease of Community Law' (1983) 8 Eur L Rev 155, 158.

What emerges from the summation of these two tendencies seems to cast doubt on some (hitherto) characteristic traits of ECtHR jurisprudence, in particular its asserted effectiveness *inter partes*, exclusively addressed to the parties involved in a specific judgment, and its foundations on the principle of individual justice.[19]

1.3. Reinforcement of Direct Effect of ECtHR Judgments

With reference to the progressive consolidation of direct effect (that is, authority over that which is judged) of its judgments, there are at least three tendencies that emerge in recent years from the jurisprudence of the ECtHR. In the first place, its judgments are accorded immediate effect under given conditions; secondly a greater importance was accorded to the execution of temporary measures; and lastly, a rather bold interpretation was given to Article 46 of the ECHR.

1.3.1. Immediate effect of ECtHR judgments and primacy of the ECHR

As has been stated, the first expression, in the post-enlargement case law of the ECtHR, of the reinforcement of the direct effect of its decisions finds its roots in innovative jurisprudence according to which the provisions of its own judgments had direct effect under certain conditions.

The brave new judicial approach is most clearly illustrated in *Vermeire*,[20] adopted when the campaign for the Council of Europe's enlargement to the east was just getting under way. This judgment could have been placed alongside the ECJ judgment *Van Gend en Loos* for its ground-breaking nature.

The background to *Vermeire* lay in the continuing inertia on the part of the Belgian legislature. It took no steps to modify several provisions of its civil law code even though in 1979[21] the ECtHR had ruled that they contrasted with Articles 8 and 14 of the ECHR. The means the Court used in its reasoning to attain the final result are more interesting than the

---

19 Since one of its first judgments (*De Beker v Belgio*, app no 214/56, 9-6-1958), the ECtHR made it abundantly clear that its privileged perspective was that of individual justice, by affirming that 'the Court is not called upon under articles 19 and 25 of the Convention, to give a decision on an abstract problem relating to the compatibility of that Act with the provisions of the Convention, but on the specific case of the application of such an Act to the applicant and to the extent to which the latter would, as a result, be prevented from exercising one of the rights guaranteed by the Convention'.

20 ECtHR, *Vermeire v Belgio*, app no 12849/1987, 29-11-1991.

21 ECtHR, *Marckx v Belgio*, app no 6833/1964, 13-6-1979.

final judgment, in which the Court ruled there had been a new violation of Convention provisions. The Belgian government maintained that the obligation to conform to the Court's previous judgment depended exclusively on the legislative body. It concluded that the internal judge had correctly applied the national law in force, even though the Strasbourg Court had declared that it contrasted with the ECHR. The European judges answered that 'It cannot be seen what could have prevented the Brussels Court of Appeal and the Court of Cassation from complying with the findings of the Marckx judgment, as the Court of First Instance had done. There was nothing imprecise or incomplete about the rule which prohibited discrimination against Astrid Vermeire compared with her cousins Francine and Michel, on the grounds of the "illegitimate" nature of the kinship between her and the deceased (paragraph 25).' Then they added, to be even more precise, that 'The freedom of choice allowed to a State as to the means of fulfilling its obligation under Article 53 (today 46) cannot allow it to suspend the application of the Convention while waiting for such a reform to be completed . . . (paragraph 26).' What the ECtHR proposed was rather innovative. It affirmed the possibility for its judgments to have immediate effect provided their provisions had a precise and unconditioned scope.

After a long period of silence, the ECtHR recently returned to this question to clarify the effect of *Vermeire*, renewing its views on this point. More precisely, in a rather significant judgment[22] in 2007, which strangely enough passed almost unobserved, the ECtHR inferred, for the first time, a general clause of primacy of Convention law over internal law, independently of the rank occupied by the Convention in internal sources of law.[23]

This is an innovation of no little account. It perfectly captures the pro-integration spirit of the new direction ECtHR jurisprudence has taken

[22] ECtHR, *Dumitru Popescu v Romania*, ricc. 49234/99 and 71525/01, 26-4-2007.

[23] This of course brings to mind the ECJ's attack in *Costa v Enel*. In particular the ECtHR affirmed that 'le statut conféré à la Convention en droit interne permet justement aux juridictions nationales d'écarter – *ex officio* ou à la demande des parties – les dispositions du droit interne qu'elles jugent incompatibles avec la Convention et ses protocoles additionnels. Le simple fait qu'elles ont choisi, en l'espèce, la voie d'un renvoi à la Cour constitutionnelle – qui statue sur la compatibilité de la loi avec le droit interne dont la Convention fait partie intégrante – et qu'elles n'ont pas elles-mêmes tranché cette question alors qu'il leur était également loisible de le faire, ne saurait en soit entraîner une méconnaissance de l'article 6. Il en va d'autant plus ainsi que ni la Convention en général, ni son article 13 en particulier, ne prescrivent aux Etats contractants une manière déterminée d'assurer dans leur droit interne l'application effective des dispositions de cet instrument' (paragraph 104) (judgment available only in French).

since enlargement. This spirit is often expressed, as it was in this case, in the tendency of the ECtHR to emulate the style and points of argument characteristic of the so-called glorious period of the ECJ's jurisprudence.

1.3.2. Binding Nature of Interim Measures

The second tendency shown in recent ECtHR case law, which seems to support the new, more aggressive stance towards the sovereignty of contracting States, has been taken by the Court after the Council of Europe's enlargement to the east and the entry into force of Protocol 11. More precisely, this tendency concerns the degree to which temporary measures are binding on contracting States that are party to ECtHR judgments. As is well known, the Court may adopt such cautionary measures to avoid having a right protected by the Convention irrevocably compromised while awaiting a decision on the merits.

Unlike other international courts, the ECtHR has the power to adopt temporary measures because contracting does not find its *ad hoc* legal basis in the text of the Convention. Such a power is only mentioned in the internal regulations that the ECtHR established for itself.[24] This 'loop hole' in the Convention's text was one of the reasons the Court at the beginning of the 1990s excluded the binding nature of temporary measures for contracting States. This binding effect, according to the ECtHR itself, could not even be enucleated by reading Article 34 of the Convention.[25]

In 2005,[26] the Grand Chamber of the ECtHR reversed this position, stating that under the Convention system, interim measures, as they have consistently been applied in practice, play a vital role in avoiding irreversible situations that would prevent the Court from properly examining the application and, where appropriate, securing to the applicant the practical and effective benefit of the Convention rights asserted. Accordingly, in these conditions a failure by a respondent State to comply with interim measures will undermine the effectiveness of the right of individual application guaranteed by Article 34 and the State's formal undertaking in Article 1 to protect the rights and freedoms set forth in the Convention (paragraph 125).

This is a true revirement which led the ECtHR to argue, some paragraphs later, that 'a failure by a Contracting State to comply with interim

---

24 See Article 39 of the ECtHR internal regulation.

25 ECtHR, *Cruz Varas and others v Sweden* app no 15576/88, 20-3-1991, paragraph 102–103.

26 ECtHR, *Mamatkulov and Askarov v Turkey*, 5-2-2005. app no 46827/99 and 46951/99.

measures is to be regarded as preventing the Court from effectively examining the applicant's complaint and as hindering the effective exercise of his or her right and, accordingly, as a violation of Article 34 (right to the individual petition)'.

The Strasbourg judges had no appropriate legal basis for temporary measures. This led them to interpret their internal regulations in the light of the Convention provisions they refer to (Articles 34 and 36). In other words, the judges 'promoted' a simple procedural regulation they themselves had introduced to the rank of primary law adopted by the Founding States in accordance with international public law.

1.3.3. Individual measures and general measures: maximum enhancement of direct effect of ECtHR judgments

A third tendency has been consolidated in recent ECtHR jurisprudence, which seems to question the condemned State's asserted discretion to decide which internal measures to adopt in order to fulfil its obligations as provided for by the Convention. This tendency finds its concretization in two distinct types of judgments, depending on whether the Court decided the claimant State had to adopt individual or general measures to fulfil its obligations under Article 46 of the Convention.

With regard to the first type identified, the Strasbourg Court judges have recently begun to specify which type of measure fully satisfies the claimant's interests. More precisely, in *Assanidze*[27] the ECtHR stated that, in the light of the particular circumstances of the case,[28] 'the respondent State must secure the applicant's release at the earliest possible date' (paragraph 203). The 'particular circumstances' reappeared some months later in *Ilascu.*[29] Here the complaint was of illegitimate and arbitrary detention accompanied by inhuman and degrading treatment. The only possible measure the State could adopt to fulfil its obligations, according to the ECtHR, was the immediate release of the prisoner. The Court added that 'any continuation of the unlawful and arbitrary detention would necessarily entail a serious prolongation . . . a breach of the respondent States'

[27] ECtHR, *Assanidze v Georgia*, app no 71503/01, 8-4-2004, paragraph 203. See V. Colandrea, 'On the Power of the European Court of Human Rights to Order Specific Non Monetary Measures: Some Remarks in Light of Assanidze, Broniowsky and Sejdovic Cases' (2007) Intl Human Rights L Rev 396.

[28] The plaintiff was a Georgian man imprisoned in Ajarina. Even though the President of the Republic pardoned him, the local authorities did not release him from prison.

[29] ECtHR, Grande Chamber, *Ilascu e al. v Moldova and Russia*, app no 48787/99, 8-7-2004.

obligation under Article 46 paragraph 1 of the Convention to abide by the Court's judgment' (paragraph 490).[30]

With regard to the second kind of judgments mentioned above, since 2004,[31] not surprisingly in a case involving a CEE Member State, the Strasbourg judges have started, by adopting the judicial technique of the so called 'pilot judgments',[32] to 'invite' the condemned state to enact all the necessary general measures needed to remedy the structural problems that had led to systemic violations of the Convention in the first place.

This tendency is rather innovative with respect to the ECtHR's past orientation. If it is true that the Court had never excluded the possibility that the effectiveness of its judgments might extend beyond the specific case,[33] nevertheless, it had always refused to indicate in them what general internal measures the condemned state should take to remedy its structural problems.

In particular, in 1995, in reply to all those claimants who wanted the Court to indicate what measures the defendant State should take to remedy a violation of the ECHR, the Court answered that 'the Convention does not empower it to accede to such a request. It is for the State to choose the means to be used in its domestic legal system in order to comply with the

---

30 See, along the same path, ECtHR, *Abbasov v Azerbaijan,* app no 24271/05, 17-1-2008, paragraph 35ff.

31 ECtHR, *Broniowski v Polonia*, app no 31443/96, 22-6-2004. See L. Garlicki, 'Broniowski and After, on Dual Nature of Pilot Judgments', in L. Caflish, J. Callewaert et al. (eds) *Human Rights, Strasbourg Views/Droits de l'homme, regards de Strasbourg: Liber Amicorum L. Widhabe*r (N.P. Engel Verlag 2007), 177; E. Lambert, 'La Cour européenne au secours du Comitè des Ministres pour une meilleure exécution des arrets "pilote"' (2005) *Revue trimestrielle de droits de l'homme* 203; J. Jackson, '*Broniowski v Poland*, a Recipe for Increased Legitimacy of the European Court of Human Rights as a Supranational Constitutional Court' (2006) Connecticut L Rev 759.

32 See P. Leach, S. Stephenson and B.K. Blitz, *An Analysis of 'Pilot Judgments' of the European Court of Human Rights and Their Impact at National Level* (Intersentia 2010).

33 Already in 1979 the ECtHR stated that 'The Court is not required to undertake an examination *in abstracto* of the legislative provisions complained of [. . .] Admittedly, it is inevitable that the Court's decision will have effects extending beyond the confines of this particular case, especially since the violations found stem directly from the contested provisions and not from individual measures of implementation, but the decision cannot of itself annul or repeal these provisions: the Court's judgment is essentially declaratory and leaves to the State the choice of the means to be utilised in its domestic legal system for performance of its obligation under Article 53 (today 46)', *Marckx*, app no 6833/1964, 13-6-1979, paragraph 58, parenthesis added.

provisions of the Convention or to redress the situation that has given rise to the violation of the Convention.'[34]

The origin of the pilot judgment goes back to the document the ECHR approved in a plenary session in 2003[35] and presented to the Steering Committee on Human Rights. Among other things, the Court requested the Convention text be revised so as to provide a legal basis for adopting this type of judgment. The proposal was rejected because, according to the Steering Committee, an *ad hoc* juridical basis was not necessary to obtain the result it requested. With a special resolution the Committee of Ministers rather innovatively invited the Court to identify '[. . .] structural problems and the source of these problems in its judgments'.

The ECtHR did not need to be invited twice. Several months later it adopted its first pilot judgment against one of the CEE countries.[36] More precisely, in a decision of 2004, the Court held that a violation of the ECHR had originated in a systemic problem connected with the malfunctioning of domestic legislation which involved 80 000 persons. The Court suspended 167 complaints pending before it on the same issue until the respondent state secured, through appropriate legal measures and administrative practices, the implementation of the fundamental rights protected by the ECHR (in that case the right to property).[37] In particular, the Court argued that:

> Although it is in principle not for the Court to determine what remedial measures may be appropriate to satisfy the respondent State's obligations under Article 46 of the Convention, in view of the systemic situation which it has identified, the Court would observe that general measures at national level are undoubtedly called for in execution of the present judgment, measures which must take into account the many people affected. Above all, the measures adopted must be such as to remedy the systemic defect underlying the Court's finding of a violation so as not to overburden the Convention system with large numbers of applications deriving from the same cause . . . In this context the Court's concern is to facilitate the most speedy and effective resolution of a dysfunction established in national human rights protection. (paragraph 193).

In *Hutten-Czapska* some Strasbourg judges expressed their doubts about the application of this judicial technique[38] but, apparently, the

---

[34] See ECtHR. *Yagci and Sargin v Turchia*, ric. 16419/90 and 16426/90, 8-6-1995, paragraphs 79–81.

[35] Steering Committee for Human Rights, *Interim Activity Report of 26 November 2003*, doc. CDDH (2003)026 Addendum 1 Final, paragraphs 20–21.

[36] ECtHR, *Broniowski v Polonia*, app no 31443/96, 22-6-2004.

[37] Ibid.

[38] See ECtHR, *Hutten-Czapska*, app no 35014/97, 19-6-2006 and 28-4-2008,

Court was not so impressed by them. Some months later, it applied the technique again, providing for the first time a peremptory term for the adoption of the general measures.[39]

It should be added finally that the Strasbourg Court, by applying this technique, and by consequently suggesting what individual or general measures the condemned state should adopt, reads into Article 46 what does not really exist in reality, at least as far as its literal interpretation is concerned. The said reading, in fact, affects not only what obligations 'in theory' the state needs to fulfil (question), but also in what manner (*quomodo* question) it should do so, an issue that is not in any way touched by Article 46.

1.4. ECtHR Jurisprudence and Enhancement of its Indirect Effect

In the last paragraphs we have seen a progressive consolidation of the direct effect of ECtHR jurisprudence and, consequently, a greater pervasiveness of the ECHR within the national legal orders that are defendants in Strasbourg.

A second, complementary attitude of the more recent, post-enlargment Strasbourg case law has the effect of reinforcing the indirect effect of the ECtHR jurisprudence. More precisely, this attitude is not specifically intended to intensify and amplify the scope of the obligations the condemned Member State had to fulfil as provided for by Article 46 of the Convention. Instead, it is related to the question of the asserted existence of the obligation for the other contracting States and their national judges to respect the *dictum* of ECtHR judgments.[40]

---

partially dissenting opinion of Judge Zagrebelsky, who stated that 'the Court is not competent (and does not have the necessary knowledge) to express a view in the abstract and in advance on the consequences of the reforms already introduced in Poland and to give a vague positive assessment of a legislative development'.

[39] See ECtHR, *Burdov v Russia*, app no 33509/04, 15-1-2009: 'The respondent State must introduce a remedy which secures genuinely effective redress for the violations of the Convention on account of the State authorities' prolonged failure to comply with judicial decisions delivered against the State or its entities. Such a remedy must conform to the Convention principles as laid down notably in the present judgment and be available within six months from the date on which the present judgment becomes final' (paragraph 141).

[40] See, for an example of the said attitude, ECtHR, *Opuz v Turchia*, app no 33401/02, 9-6-2009, where it has stated that 'the Court will consider whether the national authorities have sufficiently taken into account the principles flowing from its judgments on similar issues, even when they concern *other* States' (paragraph 163). Along the same path the memorandum of the President of the ECtHR prepared for the Conference on the Future of European Court of Human Rights, Interlaken, on 3 July 2009. In particular, Jean-Paul Costa remarked that 'consensus

Although Article 46, as we have seen in the above, is used to provide a not too solid legal basis for extending the direct effect of Strasbourg judgments, the same provision, by attributing, in fact, the obligation of conformity to ECtHR judgments *exclusively* to the state against which the judgment of condemnation is delivered, is decidedly contrary to the enhancement of the indirect effect of the Strasbourg case law. It was recently proposed[41] to link this extension to the principle of solidarity. Solemnly provided in Article 3 of the Statute of the Council of Europe, this is one of the founding principles of the entire ECHR legal order.

Now we will analyze the most evident expression of the said attitude: the emerging indifference of the ECHR case law towards the constitutional structures of the Member States.

1.4.1. The new indifference of the ECtHR case law towards the constitutional structure of the Member States and their consequent reduction of their national margin of appreciation

Even with regard to the above mentioned trend, the strong stance of the ECtHR seems to represent an answer, years later, to one of the best known passages of EC jurisprudence. In 1970 the ECJ stated that 'the validity of a Community measure or its effect within a Member State cannot be affected by allegations that it runs counter to either fundamental rights as formulated by the constitution of that State or the principle of a national constitutional structure'.[42]

Twenty-eight years later a provision of the Turkish Constitution as interpreted by the Turkish Constitutional Court was brought to the attention of the ECtHR because it contrasted with the Convention. The ECtHR pointed out that

> The political and institutional organisation of the member States must accordingly respect the rights and principles enshrined in the Convention. It matters little in this context whether the provisions in issue are constitutional [. . .] or merely legislative [. . .] From the moment that such provisions are the means by

---

could make it possible to give binding effect to the Court's judgments in respect of their interpretation of the Convention. This would strengthen the States' obligation to prevent Convention violations. It is no longer acceptable that States fail to draw the consequences as early as possible of a judgment finding a violation by another State when the same problem exists in their own legal system. The binding effect of interpretation by the Court goes beyond *res judicata* in the strict sense.'

41 V. Esposito, *La liberté des Etats*, 848.

42 ECJ C-11/70, *Internationale Handelsgesellschaft Gmbh v Einfuhr-und Vorratsstelle für Getreide und Futtermittel,* (1970) ECR I-1125, 17 December 1970, paragraph 3.

> which the State concerned exercises its jurisdiction, they are subject to review under the Convention.[43]

Here the ECtHR attempted to legitimate *ex post* a series of assumptions that had begun to emerge in its case law some time previously. These assumptions led it to question the legitimacy of constitutional provisions and/or orientations of contracting States' constitutional courts.

Already in the early 1990s,[44] the Court had ruled that Article 40, paragraph 3, of the Irish Constitution, as interpreted by the Supreme Court of Dublin, contrasted with the Convention and in particular Article 10, paragraph 1, regarding freedom of expression. Pursuant to the provisions of Article 40, in fact, it was prohibited to give Irish women information about the possibility of having an abortion abroad. In the second half of the 1990s, following the Strasbourg judgment in *Vogt*,[45] the German Constitutional Court was obliged to modify its constitutional provisions whereby active members of 'extremist parties', such as Communists or the far right, were excluded from any job in the public services sector. In 1999[46] in a case that concerned France as the defendant state, the claimants complained that the intervention of the state in a pending procedure in which they were involved due to the retroactivity of the law, violated the principle of equality and of legal certainty. Even though the *Conseil Constitutionnel* found no violation of the French Constitution, the ECtHR ruled that French law contrasted with Article 6 of the Convention.

Some years later, the ECtHR has adopted an even bolder orientation. In the famous case of Princess Caroline of Monaco, its evaluation was antithetical to the one adopted by Europe's most prestigious and feared Constitutional Court. According to the German Federal Constitutional Tribunal, photographs of Princess Caroline taken in a public place came under the constitutionally guaranteed right of freedom of the press (Article 5 of the German Constitution). Because she was a public figure, the German court decided that the photographs did not violate her right to privacy. The Strasbourg judges interpreted the case differently and ruled instead that there had been a breach of Article 8 of the ECHR.[47]

---

43 ECtHR, *United Communist Party of Turkey v Turkey,* ric. 19392/92, 30-1-1998, paragraph 30.

44 ECtHR, *Open Door and Dublin Well Woman v Ireland*, app no 14234/88 and 14235/88, 29-10-1992.

45 ECtHR, *Vogt v Germania*, app no 17851/91, 26-9-1995.

46 ECtHR, *Zielninsky and Pradal v Francia*, app no 24846/94, and from 34165/96 to 34173/96, 28-10-1999

47 ECtHR, *Von Hannover v Germany*, app no 59320/00, 24-6-2004. More

Jean-Paul Costa, President of the ECtHR, gave an authentic interpretation of the described orientation that confirms its tendency to raise the constitutional tone of the Court's jurisprudence. As a consequence this also increases the impingement of the ECHR on legal orders. In fact, commenting on some of the aforementioned judgments, he stated that 'this reasoning is important because it suggests that the Convention prevails over national constitutions, even if it does not state it as directly as the Luxembourg Court has done in relation to the primacy of Community law (here I would refer, for example, to its 1970 *Internationale Handelsgesellschaft* judgment)'.[48]

Italy recently saw its margin of appreciation initially reduced,[49] and then again amplified,[50] in the well known *Lautsi* saga. In *Lautsi 1*, delivered in November 2009, the ECtHR ruled that the obligation to place a crucifix in school classrooms violated Article 2 of ECHR Protocol No. 1, which provided for the right to education, and Article 9, which safeguards freedom of conscience, thought and religion. Here it is only important to note that the Court kept its distance from its precedent related to the relationship between religious symbols and principle of secularism.[51] In particular, the ECtHR, in this respect, had previously recognized, in *Sahin*, with regard to the issue related to the right for a female student to wear a veil in class, that 'it is not for the Court to substitute its view for that of the university authorities. By reason of their direct and continuous contact with the education community, the university authorities are in principle better placed than an international court to evaluate local needs and conditions or the requirements of a particular course.'[52]

It was no accident that the ECtHR failed, in *Lautsi 1*, to include an

---

recently, in the decision Von Hannover 2, the ECtHR noted that the Court noted that private individuals may have a particular protection under Article 8 because there is a 'fundamental distinction' between 'reporting facts capable of contributing to debate in a democratic society, relating to politicians in the exercise of their official functions for example, and reporting details of the private life of an individual who does not exercise such functions.' (Paragraph 110) and concluded that Germany had not failed in its obligation to respect the applicants' Article 8 rights when it refused to grant an injunction against the publication of a photograph taken of Princess Caroline and her husband while on holiday at a ski resort in Switzerland. See ECtHR, *Von Hannover v Germany (no 2)*, app no 40660/08, 7-2-2012.

48 Inaugural speech of Jean-Paul Costa during the visit of the ECtHR judges to the Russian Constitutional Court, 10–11 May 2007.

49 ECtHR, II section, *Lautsi v Italy*, app no 30814/06, 3-11-2009.

50 *Lautsi v Italy*, Grand Chamber, 18-3-2011.

51 ECtHR, *Sahin v Turchia*, app no 44774/98, 10-11-2005, and ECtHR, *Dahlab v Svizzera*, app no 42393/98, 15-2-2001.

52 *Sahin v Turchia*, paragraph 121.

analysis of comparative law, which in general characterizes the reasoning of its judgments dealing with the ECHR and of religious symbols. Such an analysis would have revealed, as in *Lautsi*, what emerged in the reasoning of the previous judgments, i.e. the lack of consensus in Europe over the matter, which meant that a conspicuous margin of appreciation was left to decisions of the local authorities.

In *Lautsi 1*, to the contrary, the ECtHR gave an anomalous evaluation of the 'local dimension' of the matter, in particular referring to the 'special' role which Christianity occupies in Italian society and, in particular, how difficult the question of a crucifix is in a country such as Italy with its strong Catholic traditions and how, consequently, it is even more difficult to protect non-believers in need of protection.

Despite the intentions of the Strasbourg Court to support, by underlining the local dimension of the problem, the persuasiveness of its reasoning, the said technique ended up having a boomerang effect because of the risk of further enhancing both the local specificity of the question and the need to evaluate and resolve conflicting interests by State decision.

It has been stated[53] that the ECtHR's anti-majoritarian role played in *Lautsi 1* was a positive factor, useful to correct some deficiencies of the majoritarian democracy. This may be, but such a role seems also not only to cause a substantial annulment of the national margin of appreciation[54] but also to radically transform the very nature of the ECtHR (from an international court to a quasi-constitutional one) and the rationale at the basis of the ECtHR system (from individual justice to constitutional justice), especially after the entry into force of Protocol 14.[55] The judgment, in *Lautsi 1*, exactly for those reasons, has been fiercely stigmatized by many constitutional scholars as disregarding the Christian roots of the Italian state and because of its intrusiveness against state sovereignty and national values which should be regulated and protected at national level.

---

[53] S. Mancini, 'The Crucifix Rage: Supra-National Constitutionalism Bumps Against the Counter-Majoritarian Difficulty' (2010) 1 Eur Constitutional L Rev.

[54] Contra also Benvenisti, 'Judicial Misgiving Regarding the Application of International Norms: An Analysis of Attitudes of National Courts' (1993) Eur J Intl L 159.

[55] Protocol 14, which entered into force on 1 June 2010, provides a new criteria according to which the ECtHR could also declare an individual petition not receivable when 'the applicant has not suffered a significant disadvantage'. This term is open to interpretation, represents an additional element of flexibility and discretion granted to the ECtHR and will require interpretation establishing objective criteria through the gradual development of the case law of the Court. In the meanwhile, the enhancement of the move from a logic of individual justice to a logic of constitutional justice could not be denied.

In particular, the decision of the Court's Second Section caused a great uproar in Italy, both at political and judicial levels. The main concern at both levels has been the alleged disregarding, by the Strasbourg Court, not only of the Christian roots of the Italian state but also of the margin of appreciation which should be left to the individual Member State. Further concern is its intrusiveness against state sovereignty and national values which should be regulated and protected at national level.

With regard to the political dimension, many declarations from various sources were made against the judgment. Basically, all political parties opposed the judgment, the Radical Party and the Green the only parties supporting the ruling. The Italian government led by Silvio Berlusconi has expressed a unified opposition, and several ministers of the PDL-Northern League coalition expressed and promoted initiatives and petitions for the maintenance of the symbol in the classroom. The Protestant churches and the Jewish Unions praised the ruling, as did the Atheist and Agnostic Association, while the Muslim community preferred to keep a low profile.

In relation to the judicial reaction, even the Italian Constitutional Court found its way to react to the new aggressive approach of the ECtHR, by arguing in its decision no. 317/2009:

> the reference to the national 'margin of appreciation' – elaborated by the Strasbourg Court in order to temper the rigidity of the principles formulated on European level – is primarily manifested through the legislative function of Parliament, though it must always be present in the assessments of this Court, which is not unaware that the protection of fundamental rights must be systematic and not broken down into a series of provisions that are uncoordinated and potentially in conflict with one another [. . .] In summary, the national 'margin of appreciation' can be determined having regard above all to the overall body of fundamental rights, the detailed and overall consideration of which is a matter for the legislature, the Constitutional Court and the ordinary courts, each within the ambit of its own jurisdiction.[56]

Not exactly a cryptic message sent to Strasbourg, in which it is made clear that the Member State is always in a better position to decide upon the right balance between national and constitutional values and that the Constitutional Courts, within each Member State, are even in the best position to assess the said balance.

The Italian Government did not accept the ECtHR's ruling, and it subsequently appealed[57] to the Grand Chamber of the ECtHR to review the

---

[56] Italian Constitutional Court, decision no 317/2009, Paragraph 5.

[57] Appeal prepared by Corrado Bile, magistrate clerk, as an expert in the

decision of 3 November 2009 in which the ECtHR found that the display of crucifixes in public school classrooms violated Article 2 of Protocol 1 of the ECHR, viewed in conjunction with Article 9 protecting freedom of thought, conscience and religion. On 1 March 2010 a panel of the Grand Chamber granted that request and the hearing before the Grand Chamber took place on 30 June 2010. Moreover, the governments of Armenia, Bulgaria, Cyprus, the Russian Federation, Greece, Lithuania, Malta and the Republic of San Marino supported, as third-party interveners, the position of the Italian government. Along with the Italian Government and these ten countries, 33 MEPs (jointly) and several NGOs were authorized as third parties to present written observations.

According to the Italian government, the Court's decision appears to have created confusion and dismay. The ECtHR held that neutrality in religious matters is a state's duty and that the obligation to display the crucifix (symbol of the Christian confession) limits not only the right of parents to educate their children according to their beliefs, but also the right of students to believe in other faiths or to have no faith at all.

On 18 March 2011 the Grand Chamber of the ECtHR announced its decision, reached by fifteen votes to two, overturning the ruling of the lower chamber. The Grand Chamber did not confirm the 2009 ruling, which condemned the compulsory presence of crucifixes in classrooms of public schools. According to the Court, the presence of the crucifix is not incompatible with the right of parents to have their children educated secularly. A crucifix as such does not amount to indoctrination and is therefore permissible. The Court held that 'by prescribing the presence of crucifixes in State schools classrooms – a sign which, whether or not it is accorded in addition a secular symbolic value, undoubtedly refers to Christianity – the regulations confer on the country's majority religion preponderant visibility in the school environment'. Furthermore, 'it is not in itself sufficient, however, to denote a process of indoctrination on the respondent State's part and establish a breach of the requirements of Article 2 of Protocol No. 1' and 'a crucifix on a wall is an essentially passive symbol and [. . .] cannot be deemed to have an influence on pupils comparable to that of didactic speech or participation in religious activities'.

The judges of the Grand Chamber in their reasoning followed, as Ferrari has pointed out,[58] these logical steps:

Department of Legal and Legislative Affairs of the Prime Minister, in www.governo.it/presidenza.

[58] G.F. Ferrari, in G.F. Ferrari and O. Pollicino, 'The Impact of Supranational Laws on the National Sovereignty of Member States, with Particular Regard to the Judicial Reaction of UK and Italy to the New Aggressive Approach of the

(1) there is no common concept of secularism in Europe and even less in relation to the issue of religious symbols (Paragraphs 26–28 and 68);
(2) therefore the maintenance of a tradition providing for the display of the crucifix falls within the margin of appreciation of the State (Paragraph 68);
(3) the Court respects the margin under the principle of subsidiarity and intervenes only when the State constitutes forms of indoctrination at the expenses of minorities (Paragraphs 69–72).

Applying such reasoning, the Grand Chamber overruled the aggressive approach characterizing the decision of 2009, thus renouncing the policy of 'white wall' (as defined by Weiler[59]).

In particular, the Strasbourg judges completely reversed the evaluation of the second chamber, holding that 'the Contracting States enjoy a margin of appreciation in their efforts to reconcile the exercise of the functions they assume in relation to education and teaching with respect for the right of parents to ensure such education and teaching is in conformity with their own religious and philosophical convictions' (paragraph 69). On this basis the Court concluded 'the decision whether crucifixes should be present in State-school classrooms is, in principle, a matter falling within the margin of appreciation of the respondent State. Moreover, the fact that there is no European consensus on the question of the presence of religious symbols in State schools' (Paragraph 70) speaks in favour of that approach.

The decision of the Court received critical commentary, especially in the Italian scholarship. Scholars criticized reasoning according to which the display of the crucifix would not compromise the religious freedom of individuals (Paragraph 74) because it is not associated with compulsory teaching about Christianity, and Italy opens up the school environment in parallel to other religions. This conclusion, in fact, would have very serious implications for the effective protection of minority religions, which are now forced to tolerate any religious symbol that does not spill over into an explicit attempt at indoctrination.[60] It has also been pointed out that in its

European Court of Human Rights', Paper presented at the Hart Workshop, Sovereignty in Question, 28–30 July 2011, London and (2011) Comparative Law Review, (2) 1–63.

[59] J.H.H. Weiler, 'Lautsi: Crucifix in the Classroom Redux', in www.ejiltalk.org/lautsi-crucifix-in-the-classroom-redux.

[60] Mancini, 'Lautsi II: la rivincita della tolleranza preferenzialista', 2011, in www.forumcostituzionale.it/site/images/stories/pdf/documenti_forum/giurisprudenza/corte_europea_diritti_uomo/0015_mancini.pdf.

ruling the Court would have marked a significant shift in the interpretation of the principle of secularism: the centrality of the self-determination of young students in matters of religion would have been abandoned in favour of an institutional perspective, focused on the relations between the different religious faiths and between them and the state.[61]

On the other hand, the reasoning of the Grand Chamber has been considered a positive step towards the role of a subsidiary international court which would act as the the physiological one for the ECtHR.[62]

It is possible to question whether such an evident change of direction of the Grand Chamber in relation to the reasoning of the Second Chamber may represent the beginning of a new season of the Strasbourg Court. After sharp criticism from the Member States for its intrusive approach, it has chosen a new path in which self-restraint and deference for the margin of appreciation granted to the contracting States are the main criteria.

The judgment in *A, B and C v Ireland*[63] seems to confirm this trend, especially where the ECtHR stated that

> since the rights claimed on behalf of the foetus and those of the mother are inextricably interconnected (see the review of the Convention case law) the margin of appreciation accorded to a State's protection of the unborn necessarily translates into a margin of appreciation for that State as to how it balances the conflicting rights of the mother. It follows that, even if it appears from the national laws referred to that most Contracting Parties may in their legislation have resolved those conflicting rights and interests in favour of greater legal access to abortion, this consensus cannot be a decisive factor in the Court's examination of whether the impugned prohibition on abortion in Ireland for health and well-being reasons struck a fair balance between the conflicting rights and interests, notwithstanding an evolutive interpretation of the Convention (paragraph 237).

---

61 A. Schillaci, 'L'ultima sentenza Lautsi: margine di apprezzamento, principio maggioritario e libertà di coscienza, 23-3-2011', in www.diritticomparati.it/2011/03/lultima-sentenza-lautsi-margine-di-apprezzamento-principio-maggioritario-e-libert%C3%A0-di-coscienza.html.

62 C. Pinelli, 'Esposizione del crocefisso nelle aule scolastiche e libertà di religione (Oss. a Corte europea dei diritti dell'uomo – Grande Chambre, Lautsi contro Italia, 18 marzo 2011', (2011) Giurisprudenza Costituzionale.

63 ECtHR, *A, B and C v Ireland*, app. no 25579/05, 16-12-2010.

6. The enlargement of Europe to the East and the reaction of the European Court of Justice

NEW CHALLENGES FOR THE ECJ

The further centralization of the ECtHR's adjudication powers, which were analyzed in the previous chapter, along with the reduction (even if, as *Lautsi 2* shows, with prominent exceptions) of the margin of appreciation of the contracting States, need not be regarded as a foolish leap into activism by the Strasbourg judges. This is because, in the words of Wojciech Sadurski: 'if there is a domain in which concern over national identity and accompanying notions of sovereignty are obviously weak in central and eastern Europe it is in the field of protection of individual rights.'[1]

It should also be added that, in support of its new post-enlargement attitude of judicial activism, the ECtHR could count on the remarkable openness of the constitutions of Central and Eastern European (CEE) Member States to international law, especially international law on human rights.[2] This openness – a reaction to the very weak, almost non-existent, role played by international law in the legal orders of CEE countries, even at constitutional level, under the Soviet dominance[3] – finds its concrete expression in the monistic vocation of the new constitutions and in the rank granted to international law, which almost everywhere occupies an

---

[1] The main reason, according to Sadurski, is that 'the legacy of Communism under which individual rights were systematically trampled on is still fresh in many people's minds'. See W. Sadurski, 'The Role of the EU Charter of Fundamental Rights in the Process of the Enlargement', in G.A. Bermann and K. Pistor (eds), *Law and Governance in an Enlarged European Union*, (Oxford University Press 2004) 61, 80.

[2] E. Stein, 'International Law in Internal Law. Toward Internationalization of Central-Eastern European Constitutions?' (1994) Am J Comparative L 427.

[3] A. Drzemczewski and M.A. Nowicki, 'Poland' in R. Blackburn and J. Polakiewicz (eds), *Fundamental Rights in Europe: The European Convention of Human Rights and Its Member States 1950–2000* (Oxford University Press 2001), 657.

intermediate position between the constitution and the ordinary domestic law.[4]

On the contrary, the ECJ could not count on the same advantages brought by the EU enlargement to the east. At least five factors, direct or indirect consequences of the said enlargement, dictate against the 'peaceful' impact of EU law on the domestic legal orders of the CEE Member States, and therefore, represent new, problematic challenges for the ECJ.

First of all, there is the risk that the taste of freedom – recently rediscovered after years of humiliation and substantial or formal subjection to the Soviet Union – made the candidate countries from Central and Eastern Europe strongly averse to a (new) transfer of sovereignty to the European Union, albeit that it was in a completely different political and historical context.[5] Against this background, it should be remarked that the protection of national identity acquires a crucial importance in the post-1989 constitutionalism. As Sadurski has pointed out, 'after the fall of communism, national identity (often perceived in an ethnic rather than civic fashion) has been either the only or the most powerful social factor, other than those identified with social foundations of the *ancien regime*, capable of injecting a necessary degree of coherence into society and of countervailing the anomie of a disintegrated, decentralised and demoralised society'.[6]

Secondly, there is a related argument concerning the 'sovereignist' nature of the CEE legal orders compared with western constitutional models.[7] Thirdly, the emphasis in the constitutions of the CEE countries on the supremacy of the constitution over all other sources of law (including

---

4 See A. Kellerman, J. De Zwan and J. Czuczai (eds), *EU Enlargement, The Constitutional Impact at EU and National Level* (Asser Press, 2001); M. Cremona (ed.), *The Enlargement of the European* Union (Collected Courses of the Academy of European Law 2003); A. Kellerman, J. Cuczai, S. Blockmans, A. Albi and W.T. Douma (eds), *The Impact of EU Accession on the Legal Order of the New EU Member States and (Pre-) Candidate Countries. Hope and Fears* (The Hague 2006).

5 W. Sadurski, 'Constitutionalization of the EU and the Sovereignty Concerns of the New Accession States: The Role of the Charter of Rights', EUI Working Paper Law, No. 2003/11, www.iue.it/PUB/Law03-10.pdf.

6 Ibid., 12.

7 In this regard it is often underlined how the CEE constitutions place much more emphasis than Western European constitutions on the values of independence and sovereignty, which recur almost obsessively in all the CEE constitutions. See A. Albi, 'Postmodern versus Retrospective Sovereignty: Two Different Discourses in the EU and the Candidate Countries', in N. Walker (ed.), *Sovereignty in Transition* (Hart 2003).

international treaties)[8] is difficult to reconcile with a radical version of the primacy of EU law. Fourthly, we should recall the role of the constitutional courts within these legal orders, as protagonists of the transition period and guardians of regained sovereignty. These courts may be tempted (indeed, it has happened[9]) to raise their voices against Brussels and Luxembourg in order to defend their crucial role, in a domestic dimension, in respect to the national political powers.[10]

Finally, it is not difficult to see that, while, as we noted above, the Council of Europe's enlargement process to the east has been characterized by a generous and benign attitude towards the CEE candidate countries, the same could not be said with regard to the European Union's enlargement to the east. For many reasons this situation was the exact opposite of the one characterizing the application of the so-called ex-post conditionality mechanism in the Council of Europe's enlargement to the east. In both cases a double standard was applied to determine the level of human rights protection between the internal and external dimensions respectively of the Council of Europe and the European Union.

In the first case, through ex-post conditionality, the standard of protection required of CEE candidate states by the Council of Europe was less stringent than the standard applied internally to states that were already members of the Council. However, a diametrically opposite situation characterized accession to the European Union of those countries. They had to supply guarantees of protection in addition to those required of the 'old' Member States by the EU and EC Treaties.

In order to join the EU, the CEE candidate Member States were required not only to adhere to a degree of scrutiny which, at that time, was not applicable to others within the EU (in the absence of a binding Charter of Fundamental Rights), but also to a system of enforcement which simply did not exist internally in the EU. In other words, the candidate countries were required to meet standards that several of the Member States did not even meet at that time, regarding, for instance, the field of minority

---

[8] See Article 8 of the Polish Constitution; Article 153 of the Slovenian Constitution; Article 7 of the Lithuanian Constitution; Article 2(2) of the Slovak Constitution; Article 77 (1) of the Hungarian Constitution; Articles 123(1) and 152 of the Estonian Constitution.

[9] See A. Lazowsky, *The Application of EU Law in the New Member States – Brave New World* (TMC, Asser Press 2010).

[10] W. Sadurski, 'Partnering with Strasbourg: Constitutionalization of the European Court of Human Rights, the Accession of Central and East European States to the Council of Europe, and the Idea of Pilot Judgments' (2009) Human Rights L Rev, 397.

protection,[11] a key element of the Copenhagen criteria but not at all an integral part of the European *acquis*.[12]

Against this background it should be emphasized that the demand for consistency and reciprocity between internal and external human rights policies, raised almost ten years ago by Philip Alston and Joseph Weiler,[13] was never so neglected at the EU level as much as it was with regard to the monitoring policy applied to the CEE candidate countries, especially in light of the criteria laid down in Copenhagen in 1993.[14] This policy was based, in the light of the reasons mentioned above, on a core discrimination.[15] In this regard, another element should be taken into account: the conditions to be fulfilled have been entirely set by the EU, without room for any negotiation or differentiation as to each candidate's peculiar position. In the end, the whole European pre-accession strategy was nothing more than a de facto 'take it or leave it' package.[16]

---

[11] See C. Hillion, 'On Enlargement of the European Union: The Discrepancy between Membership Obligations and the Accession Conditions as regards the Protection of Minorities' (2004) Fordham Intl L J, 715.

[12] See A. Wiener and G. Schwellnus, 'Contested Norms in the Process of EU Enlargement: Non-discrimination and Minority Rights', *Constitutionalism Web-Papers*, ConWEB No. 2/2004; Sadurski, 'Constitutionalization', 6; G. de Búrca, 'On Enlargement of the European Union: Beyond the Charter: How the Enlargement Has Enlarged the Human Rights Policy of the European Union' (2004) Fordham Intl L J, 679, 683.

[13] Philip Alston and Joseph Weiler have in 'not suspicious times' argued that 'a credible human rights must assiduously avoid unilateralism and double standard, and that can only be done by ensuring reciprocity and consistency'. See P. Alston and J.H.H. Weiler, 'A European Union Human Rights Policy', in P. Alston (ed.), *The European Union and Human Rights* (Oxford University Press 1999), 8–9.

[14] Which, *inter alia*, required the candidate countries to demonstrate the stability of the institutions guaranteeing democracy, rule of law, human rights, and the protection of minorities.

[15] A. Williams, 'Enlargement of the Union and Human Rights Conditionality: A Policy of Distinction?' (2001) Eur L Rev, 601, 616.

[16] András Sajó has observed, making clear that the enlargement was mainly a unilateral process, that 'the accession process was, objectively and subjectively, a process of submission – one that may well have been in the best interest of the new Member States, but a submission nonetheless'. See A. Sajó, 'Constitution without the Constitutional Moment: A View from the New Member States' (2005) Intl J Constitutional L, 243, 252.

THE REACTION OF THE ECJ

Against this background, the relevant question is whether (and if so, in which direction) the European Court of Justice has somehow developed a new judicial sensitivity after the 2004 and 2007 enlargements in order to respond to the change of the dynamic nature of constitutional tolerance. In this respect it has been argued[17] that, in order to prevent potential 'sovereignist' reactions by Member States, and namely in order to enhance this miraculous 'voluntary obedience', in the last few decades the ECJ has resorted to applying the 'majoritarian activist approach'.[18] According to this approach, among the various solutions to a case, the European judges may opt for the final ruling that is most likely to meet the highest degree of consensus in the majority of Member States.[19] The European judges seem to have understood that if such an approach had been partially[20] able to convince Germans and Italians when they were 'invited' to obey the European discipline in the name of the peoples of Europe, the same 'invitation' would have proven much less successful when applied to Estonians or Hungarians.

The post-2004 era has called, then, for a new *ad hoc* judicial strategy to

---

17 G. Martinico and O. Pollicino, 'Between Constitutional Tolerance and Judicial Activism: The "Specificity" of the European Judicial Law' (2008) Eur J Law Reform, 99.

18 Miguel Maduro identifies the same judicial approach in the different field of European economic constitution. See M. P. Maduro, *We, the Court. The European Court of Justice and Economic Constitution* (Hart, 1998), 72–78.

19 In particular, in a previous work we have tried to prove how the reference to the majoritarian approach has been able to explain how it is not unusual in European case law that a couple of cases, which are very similar in their factual and/or legal background, are decided in an opposite, thus almost schizophrenic, way by the ECJ. The key to the apparent enigma has been found by reflecting upon the impact that a decision can have on the national legal systems by the application of the majoritarian activism approach, as is proved by the analysis of two decisions in the field of protection of sexual minorities. See O. Pollicino, *Discriminazione sulla base del sesso e trattamento preferenziale nel diritto comunitario. Alla ricerca del nucleo duro del 'new legal order'* (Giuffrè 2005) 283.

20 Doubts about the real persuasive attitude of the mentioned judicial strategy have been advanced by Matey Avbelj, arguing that 'The damaging effect of the "supranational" counter-majoritarian difficulty on legitimacy appears to be doubled: the whole "national demos" is turned into minority and the prevailing value-based view – the identity of the majority of the "national demos", is compromised in favour of a distinct European demos.' See M. Avbelj, *European Court of Justice and the Question of Value Choices: Fundamental Human Rights as an Exception to the Freedom of Movement of Goods*, Jean Monnet Working Papers 6/2004, Jean Monnet Chair.

combine with the pre-2004 majoritarian activist approach. After all, what new Member States need to be reassured about seems to be that even if, with regard to those national values relating to a peculiar identity that their constitution protects, they found themselves in a minority or isolated position, the European judges would not sacrifice them on the altar of the majoritarian-activist approach. It does not seem a coincidence, indeed, that some months after the 2004 enlargement, the Court stated, against an exclusively majoritarian logic, for the very first time, that 'it is not indispensable in that respect for the restrictive measure issued by the authorities of a Member State to correspond to a conception shared by all Member States as regards the precise way in which the fundamental right or legitimate interest in question is to be protected'.[21]

The factual background of the *Omega* decision is too well known to be narrated here. It is sufficient to recall that the question was whether the aim of protecting a constitutional right, in that case the right of human dignity, representing an issue of high priority, especially for one Member State (in that case, Germany), could possibly justify a restriction of freedom to provide services, a fundamental freedom but also a fundamental right of the European 'economic constitution'. The outcome of the decision is even more famous: 'Community law does not preclude an economic activity consisting of the commercial exploitation of games simulating acts of homicide from being made subject to a national prohibition measure adopted on grounds of protecting public policy by reason of the fact that that activity is an affront to human dignity'.[22]

What seems instead to have been undervalued in several commentaries on the case is the circumstance that the European judges, in order to acknowledge the protection of the single Member State's constitutional values, had to manipulate their previous judgment which clearly reflected the then prevailing approach of the majoritarian (if not unanimous) logic at the heart of the justification grounds for the restriction of fundamental freedoms.[23] The ECJ was then able to give an authentic (manipulated) interpretation of its precedent, explaining how:

> Although, in paragraph 60 of *Schindler* the Court referred to moral, religious or cultural considerations which lead all Member States to make the organisation of lotteries and other games with money subject to restrictions, it was not its intention, by mentioning that common conception, to formulate a general

21 ECJ, C-36/02, *Omega* [2004] ECR I-9609, paragraph 37.
22 *Omega*, paragraph 41.
23 ECJ, C-275/92, *Schindler* [1994] ECR I-1039.

> criterion for assessing the proportionality of any national measure which restricts the exercise of an economic activity.[24]

In other words, a shift emerged in the judicial reasoning of the ECJ, from a pre-enlargement majoritarian activist approach to a post-enlargement reference to the needed protection, at least in the most sensitive cases, of the fundamental rights peculiar even to a single Member State's constitutional identity. The same vision, even more clearly expressed, was confirmed in *Dynamic Medien*, in a judgment of 14 February 2008[25] which has gone strangely unnoticed.

The dispute in the main proceedings concerned the importation by a German company of Japanese animé cartoons in DVD or video cassette format from the United Kingdom to Germany. The cartoons were examined before importation by the British Board of Film Classification (BBFC). The latter checked the audience targeted by the image storage media by applying the provisions relating to the protection of young persons in force in the United Kingdom and classified them in the category 'suitable only for 15 years and over'. The image storage media bear a BBFC label stating that they may be viewed only by persons aged 15 years or older.

Dynamic Medien, a competitor of Avides Media, brought proceedings for interim relief before the *Landgericht* (Regional Court) of Koblenz (Germany) with a view to prohibiting Avides Media from selling such image storage media by mail order. Dynamic Medien submitted that the legislation on the protection of young persons prohibits the sale by mail order of image storage media which have not been examined in Germany in accordance with that law, and which do not bear an age-limit label corresponding to a classification decision from a German higher regional authority or a national self-regulation body ('competent authority'). By decision of 8 June 2004, the Koblenz *Landgericht* held that mail-order sales of image storage media bearing an age-limit label from the BBFC alone was contrary to the provisions of the law on the protection of young persons and constituted anti-competitive conduct.

On 21 December 2004, the *Oberlandesgericht* (Higher Regional Court) of Koblenz, ruling in an application for interim relief, confirmed that decision. The Koblenz *Landgericht*, called to rule on the merits of the dispute and unsure whether the prohibition provided for by the law on

---

24 *Omega*, paragraph 37.

25 ECJ, C-244/06, *Dynamic Medien Vertriebs GmbH*, 14 February 2008, in www.curia.eu.int.

the protection of young persons complied with the provisions of former Article 28 EC, decided to stay the proceedings and to refer to the ECJ for a preliminary ruling. The German court asked the ECJ whether the principle of free movement of goods laid down in former Article 28 EC precludes the German law prohibiting the sale by mail order of DVDs and videos that are not labelled as having been vetted by the German authorities as to their suitability for young people. The German court also asked whether the German prohibition could be justified under former Article 30 EC.

The ECJ held, in the first place, that the German rules constitute a measure having equivalent effect to quantitative restrictions within the meaning of former Article 28 EC, which in principle is incompatible with the obligations arising from that article unless it can be objectively justified. The Court then considered whether the German measures could be justified as being necessary to protect young people, being an objective linked to public morality and public policy, which are recognized as grounds for justification in former Article 30 EC. The ECJ held that the German measures were so justified, and stated in particular:

> that it is not indispensable that restrictive measures laid down by the authorities of a Member State to protect the rights of the child, correspond to a conception shared by all Member States as regards the level of protection and the detailed rules relating to it (see, by analogy, Omega, paragraph 37). As that conception may vary from one Member State to another on the basis of, inter alia, moral or cultural views, Member States must be recognised as having a definite margin of discretion[26]

Despite the reference to the analogy of the *Omega* case, in *Dynamic Medien* the ECJ seems have gone further with the appraisal of the national constitutional values of the particular Member State, in the direction of indirect reassurance towards the new Member States. The case presents a twofold innovation. Firstly, by making express reference to different levels of the protection of fundamental rights within Member States (rather than *way of protection* as in *Omega*), and by acknowledging for the first time a definite margin of discretion to the individual Member State, the ECJ has achieved a double objective. On one hand, the Court refused to follow the highest standard-based conception of fundamental human rights[27]

---

26 *Dynamic Medien Vertriebs GmbH*, paragraph 48.

27 See L.F.M. Besselink, 'Entrapped by the Maximum Standard: On Fundamental Rights, Pluralism and Subsidiarity in the European Union' (1998) CML Rev, 629, 636.

whilst, on the other, it has explicitly confirmed its willingness to adhere to the substantive nature of the fundamental rights. In Alexy's words,[28] they are substantively fundamental because they enshrine the basic normative structures of state and society.[29] It would be difficult not to perceive the link between, on one hand, the Court's step back, facing the fundamental boundaries[30] of basic value-oriented choices of the Member States, in its obsessive enhancement of European law uniformity and, on the other hand, the aim to reassure (also) CEE States that their constitutional identity will not be sacrificed in the name of the achievement of European economic values. Secondly, the reference to the European Charter of Fundamental Rights is also very innovative in this regard. Departing from other cases where the ECJ has made explicit reference to the Charter,[31] here the mentioned reference is the sole means to assert European primary law protection of the fundamental right in question.[32]

It is not a coincidence that, in light of this judicial strategy of reassurance being put in place, the ECJ started to make express reference in its reasoning, after years of indifference, to the Charter almost immediately after the accession of the CEE Member States. As has been astutely argued: 'There is a high degree of congruence between the structure of constitutional rights in the post-communist countries of Central and Eastern Europe and the structure of the rights as displayed in the EU Charter.'[33]

Upon closer inspection, the attention to national values, far from being a post-2004 accession novelty, has always been a main feature of the ECJ case law related to the achievement of a European single market. This is true in particular with regard to consumer protection and the preservation of public order as legitimate justification for the hindrance to fundamental

---

[28] See R. Alexy, *A Theory of Constitutional Rights* (Oxford, 2002), 349, 350.

[29] Avbelj, *European Court of Justice and the Question of Value Choices*, 42.

[30] See J.H.H. Weiler, 'Fundamental Rights and Fundamental Boundaries: On Standards and Values in the Protection of Human Rights', in N. Neuwahl and A. Rosas (eds), *The European Union and Human Rights* (Clarendon Press 1995), 51, 52.

[31] ECJ, C-540/03, 27-6-2006, paragraph 38; C-432/05, 13-3-2007, paragraph 37; C-303/05, 3-5-2007; C-438/05, *Viking*, 11-12-2007, and C-341/05, Laval, 18-12-2007.

[32] The Court of Justice (*Dynamic Medien Vertriebs GmbH*, paragraph 41) stated that 'the protection of the child is also enshrined in instruments drawn up within the framework of the European Union, such as the Charter of Fundamental Rights of the European Union, proclaimed on 7 December 2000 in Nice (OJ 2000 C 364, p. 1), Article 24(1) of which provides that children have the right to such protection and care as is necessary for their well-being'.

[33] Sadurski, 'Constitutionalization', 12. See, for arguments supporting this point, W. Sadurski, 'Charter and Enlargement' (2002) Eur L J, 340, 348.

freedoms in national laws, especially the freedom of establishment and the freedom to provide services.

It is sufficient to consider the case law related to gambling where the ECJ has admitted that moral, religious and cultural factors, and the morally and financially harmful consequences for individuals and societies associated with gambling, could serve to justify the existence, in the hands of the national authorities, of a margin of appreciation sufficient to enable them to determine what kind of consumer protection and public order preservation they should apply.[34]

The innovative element of the post-enlargement phase of the ECJ case law, mainly connected with the need to provide reassurance for the strong, identity-based demands for recognition coming from the new CEE Member States, is instead the willingness of the ECJ to take a step back if the protection of a national constitutional right is at stake. If it is true, as it has been objected,[35] that: 'the phase of justification before the ECJ is a phase in which the Court strikes a balance between the competing values of the Member States and the economic values of the Union and makes the final determination', the added value of the relevant post-enlargement case law[36] is that fundamental rights become a legitimate justified obstacle to the further enhancement of the European economic constitution even if that ground of justification is not at all enshrined in the founding Treaties.

In light of the scenario that we have just tried to delineate, it is perhaps possible to advance further in the attempt to systematize the reactions to the enlargement that have characterized the judicial approach of the ECJ. The ECJ, in fact, seems increasingly committed to work on a self-restriction of the principle of EU primacy when it comes to the protection of identity-based constitutional dimensions of one or more Member States. A precise

---

34 C-124/97 *Läärä and Others* ECR I-6067. Along the same lines, more recently, see C-243/01, *Gambelli*, 6-11-2003, and, Joined Cases C-338/04, C-359/04 and C-360/04, *Placanica,* 6-3-2007, where the Court expressly states that 'context, moral, religious or cultural factors, as well as the morally and financially harmful consequences for the individual and for society associated with betting and gaming, may serve to justify a margin of discretion for the national authorities, sufficient to enable them to determine what is required in order to ensure consumer protection and the preservation of public order' (paragraph 47).

35 See Avbelj, *European Court of Justice and the Question of Value Choices.*

36 *Omega*, anticipated by Case C-112/00, *Eugen Schmidberger Internationale Transporte Planzüge v Republik Österreich* [2003] ECR I-565. See, for an analysis of the two decisions, A. Alemanno, 'A la recherche d'un juste èquilibre entre libertés fondamentales et droits fondamentaux dans le cadre du marché intérieur. Quelques reflexions à propos des arrêts "Schmidberger" et "Omega"' (2004) Revue du droit de l'Union europeenne, 1.

strategy of the ECJ, whose aim seems, in line with the *Solange* approach, to prevent further positions (also) of the European constitutional courts by somehow 'internalizing', the '*controlimiti*' (counterlimits) doctrine in its case law.

In other words, the 'evolutionary nature of the doctrine of primacy'[37] seems to have undergone another transfiguration phase after the 2004 enlargement, from an uncompromising version[38] to a compromising one. It is not a coincidence that the Treaty establishing the European Constitution[39] of 2004 provided, immediately prior to the codification of the principle of EU primacy, at I-6, the following complementary principle:

> The Union shall respect the equality of the Member States before the constitution as well their national identity, inherent in their fundamental structures, political and constitutional, inclusive of regional and local self-government. It shall respect the entire state functions, including the territorial integrity of the state, maintaining law and order and safeguarding national security.

Moreover, it does not appear to be coincidence either that in the 'substantial reincarnation' of the Treaty establishing a Constitution for Europe, whereas the Lisbon Treaty entered into force on 1 December 2009, notwithstanding the lack of an express codification of the principle of the primacy of EU law, the principle enshrined in Article 1-5 of the Treaty establishing the European Constitution has been textually provided by Article 4.2[40] of the Treaty on European Union as amended by the Treaty of Lisbon.[41] Despite the undeniably high potential of the identity clause

---

[37] See J.H.H. Weiler, 'The Community System, the Dual Character of Supranationalism', (1981) Ybk Eur L, 268, 275.

[38] J.H.H. Weiler, 'The Transformation of Europe' (1991) Yale L J, 2403, 2414.

[39] For an in-depth analysis of the element of identity in the Constitutional Treaty, see Armin von Bogdandy, 'The European Constitution and the European Identity: Text and Subtext of the Treaty establishing a Constitution for Europe' (2005) Intl J Constitutional Law, 295, 299.

[40] See I. Aronstein, '"The Union shall respect cultural diversity and national identities". Lisbon's Concessions to Euroscepticism – True Promises or a Booby-trap?' 2010 Utrecht L Rev, 89.

[41] It is true that the Treaty of Maastricht included in the former Article 6.4 of the former (pre-Lisbon) TEU the reference to the respect for national identity by providing that 'The Union shall respect the national identities of its Member States'. It is also true that, comparing this succinct formulation with the very wordy formulation in the Lisbon version ('shall respect their national identities, inherent in their fundamental structures, political and constitutional, inclusive of regional and local self-government') it is quite clear that the political and

with regard to its enhancement of the ECJ's new interest in the margin of appreciation of the single Member State, there was some scepticism in the scholarship[42] about the effective use of the clause in the case law of the Luxembourg Court. Against these pessimistic predictions, 'only' one year after the entry in force of the Lisbon Treaty, the ECJ, for the first time, in the seminal judgment *Sayn-Wittgenstein*,[43] expressly referred to the new 'identity clause' provided by Article 4(2) of the TEU. In this case, the ECJ, recalled, in the light of the *Omega* doctrine, that:

> it is not indispensable for the restrictive measure issued by the authorities of a Member State to correspond to a conception shared by all Member States as regards the precise way in which the fundamental right or legitimate interest in question is to be protected and that, on the contrary, the need for, and proportionality of, the provisions adopted are not excluded merely because one Member State has chosen a system of protection different from that adopted by another State. (Paragraph 92).

It also felt the need to add: 'It must also be noted that, in accordance with Article 4(2) TEU, the European Union is to respect the national identities of its Member States, which include the status of the State as a Republic' (paragraph 93). In this regard, it has been correctly pointed out that 'Constitutional identity still seems to be an element to be taken into account in operations of balancing. The weight of arguments based on it is perhaps different from what normally happened before the last wave of modifications of the Treaties.'[44]

---

constitutional aspect is much enhanced in the Lisbon version. To the extent that the Lisbon Treaty here focuses on state structures, there is a shift in emphasis from national identity as such to '*constitutional* identity'. See L. Besselink, 'National and Constitutional Identity before and after Lisbon' (2010) Utrecht L Rev 36, 45.

42 See, for instance, the reactions after the *Zambrano* and *Elchinov* cases: E. Guild, 'The Court of Justice of the European Union and Citizens of the Union: A Revolution Underway? The Zambrano judgment of 8 March 2011', EUDO, http://eudo-citizenship.eu/citizenship-news/453-the-court-of-justice-of-the-european-union-and-citizens-of-the-union-a-revolution-underway-the-zambrano-judgment-of-8-march-2011; C. Backes and M. Eliantonio, 'Taking Constitutionalization One Step Too Far? The Need for Revision of the *Rheinmühlen* Case Law in the Light of the AG Opinion and the ECJ's Ruling in *Elchinov*', Maastricht Faculty of Law Working Paper No. 2010/9, http://papers.ssrn.com/sol3/papers.cfm?abstract_id=1722631.

43 ECJ C-208/09, *Sayn-Wittgenstein*, 22-12-2010.

44 See G. Delledonne, 'Dealing with National Identities: Article 4 TEU', paper presented at Joint Workshop (STALS, EUDO, Max Weber Programme, CSF) 'Treaty Reform beyond Lisbon?', San Domenico di Fiesole, 18 March 2011. As an example of the new approach taken by the ECJ, Delledonne quotes the passage

In a different context, Mattias Kumm has stated that the primacy principle's new 'season' following the 2004 enlargement, with a view to the new Lisbon Treaty, requires that: 'When EU law conflicts with clear and specific national constitutional norms that reflect a national commitment to a constitutional essential, concerns related to democratic legitimacy override considerations relating to the uniform and effective enforcement of EU law.'[45] If this impression is to be confirmed, *Sayn-Wittgenstein* seems to suggest, in the future, the ECJ would have found, thanks to the new parameter provided by Article 4(2) of the TEU as amended by the Treaty of Lisbon, the appropriate judicial mechanism to prevent the occurrence of the most frequent constitutional conflict between the EC and the national levels – the dualistic tension between the irresistible, overriding vocation of the ECJ's *Simmenthal* mandate and the equally monolithic national constitutional mandate to preserve the core of fundamental domestic values from EC 'invasion'.

As a matter of example, an EU norm, which would take precedence over a Member State's constitutional provision which asserts its constitutional identity, would clash, in fact, with EU law itself, and with Article 4(2) of the Lisbon Treaty, which requires, as we have seen, that EU law respects the national identity of the Member States. Consequently, in case of such a conflict, the hypothesis of annulment of a piece of EC law by a Member State's Constitutional Court would appear, beside its clear contrast with the *Foto-Frost* doctrine,[46] even less realistic. The intervention of constitutional courts in this case would in fact be prevented by the annulment of the piece of EU legislation by the ECJ itself because of its contrast with a provision of the EU Treaty.[47]

---

in *Sayn-Wittgenstein* in which the Court stated: 'It must be accepted that, in the context of Austrian constitutional history, the Law on the abolition of the nobility, as an element of national identity, may be taken into consideration when a balance is struck between legitimate interests and the right of free movement of persons recognised under European Union law' (paragraph 83). See more recently now A. Von Bogdandy and S. Schill, 'Overcoming absolute primacy: Respect for national identity under the Lisbon Treaty', (2011) CML Rev 105,

45 M. Kumm, 'The Jurisprudence of Constitutional Conflict: Constitutional Supremacy in Europe before and after the Constitutional Treaty' (2005) Eur L J, 262, 286, 298.

46 ECJ C-314/85, *Foto-Frost* (1987) ECR I-4199, 22-10-1987.

47 The proposed hypothesis has disadvantages: in this way the ECJ would have a high discretion to decide what is a national identity and when it would be put in danger by EU legislation. It should be also added, as it has been pointed out, that: 'Strictly legally, the ECJ lacks the formal competence to do so, as adjudicating an alleged infringement of Article 4(2) EU would involve an interpretation of national constitutional law. This is incompatible with Article 19 EU (formerly 220

A last consideration regards Article 53 of the European Charter of Fundamental Rights, according to which:

> Nothing in this Charter shall be interpreted as restricting or adversely affecting human rights and fundamental freedoms as recognised, in their respective fields of application, by Union law and international law and by international agreements to which the Union, the Community or all the Member States are party, including the European Convention for the Protection of Human Rights and Fundamental Freedoms, and by the Member States' Constitutions.

By taking this provision seriously, its effect can only support and accelerate the new direction ECJ jurisprudence has taken to make effective the primacy of EU law over national law with relation to human rights protection. The Charter of Nice is in fact explicitly binding when it provides that the standard of protection characterizing Member States' constitutions may not be lowered by the application of the Charter.

Some scholars have taken this a step farther by recognizing that the binding nature, with the entry in force of the Lisbon Treaty, of this provision of the Charter 'would mean an official recognition of the exception to Community law supremacy'.[48]

THE NATIONAL JUDICATURES AS ECJ INTERLOCUTORS

In the previous pages we have pointed out the changes that, following the 2004 and 2007 enlargements, have characterized the new approaches of the ECJ towards Member States' political powers. It now remains to consider if something has changed – or still needs to be changed – at European judicial level, with regard to the relationship between the European legal order and Member States' judiciaries, with particular reference to the CEE Member States.

As we said at the end of Chapter 3, the particular relationship between national judges and the ECJ via the preliminary ruling mechanism is one

---

EC) which limits the jurisdiction of the ECJ to the interpretation of EU law, which according to continuous standing case law excludes the interpretation of national law'. See Besselink, 'National and constitutional identity before and after Lisbon', 45.

[48] L.F.M. Besselink, 'The Member States, the National Constitutions and the Scope of the Charter' (2001) Maastricht J European and Comparative Law, 28. See also P. Eeckhout, 'The EU Charter of Fundamental Rights and the Federal Question' (2002) CML Rev 945.

of the characteristic features of the EU legal system. In contrast, the relationship between the ECtHR and national interlocutors has never had the opportunity to rely on such a powerful engine. In this regard, a distinction has to be made between the constitutional courts and the ordinary judges in CEE Member States. The former, as indicated above, seem well prepared to play a leading role in the new season of European cooperative constitutionalism through a creative and often activist approach. Further, as third-generation constitutional courts, they are characterized by being born into the global constitutional movement which favours the interaction between legal regimes, but the same does not apply to the ordinary courts. It has been rightly observed, in fact, that the judiciary in CEE countries is still enslaved by textual positivism.[49] In other words, the CEE ordinary judges still maintain a rather formalistic approach, almost mechanical and deferential to the national legislature, not enthusiastic about the new chances of judicial communication offered by European law and, in particular, by its preliminary ruling procedure. They are almost allergic to creativity as well as judicial activism, and far from having any intent to participate in a transnational discourse. This is not exactly the best start to building a virtuous process of mutual assistance between the legal constitutional dimension and the European one.

Against this background, our assumption is that the ECJ has already put forward actions aimed at urging CEE ordinary courts to cooperate, but that a lot still remains to be done, especially with regard to judicial style, in order to improve the virtuous cycle of reciprocal influence between the European and the national courts, including Constitutional Courts. With regard to the achievements, we refer to the need, strongly felt in the pre-enlargement period, for a rule that CEE national judges might have perceived as an incentive not to disregard the correct domestic application of European law. The solution was found, one year before the major 2004 enlargement, in the *Köbler* case.[50] There the ECJ extended the case law in *Francovich*[51] and *Brasserie*[52] related to State liability in case of actions

---

49 Z. Kühn, 'Words Apart, Western and Central European Judicial Culture at the Onset of the European Enlargement' (2004) Am J Comparative L, 531, 549.

50 ECJ, C-224/01, *Köbler*, 30-9-2003. For an early, critical assessment of *Köbler*, see P.J. Wattel, '*Köbler*, *CILFIT* and *Welthgrove*: We Can't Go On Meeting Like This' (2004) CML Rev 177. For a more balanced appraisal, see M. Breuer, 'State Liability for Judicial Wrongs and Community Law: The Case of *Gerhard Köbler v Austria*' (2004) Eur L Rev, 29.

51 Joined cases C-6/90 and C-9/90, *Andrea Francovich and Danila Bonifaci v Italian Republic* (1991) ECR I-5357.

52 Joined cases C-46/93 and C-48/93, *Brasserie du Pecheur SA v Germany* and *R v Secretary of State for Transport ex parte Factortame Ltd* (1996) ECR I-1029.

taken in breach of the national obligations stemming from European law to the judiciary of the Member States. In other words, the ordinary courts of the new Member States, at the moment of their entrance into the European judicial arena, have been welcomed by the updating of the ECJ's doctrine of Member State liability, which now enables an individual to bring suit for damages on a claim that a prior decision of a Member State's court violated European law.[53] It is difficult to deny that the decision's effect (or at least intention) was to motivate (also) the CEE Member States' courts, which will have an obvious incentive for making referrals concerning doubtful questions of EU Law to the ECJ, in the attempt to avoid any possible subsequent liability.

This is what we should also read between the lines of the ECJ's decision of December 2003, where the ECJ found the infraction procedure brought by the Commission against Italy as legitimate, due, *inter alia*, to the persisting practice of the Italian *Corte di Cassazione* in breach of Community law.[54] As has been noted,[55] the possibility of infringement proceedings against the judicial misapplication of European law has been regarded with suspicion by the ECJ and excluded by mainstream scholarship:[56] 'by the argument the co-operation and the trust between the Court of Justice and national Courts would have been disrupted. We may see this infringement procedure as a warning to national Courts in the new Member States to take Community law seriously.'[57]

With regard to the post-enlargement period, we present the European

---

53 See J.E. Pfander, '*Köbler v. Austria:* Expositional Supremacy and Member State Liability' (2006) European Business L Rev, 275. Along the same lines, the Court of Justice, in its subsequent decision in *Traghetti del Mediterraneo* held that 'Community law precludes national legislation which excludes State liability, in a general manner, for damage caused to individuals by an infringement of Community law attributable to a Court adjudicating at last instance, by reason of the fact that the infringement in question results from an interpretation of provisions of law or an assessment of facts or evidence carried out by that Court. Community law also precludes national legislation which limits such liability solely to cases of intentional fault and serious misconduct on the part of the Court, if such a limitation were to lead to exclusion of the liability of the Member State concerned in other cases where a manifest infringement of the applicable law was committed' (paragraph 46). See ECJ C-173/03, *Traghetti del Mediterraneo* (2006) ECR I-5177.

54 ECJ C-129/00, *Commission v Italy* (2003) ECR I-14637.

55 J. Komarek, 'Inter-Court Constitutional Dialogue after the Enlargement – Implication of the Case of Professor Köbler' (2005) Croatian Ybk Eur L, 75, 87.

56 See H.G. Schermers and D.F. Waelbroeck, *Judicial Protection in the European Union* (Kluwer Law International 2001), 630 ff.

57 Komarek, 'Inter-Court Constitutional Dialogue', 87.

Arrest Warrant saga as a case study, in order to examine how the constitutional courts in Europe are actually settling EU law disputes in the field of criminal matters.[58] More generally, we question whether certain general trends might be identified and injected into the current 'season' of European cooperative constitutionalism. In this context, the European Arrest Warrant (hereafter EAW) saga seems to be the most suitable example, not only because it implied a confrontation between 'Western' and 'Eastern' constitutional courts, but also because it appears a paradigmatic case to study the reactions to lack of coordination and, consequently, the conflicts arising between the European and national legal systems in relation to multilevel protection of fundamental rights, with particular regard to the right to security in criminal proceedings.

As we have mentioned above, there are few doubts that the potential grounds for such lack of coordination and the consequent arising of conflicts were inherent in the legal orders of the CEE countries at the time of their accession and the reasons for such are too obvious to be further analysed here. It is sufficient to recall the early (and later) predictions warning of:

(1) the risk that the taste of freedom – recently rediscovered after years of humiliation and substantial or formal subjection to the Soviet Union would make the CEE candidate countries strongly adverse to a (new) transfer of sovereignty (even if in a complete different political and historical context) to the European Union;[59]
(2) the related principle of the 'sovereignist' nature of CEE legal orders compared with Western constitutional models;[60]
(3) the emphasis in the jurisprudence of CEE legal orders on the supremacy of the constitution over all other sources of law (including international treaties)[61]; and

---

[58] This is the main criticism that Alec Stone Sweet made of the reports published in the volume, *The European Court and National Courts – Doctrine and Jurisprudence*, when he stated, 'however excellent on their own terms, the national reports (and studies like them) collectively suffer from a fatal flaw: the privileged focus on formal doctrine. Far more important what is ignored: how the Courts are actually resolving legal disputes'. A. Slaughter, A. Stone Sweet and J.H.H. Weiler (eds) *The European Court and National Courts – Doctrine and Jurisprudence. Legal Change in its Social Context* (Hart 1997), 325.

[59] Sadurski, 'Constitutionalization'.

[60] Albi, 'Postmodern versus Retrospective Sovereignty'; and more generally A. Albi, *EU Enlargement and the Constitutions of Central and Eastern Europe* (Cambridge University Press 2005).

[61] See Article 8 of the Polish Constitution; Article 153 of the Slovenian Constitution; Article 7 of the Lithuanian Constitution,; Article 2 (2) of the Slovak

(4) the role of the constitutional courts within CEE legal orders, as protagonists of the transition period and guardians of regained sovereignty, who are empowered to interpret and annul international treaties that conflict with national constitutions.[62]

Against all the negative predictions[63] about their lack of the necessary amount of 'constitutional tolerance' the judicial approach of the CEE constitutional courts in the EAW saga seems to demonstrate mainly encouraging signs of an increasing judicial dialogue that is crucial to maintain the delicate balance underlying the mechanism of mutual support between the national and supranational levels. One reason for this unexpected result, which will be confirmed by the analysis of case law below, might be that, as it has been argued,[64] these post-Communist Constitutional Courts developed in a favourable international environment where, as opposed to the history of the 'ancient' European constitutional courts, there already was (and is) a common European language of constitutionality and fundamental rights.[65]

There is another factor which makes very interesting the analysis of the judicial reactions to the EAW Framework Decision[66] in the Member States. This analysis aims to show that, in the relationship between interacting legal systems, a growing distance is emerging between the lower degree of openness of constitutions of the CEE Member States towards EU law and the more generous tendency to accept the penetration of European law into domestic law shown by their national courts, which

---

Constitution; Article 77 (1) of the Hungarian Constitution Articles 123 (1) and 152 of the Estonian Constitution. See A. Albi, '"Europe" Articles in the Constitutions of the Central and Eastern European Countries' CML Rev (2005) 421.

62 As it has been noted by Sadurski, all the Constitutional Courts of CEE Member States have the power of preliminary review of the constitutionality of the Treaties and, in addition, the Constitutional Courts of Hungary, Poland and Estonia have the power of ex-post review of Treaties. See W. Sadurski, 'Accession's Democracy Dividend: The Impact of the EU Enlargment upon Democracy in the New Member States of Central and Eastern Europe' (2004) Eur L J, 371, 392.

63 M. Aziz, 'Constitutional Tolerance and Enlargement: The Politic of Dissent?' in W. Sadurski, A.W. Czarnota and M. Krygier (eds), *Spreading Democracy and the Rule of Law?* (Springer 2006), 237.

64 L. Sólyom, 'Constitutional Justice, Some Comparative Remarks', Conference on 'Constitutional Justice and the Rule of Law' on the occasion of the tenth anniversary of the Constitutional Court of Lithuania (Vilnius, 4–5 September 2003) in http://www.venice.coe.int/docs/2003/CDL-JU(2003)030-e.asp.

65 L. Sólyom, 'The Role of Constitutional Courts in the Transition to Democracy' (2003) International Sociology, 133.

66 Council Framework Decision 2002/584/JHA of 13 June 2002 on the European arrest warrant and the surrender procedures between Member States.

contrast with the attitude toward EU law characteristic of the case law of many 'western' constitutional courts.

It is evident, as Advocate General Dámaso Ruiz-Jarabo Colomer pointed out in an Opinion in 2005,[67] that there are substantial differences between extradition and the EAW. The extradition procedure implies a relationship between two sovereign states: the first one requesting cooperation from the other, which in turn decides to grant it or not on the grounds of reasons that are not eminently judicial. Rather they lie, in fact, in the international relations framework, where the principle of political opportunity plays a predominant role.[68] The EAW falls instead into an institutional scenario where judicial assistance is requested and granted within an integrated transnational judicial system. In so doing, the Member States, by partially giving up their sovereignty, transfer their competences to foreign authorities which have been endowed with regulatory powers. Furthermore, the Advocate General argued that such a mechanism 'which falls within the scope of the first pillar of the Union, also operates in the third, intergovernmental, pillar – albeit with a clear Community objective, as was demonstrated in *Pupino* – by transferring to framework decisions certain aspects of the first pillar and a number of the parameters specific to directives'.[69]

In spite of all the differences that commentators[70] may emphasize, also highlighted in certain national legislations for the adoption of the Framework Decision,[71] it is clear that both measures have as their goal

---

67 See Opinion in C-303/05 *Advocaten de Wererd VZW v Leden Van de Ministerraad*, paragraph 45, fn. 40.

68 For an in-depth study on the extradition principle at both national and international levels, see M. Plachta, '(Non) Extradition of Nationals: A Never Ending Story?' (XXXX Emory International Law Review, 77XXXX). In particular, Plachta points out how 'the justification of the rule of non extradition of nationals largely derives from a jealously guarded conception of national sovereignty, and it presupposes the existence of sharp contrasts in the administration of criminal justice between states, resulting in potentially unfair treatment' (99–100).

69 AG's Opinion in C-303/05 *Advocaten de Wererd VZW v Leden Van de Ministerraad*, Point 44.

70 M. Plachta, 'European Arrest Warrant: Revolution in Extradition' (2003), *Journal of Crime, Criminal Law and Criminal Justice*, 193; O. Lagodny, 'Extradition Without a Granting Procedure: The Concept of Surrender', in T. Blekxtoon and W. Van Ballegooij (eds), *Handbook of the European Arrest Warrant* (T.M.C. Asser 2005), 41; I. Jegouzo, 'Le mandate d'arret européen ou la première concretisation de l'espace judiciaire européen' (2004) Gazette du Palais, 2311.

71 As the Advocate General pointed out in the mentioned Opinion, the preamble to the Spanish law dated 14 March 2003, on the EAW and surrender procedures (BOE n. 65 of 17-3-2003, 10244), highlights how: 'the EAW changes the classical extradition procedures so radically that one can safely say that extradi-

the surrender of a requested person to a Member State authority for the purposes of prosecution or the carrying out of a criminal sentence.

A number of Member States have sought to avoid the application of such a measure to one of their own citizens. In fact, before adoption of the EAW Framework Decision, 13 of the (then) 25 Member States provided for constitutional dispositions forbidding,[72] or somehow limiting,[73] the extradition of nationals. No wonder, then, that the innovations of the EAW provisions caused, at the time of their adoption[74] by Member States, unavoidable 'constitutional disturbance'.

---

tion as it once was no longer exists in the framework of the relationships between Member States in matters of justice and cooperation'.

[72] In the pre-amendment version of the constitutional texts, the inadmissibility of extradition of nationals was ratified by the constitutions of Germany (Article 16, para 2), Austria (Article 12, para. 1), Latvia (Article 98), Slovakia (Article 23, para. 4), Poland (Article 55), Slovenia (Article 47), Finland (Article 9.3), Cyprus (Article 11.2) and to a lesser extent, the Czech Republic (Article 14 of the Fundamental liberties and rights' Charter) and Portugal.

[73] Other constitutional texts provide, as sole exception to the extradition ban, that a different measure be imposed by an international treaty (Estonia, Article 36.2; Italy, Article 26,1; Lithuania, Article 13).

[74] Italy was the last European country to transpose the Framework Decision through its adoption, on 22 April 2005, of the law no. 69/2005. See F. Impalà, 'The European Arrest Warrant in the Italian Legal System between Mutual Recognition and Mutual Fear within the European Area of Freedom, Security and Justice' (2005) Utrecht L Rev, 56. It is worth noting how some very authoritative doctrine had already highlighted, before the adoption of the final version of the Framework Decision, its incompatibility with the constitutional principle, among others, of the peremptory nature of crime. See V. Caianello and G. Vassalli, 'Parere sulla proposta di decisione quadro sul mandato di arresto europeo' (2002) Cassazione penale, 462. Recently, the Italian Constitutional Court has also ruled on the EAW, with decision no. 227/2010. In the claim, the plaintiff invoked the violation of Article 117, paragraph 1, of the Constitution for the alleged wrong implementation in national law of Article 4 of the EAW Framework Decision related to the grounds for optional non-execution of the EAW. In particular according to Article 4, paragraph 6 of the Framework Decision, 'the executing judicial authority may refuse to execute the European Arrest Warrant: if the European Arrest Warrant has been issued for the purposes of execution of a custodial sentence or detention order, where the requested person is staying in, or is a national or a resident of the executing Member State and that State undertakes to execute the sentence or detention order in accordance with its domestic law'.

Italy implemented this provision by adopting Article 18, 1 (*r*) of law no. 69 of 2005, according to which 'if the European arrest warrant has been issued for the purposes of execution of a custodial sentence or detention order the Italian judicial authority can decide that the execution will be in Italy, in conformity to Italian law, if the requested person is a national citizen'.

It is evident that the implementation legislation has omitted reference to the stay

Some countries, such as Portugal,[75] Slovakia,[76] Latvia[77] and Slovenia,[78] revised their respective constitutions before their respective constitutional

---

or the residence of a non-citizen person in the state. Such a reference was however expressly included in the Framework Decision.

Even if the plaintiff, in relation to the violation of EU legislation invoked the breach of Article 117, paragraph 1, the ICC concluded that national legislation was in violation of Article 117, paragraph 1, taken together with Article 11.

In particular the ICC stated that the EAW Framework Decision allows the national legislator to refuse to deliver the requested person under certain circumstances, in a case where the requested person is staying in, or is a national or a resident of the executing Member State. The ICC added that the same instrument does not limit the hypothesis of a refusal only to the case of Italian citizenship, as is provided by the implementing Italian law, which is thus to be considered in breach of the ban on discrimination on the ground of nationality now provided by Article 18 of the TFEU.

There are at least three remarks that could be made with regard to the reasoning of the ICC in the above mentioned decision. The first one is related to the activation of centralized control of constitutionality in the hypothesis of wrong implementation of a framework decision and of a breach of the ban of non-discrimination on the ground of nationality provided by the above mentioned provision of the TFEU; the second has to do with the relationship between Article 11 and Article 117, paragraph 1; the third one is instead focusing on the merit of the decision, in which the formal status of citizen is postponed in favour of the substantial evaluation of the effective link between a person and a Member State.

With regard to the first issue, the ICC quoted extensively the ECJ case law related to the effects (C-105/03, *Pupino*) and the validity of the EAW decision (C-303/05, *Advocaten voor de Wereld*). The ICC also recalled that with the entry in force of the Lisbon Treaty the judicial cooperation in criminal matters is no longer founded on an inter-governmental method but, in contrast, is based, under part 4 of the Title V of the TFEU, on the community method and, in particular, that the legislative act which is entitled to regulate the field is a directive, adopted under the ordinary discipline. Against this background, the ICC has confirmed the (artificial) difference of judicial treatment between the hypothesis of contrast of national law with, respectively, directly or not directly applicable EU legislation. In particular the constitutional judges, after having clarified how the contrast between the Framework Decision and the national implementation legislation could not have been solved in interpretative terms, because it would have led to a *contra legem* interpretation of the latter, specifies that the EU legislation at stake, due to its lack of direct effect, could have been disapplied by the common judges. Only the ICC itself is then competent, according to the constitutional judges, to assess the constitutionality of the implementation legislation for its alleged contrast with Article 117 paragraph 1, in the guise of an interposed parameter. If this reasoning, with regard to the violation of the Framework Decision, was largely foreseeable, what is much more surprising is the continuation of the reasoning of the ICC with regard to the contrast of the implementation legislation also with the principle, provided before by Article 12 TCE and now by Article 18 TFUE, of the ban on discrimination on the ground of nationality. In this case it would have been

courts had a chance to rule on the alleged unconstitutionality of the implementing act, which is what actually occurred in Poland, the Czech Republic and Cyprus. Germany, instead, faced quite an unusual scenario: a constitutional amendment[79], in fact, was introduced shortly before the

---

difficult to deny, and the ICC does not, that the ECJ has recognized a direct effect to the said provision. Despite this admission, the ICC, in quite an apodictic way, added that the contrast of a national legislation with the ban on discrimination on the grounds of nationality it is not always sufficient to disapply the said legislation. What is evident, in the said approach, is the fear of the constitutional judges of being marginalized by its privileged position of judge of the constitutionality of supranationality law.

The second relevant issue emerging from this EAW decision of the Italian Constitutional Court is related to the clarification of the relationship between Article 117, paragraph 1, and Article 11, with particular regard to the margin of autonomy of the former from the latter. The Court, despite the fact that the plaintiff called into consideration only the alleged violation, by the implementing legislation, of Article 117, found the way to add some clarification in respect to the above mentioned relationship.

[75] Under Article 33 paragraph 3, of the Portuguese Constitution, which followed the review: 'the extradition of Portuguese citizens from Portuguese territory shall only be permissible where an international agreement has established reciprocal extradition arrangements, or in cases of terrorism or international organised crime, and on condition that the applicant state's legal system enshrines guarantees of a just and fair trial'.

[76] Before the revision of 2001, Article 23 paragraph 4, provided the right for the Slovak citizens: 'not to leave their homeland, be expelled or extradited to another state'. The said revision led to the elimination of the reference to the right not to be extradited.

[77] In Latvia, as Balbo was among the first to point out, two acts promulgated respectively on 16 June 2004 (in force as of 30 June 2004) and 17 June 2004 (in force as of 21 October 2004) introduced the necessary amendments to implement the constitutional modifications to Article 98 and the other relevant parts of the code of criminal law, in order to execute the EAW against Latvian citizens. See P. Balbo, *I sistemi giurisdizionali nazionali di fronte all'interpretazione del mandato di arresto europeo*: www.giurcost.org/studi.

[78] In the original version, Article 47 of the Slovenian Constitution provided the ban on extradition of its citizens. Following its review, with the Constitutional Act 24-899/2003, the notion of surrender was added, as an autonomous constitutional concept, compared to extradition. Today, Article 47 of the Slovenian Constitution provides that: 'no Slovenian citizen may be extradited or surrendered (in execution of a EAW), unless the said extradition or surrender order stems from an international Treaty, through which Slovenia has granted part of its sovereign powers to an international organisation'.

[79] The German Constitution, in its original wording, utterly banned the extradition of a German citizen. The 47th review to the fundamental act, of 29 November 2000, added to the unconditional ban provided for by Article 16 (2), the disposition according to which: 'no German may be extradited to a foreign

adoption of the EAW Framework Decision to allow, under certain circumstances, the extradition of a citizen, previously utterly banned.[80] However, this did not prevent the intervention of the Federal Constitutional Court at Karlsruhe[81] over the national legislation for the adoption of the EAW Framework Decision.

The German Case

As mentioned above, thanks to a prophetic intuition in 2000 and shortly before the implementation of the EAW Framework Decision, Article 16 (2) of the Basic Law was revised. The amendment permitted an exception to the ban on the extradition of a German citizen to allow his or her surrender to an EU Member State or an international court, on condition that the fundamental principles of the rule of law are respected.

In 2003 the German Minister of Justice rejected a request for extradition to Spain submitted by the Spanish police authority against an individual with both German and Syrian nationality who was accused by the Spanish authorities of participation in a criminal association and terrorism committed on Spanish territory. Following Germany's adoption of Framework Decision 2002/584, through the *Europänisches Haftbefehlsgestz* on 21 July 2004, the Hamburg authorities granted Spain's request for surrender of the individual pursuant to an EAW. After appealing against this decision before the competent national constitutional courts in vain, the German citizen subject to the EAW appealed to the Constitutional Court asserting, *inter alia*, the alleged violation Article 16 (2) of the Basic Law. He claimed that the transposition act for Framework Decision 2002/584 lacked democratic legitimacy for having introduced into national legislation a provision potentially depriving the individual of personal liberty and the principle of legal certainty, such as, for instance, the derogation rule to the principle of double criminality.

The German federal government intervened, stating that the constitutional complaint was to be considered groundless, above all due to the binding nature of framework decisions pursuant to the EU Treaty which, strikingly enough, when expressed by the German government, 'must have unconditional supremacy over national law, including constitutional

country. The law can provide otherwise for extraditions to a Member State of the European Union or to an international Court of Justice, as long *as the rule of law is upheld*'.

[80] Prior to the 2000 revision, Article 16 of the Basic Law was rather strict: 'no German citizen may be extradited abroad'.

[81] Decision of 18 July 2005.

principles'. Moreover the German government pointed out three important arguments.

Firstly, the procedure for surrender, with no particular limitations, of Member State citizens pursuant to the EAW Framework Decision was an innovation compared with the extradition procedure pursuant to Article 16 (2) of the Constitution. Secondly, this innovation determined the inapplicability of Article 16 (2) as a constitutional parameter of the Framework Decision and its implementing act. Thirdly, the federal government noted that in case of any doubt about interpretation, the Federal Constitutional Court could always make a preliminary reference, although it had always refrained from doing so.

The judges of Germany's highest Constitutional Court[82] seem to have been of a very different opinion. After having deemed the constitutional parameter pursuant to Article 16 (2) perfectly applicable to the implementing national law, they declared the latter unconstitutional since the German legislature did not conform to the provision pursuant to which the extradition of a German national is only permissible as long as the rule of law is upheld.

Their reasoning started with the historical background ratio of the relevant constitutional principle. In the Karlsruhe Court's opinion, the right to be tried in the country of origin, interwoven with the protection of citizens, has its foundations in Germany's tragic modern history when, after the 1933 coup, all citizens of Jewish origin and religion were denied, by the National Socialist dictatorship, their citizen status, and protection was granted instead to German citizens. Further, the Court added, the 2000 revision of Article 16 (2) allowing extradition of a German citizen proved necessary to ensure conformity of the national regulation to recent developments in the third pillar's integration process within the European Union, and to the requests for harmonization coming from the United Nations International Court of Justice.

---

[82] For interesting comments on this decision, see: F. Palermo, 'La sentenza del Bundesverfassungsgericht sul mandato di arresto europeo' (2005) Quaderni Costituzionali 897. See also C. Tomuschat, 'Inconsistencies. The German Federal Constitutional Court on the European Arrest Warrant' (2006) European Constitutional L Rev 209; J.P. Pierini, 'Il mandato d'arresto europeo alla prova del *Bundesverfassungsgericht* tedesco: "schiaffo" all'Europa o cura negligente dei diritti del nazionale da parte del legislatore?' (2006) Cassazione penale, 237; J. Woelk, 'Parlare a nuora perché suocera intenda: il BVerfG dichiara incostituzionale la legge di attuazione del mandato d'arresto europeo' (2006) Dir. pubblico comparato ed europeo, 160; S. Molders, 'Case note, The European Arrest Warrant in the German Federal Constitutional Court' (2006) German Law Journal 45; N. Nohlen, 'Germany: The European Arrest Warrant Case' (2008) International J Constitutional L, 153.

Despite these overtures, the German judges made it clear that the third pillar's intergovernmental dynamic may, in no event, fall within the EC *acquis* of the first one. They thus recalled how the EU Treaty's express provisions on the absence of direct effect of framework decisions is due precisely to the Member States' wish to avoid the ECJ conferring direct effect on these legal acts, as it had determined for the interpretation of EU directives. Furthermore, the constitutional judges maintained that, notwithstanding the high level of integration, the EU still embodies a partial legal system pertaining to the field of international public law. Accordingly, from a constitutional point of view and directly pursuant to Article 16 (2) of the Basic Law, a concrete review on a case-by-case basis should be made to ascertain that the prosecuted individual is not deprived of the guarantees or fundamental rights he would have been granted in Germany, and that except for obvious language problems and a lack of familiarity with the criminal law of the destination country, this may in no event lead to the worsening of the individual's situation.

Seemingly, the underlying theme of the whole reasoning about the decision is a sense of ill-concealed distrust of the legal systems of other Member States as to the safeguarding of the accused person. Therefore, the German legislature is blamed for infringing, by implementing the Framework Decision, the principle of proportionality, therefore not choosing the least restrictive among the possible options of the right for German citizens to be prosecuted and to serve the sentence passed against them in their native land. The German law thus underestimated the citizens' special connection to their own state's legal order.

Apparently, according to the German constitutional judges, the legislature did not fully use the discretion allowed by the Framework Decision, which permitted judicial authorities to refuse execution where the EAW relates to offences that 'are regarded by the law of the executing Member State as having been committed in whole or in part in the territory of the executing Member State or in a place treated as such; or having been committed outside the territory of the issuing Member State and the law of the executing Member State does not allow prosecution for the same offences when committed outside its territory'.[83] In such circumstances, according to the Federal Constitutional Court, a significant *domestic connecting factor* is established and 'the trust of German citizens in their own legal order shall be protected' (paragraphs 86–87).

By reading the ruling from a different perspective, it is rather evident how, behind the attempt to verify the responsibility of the German

[83] Article 4 paragraph 7 of decision 2002/584/JHA.

legislature in the transposition activity, the Federal Constitutional Court's actual aim was to halt the acceleration process, which followed the adoption of the EAW Framework Decision, of European integration concerning the third pillar which, according to the same Court, 'cannot overrule, given its mainly intergovernmental character, the institutional dynamic peculiar to a system of international public law'.

It was the opinion of the Karlsruhe judges that in light of the safeguards of the subsidiarity[84] principle, 'the cooperation in criminal matters established within the third pillar on the basis of a *limited* mutual recognition of criminal decisions, does not presuppose general harmonization of criminal laws of the Member States; conversely, it is a way to preserve national identity and statehood within the uniform European legal space' (paragraph 77). It has been correctly pointed out[85] that the key word in this crucial part of the reasoning is the adjective 'limited', through which the Constitutional Court has precisely set a limit to the 'optimism' of European judges who, in the first ruling[86] dealing directly with the third pillar's integration scope, expressly stated how 'the *ne bis in idem* principle necessarily implies a high level of confidence between Member States and that each of them recognises the criminal law in force in the other Member States even when the outcome would be different if its own national law were applied' (paragraph 33).

The message sent from Karlsruhe proved, beyond all doubt, that any Member State's attempt to emulate the first pillar's procedures in such a constitutionally sensitive context, by definition part of their (remaining) hard core of sovereignty, would not have been tolerated by the *Solange* judges. Although the majority of the Federal Constitutional Court made no mention of the ECJ ruling of 16 June 2005, the decision seems to be

---

[84] As Francesco Palermo observed, the constitutional judges consider this principle as having been complied with, thus sorting out a difficult situation: 'in fact, the non-recognition of subsidiarity, therefore of the urgent need for a European discipline on the European arrest warrant, would have hampered it forever. Conversely, the judges deem Germany's participation in European judicial cooperation a significant step towards the administration of justice within an integrated context, which makes it not only possible, but desirable as well'. See Palermo, 'La sentenza del Bundesverfassungsgericht sul mandato di arresto europeo', 899.

[85] J. Komarek, 'European Constitutionalism and the European Arrest Warrant: In Search of the Limits of the "Contrapunctual Principles"' (2007) CML Rev, 9, 24.

[86] ECJ, Joined cases C-187/01 and C-385/01, *Hüseyin Gözütok* and *Klaus Brügge*, 11-2-2003.

a direct response to the 'acceleration' represented by the ECJ decision in *Pupino* delivered 30 days before.[87]

A Comparison Between the Polish and the Czech Cases

To fully understand the implications related to the relationship between the European and the constitutional legal systems by the adoption of the EAW Framework Decision in Poland and the Czech Republic, as well as the reactions of the Warsaw and Brno Constitutional Courts to the risk of collision between the constitutional and European dimensions, it is necessary to take a step back to the process which led to the adoption of the Czech and Polish Constitutions in 1992 and 1997, respectively. Both constitutions are characterized by a number of clauses aimed at the protection of the long sought-after sovereignty, attained after decades of subjugation to Communist regimes, which make a distinction, as is the case for the constituent documents of most CEE countries, between internal and external sovereignty.[88] Another aspect to be taken into account is the 'low profile approach' typical of all CEE countries as regards the constitutional amendments leading to their accession to the European Union.

Some scholars maintain there is a difference between the two countries, qualifying as remarkable the level of 'Euro' constitutional amendment reached by the Czech Republic and Poland's as only average.[89] However, it must be asserted how – owing as well to hostile response in public opinion to their accession – with regard to the sensitive issue of the supremacy between EU law and the Constitution, both legislatures only slightly amended the relevant constitutional parameters, leaving to the respective constitutional courts the heavy and ungrateful burden of finding solutions to the inevitable conflicts between the constitutional and European dimensions that such relaxed 'super primary' parameters could only worsen.[90]

---

[87] ECJ, C-105/03, [2005] ECR I-5285, among which, see, at least: V. Mazzocchi, 'Il caso Pupino e il principio di interpretazione conforme delle decisioni quadro' (2005) Quaderni Costituzionali, 884; E. Spaventa, 'Opening Pandora's Box: Some Reflections on the Constitutional Effect of the Decision in *Pupino*' (2007) European Constitutional L Rev, 5.

[88] For a cross-reference to independence, see the preamble to the Czech Constitution and Articles 26 and 130 of the Polish Constitution; for the emphasis on State sovereignty, see Article 1 of the Czech Constitution, the preamble and Articles 104 paragraph 2 and 126 paragraph 2, of the Polish Constitution. For further references, see also: Stein, 'International Law in Internal Law', 427.

[89] See: Albi, *EU Enlargement*.

[90] As for the Czech Republic, in the 2001 revision of Article 10a, a general and undifferentiated clause of openness to international organizations was intro-

As to the specific question relating to the alleged constitutional invalidity of the implementing acts of the EAW Framework Decision, the Constitutional Courts of Warsaw and Brno have delivered direct judgments. The implementing regulations in both jurisdictions were similar, and the relevant constitutional parameters, as to the ban on extradition of nationals, were also very similar.

The Polish Constitution is lapidary: Article 55 states, in fact, that 'the extradition of a Polish citizen shall be forbidden'. Article 14 (4) of the Charter of Fundamental Rights and Liberties, which encompasses all rights and liberties protected by the Constitution of the Czech Republic, states more generally that: 'no Czech citizen shall be removed from his/her homeland'.

One notable distinction between the two systems has been the extent of the debate on the opportunity to amend the two constitutional provisions in view of the, then, future accession to the European Union. If the Czech Republic never granted priority to the issue, in Poland, on the contrary, revision of Article 55 of the Constitution had already been envisaged by some insiders who stressed how an unconditional ban on the extradition of nationals could potentially represent a hindrance to the European integration process within the third pillar, which in turn – as already emphasized – had been gaining strength since the enforcement of the Amsterdam Treaty. Conversely, others thought that the conflict could be settled by discussions. Finally, it was the second possibility to be opted for, given the highly symbolic value of Article 55 which, in the Polish Constitution, enshrines those ideals of identity and sense of belonging deeply rooted within an ethnocentric-oriented *demos* still bound to nationalistic[91] memories, which characterizes the predominant view in Central and Eastern Europe.

---

duced, which made no mention of the EC system's peculiar features, or stressed, in any way, how the supremacy given to the Constitution could be combined with the doctrine of the primacy of EC law over domestic laws, as extrapolated, some decades ago, by the ECJ caseload which, as the rest of the European *acquis*, all the CEE countries have undertaken to follow, pursuant to the Athens Accession Treaty of 2003. The same, more or less, applies to the 1997 Polish Constitution, the most recent Constitution among CEE countries, therefore already inclusive *ab origine* of the European clauses. Conversely, Article 91 paragraph 3, as opposed to the more international approach of the Czech Constitution, makes express reference to the EC system and particularly to the off-shoot European law, stressing its direct effect and supremacy over ordinary national regulations. Again, no mention is made of the relationship between the Constitution and EU law, especially primary law.

91 See A. Sajó, 'Protecting Nation States and National Minorities: A Modest

These clarifications having been made, it is interesting to move on to draw a parallel of the actual *reasoning* of the Constitutional Courts of Warsaw and Brno which, while starting from similar constitutional parameters, and a practically equivalent object of the matter, reached opposite outcomes. The first, in fact, annulled the national regulation, while the second did not detect any constitutional illegitimacy.

The Polish judges[92] had to establish whether surrender, the substantive issue of the EAW, could anyhow be regarded as a subset of extradition, the latter being expressly forbidden by Article 55 of the Constitution if the person concerned is a Polish national. The Constitutional Tribunal, answering positively to the interpretative dilemma, holding that the constitutional concept of extradition was so far reaching as to encompass even the surrender of a Polish citizen, a necessary provision to implement the EAW, whose purpose, at least at the Framework Decision level, is to replace within the European legal space, the bilateral, intergovernmental dynamic typical of the extradition mechanism.

After grouping under the same legal notion the two concepts of extradition and surrender, the second argument of the Polish Constitutional Tribunal was to point out how the admissibility of a national's surrender, provided for by the Framework Decision, undermined the rationale behind the ban in Article 55 of the Polish Constitution, pursuant to which the essence of the right not to be extradited is that a Polish citizen should be prosecuted before a Polish court. According to the Warsaw Constitutional Tribunal, Poland's accession to the EU brought about a radical change. Namely, its accession not only accounts for, but also necessarily implies, a constitutional revision of Article 55 so that the constitutional requirements conform to EU provisions. The said constitutional revision, however, according to the Polish judges, could not be carried out using a manipulative and dynamic interpretation of the relevant constitutional principle but needs an *ad hoc* constitutional action by the legislature.

The *Pupino* judgment, which reasserts the obligation on national courts to make consistent interpretations of framework decisions pursuant to Article 34 (b) EU, was yet to be delivered by the ECJ. Nevertheless, AG

Case for Nationalism in Eastern Europe' (1993) University of Chicago Law School Roundtable, 53.

[92] One of the first studies on the decision is that by S. Sileoni, 'La Corte costituzionale polacca, il mandato arresto europeo e la sentenza sul trattato di Adesione all'UE' (2005) Quaderni Costituzionali, 894; more recently, A. Nußberger, 'Poland: The Constitutional Tribunal on the Implementation of the European Arrest Warrant' (2008) International J Constitutional Law 162.

Kokott's opinion regarding the judgment had already been published.[93] The Polish constitutional judges, without directly mentioning it, considered the possibility of an obligation of consistent interpretation. However, they did not find it relevant in the current situation since, according to them, the obligation was limited by the ECJ itself, as it may not worsen an individual's condition, especially as regards the sphere of criminal liability.[94]

According to the Polish constitutional judges, on the other hand, while national legislation is bound under Article 9 of the Constitution to implement secondary EU legislation, a presumption of the implementing act's compliance with constitutional norms cannot be inferred *sic et simpliciter*. The Constitutional Tribunal easily concluded how, by permitting the prosecution of a Polish citizen before a foreign criminal court, the national regulation implementing the EAW Framework Decision would have prejudiced the constitutional rights granted to Polish citizens, and therefore, it could only be found to be unconstitutional.

In spite of clarifying unconstitutionality of the matter, the Tribunal found that the mere annulment of the provision would have led to breach of Article 9 of the Constitution, according to which 'Poland shall respect international law binding upon it' and whose application, according to the constitutional judges, also encompasses Poland's obligations stemming from accession to the European Union. Therefore, in order to comply fully with such obligation, an amendment of Article 55 was considered necessary to provide for the possibility, departing from the general ban on extradition of nationals, of enabling the surrender of such persons to other Member States in execution of an EAW. Meanwhile, the Tribunal, by enforcing Article 190(3) of the Constitution, set a deadline for the decision's effects – 18 months – to give the constitutional legislators time to pass the necessary amendments while the provision remained temporarily in force, and for the constitutional revision to be in line with the EAW Framework Decision.[95]

One year later, the Czech constitutional judges founded their reasoning on a completely different set of grounds. After recalling the decision issued

---

93 A.G. Kokott's opinion in case C-105/03, *Pupino* (2005) ECR, I-5285.

94 Polish Constitutional Tribunal.

95 Amendments to Article 55 of Constitution were made within the deadline provided for in the decision, and as of 7 November 2006, Poland has agreed to the execution of EAWs against its nationals, subject to two conditions, which do not appear to be in line with the EU regulation: the fact that the crime has been committed outside Polish territory and that it is recognized under and also capable of being prosecuted under Polish criminal law.

barely two months earlier (judgment of 8 March 2006), where they had carried out an express *revirement* of their own jurisprudence in order to meet the interpretation criteria required by the application of the equality principle as interpreted by the ECJ,[96] the judges were faced with the sensitive issue of the binding nature, and related margin of discretion left to the legislature regarding cooperation in criminal justice matters, which were to be attributed within the scope of the framework decisions pursuant to former Article 34 EU.

Showing a further degree of openness to (and extensive knowledge of) EU law, the Czech constitutional judges broadly touched upon the *Pupino* judgment, and although perhaps underestimating its added value, they pointed out how the obligation of national judges to interpret, *as far as possible*, national law in conformity with framework decisions adopted under the third pillar – and pursuant to such jurisprudence – would leave unprejudiced the issue relating to the enforcement of the principle of primacy of the EU law over (all) national legislation. The issue was the latter, which most of the scholars[97] have instead maintained as inextricably linked to the obligation of consistent interpretation.

The Brno Court, taking into account the doubts concerning the interpretation of the nature and scope of the Framework Decision, seriously considered the possibility – evidencing once again[98] its will to engage in dialogue with the EC's supreme judicial body – of referring a preliminary question to Luxembourg, although later it ruled out the option due to the fact that the Belgian *Cour d'Arbitrage*, as anticipated,[99] had already addressed the ECJ regarding the same issue.

The Czech constitutional judges, faced with the dilemma of whether they should suspend judgment concerning constitutionality while 'awaiting' the ECJ's answer, or rather rule on the matter themselves, chose the second option. Thus they attempted, and this is the most interesting aspect, to find amongst all the potential interpretations of the relevant constitutional

---

[96] See O. Pollicino, 'Dall'Est una lezione sui rapporti tra diritto costituzionale e diritto comunitario' (2006) Diritto dell' Unione Europea, 819.

[97] See D. Piqani, 'Supremacy of European Law Revisited: New Developments in the Context of the Treaty Establishing a Constitution for Europe', paper presented at the VII World Conference of the Constitutional Law International Association held in Athens, 11–15 June 2007; C.W. Herrmann, 'Much Ado about Pluto? The Unity of the Legal Order of the European Union Revisited', EUI Working paper, 2007/05, in www.iue.it.

[98] They have already shown the same attitude with decision PI US 50/04, 8-3-2006. See Pollicino, 'Dall'Est una lezione sui rapporti tra diritto costituzionale e diritto comunitario'.

[99] Preliminary reference by the *Cour d'Arbitrage* dated 29 October 2005.

norm – Article 14 (4) of the Czech Charter of Constitutional Rights – one not that did not clash with EU Law.

In particular, the judges highlighted how, without the support of an interpretation effort, the provision's wording of Article 14 (4), according to which no Czech citizen shall be removed from his homeland, does not fully account for[100] the actual existence of a constitutional ban on the surrender of a Czech citizen to a foreign state, in execution of an arrest warrant, for a set period of time. In the view of the Czech Constitutional Court, two plausible interpretations exist. The first and literal one, even though it might lead to the ban's provision within the constitutional norm, would have at least two disadvantages.

Firstly, it would not take into account the 'historical impetus' underlying the adoption of the Czech Charter of Fundamental Rights, and especially of Article 14 (4). The Constitutional Court stressed, in fact, how a historical interpretation of the criterion under discussion clearly explained that, based on the wording of the Charter between the end of 1990 and the beginning of 1991, the authors who drafted the ban on a Czech citizen being removed from his homeland, far from considering the effects of the implementation of extradition procedures, had in mind 'the recent experience of communist crimes' and especially of the 'demolition operation' that the regime had perpetrated in order to remove from the country anyone who represented an obstacle to the hegemony of the regime itself.

Secondly, an interpretation of that sort would lead to a violation of the principle, clearly expressed for the first time by the constitutional judges, according to which all domestic law sources, including the Constitution, must be interpreted as far as possible in conformity with the legislation implementing the evolutionary process of European integration. Under such an obligation the constitutional provisions should be interpreted consistently in light of EU law, which the constitutional judges derived from the combined provisions of Article 1 (2) of the Constitution, added in light of the accession to the European Union and pursuant to which 'the Czech Republic is compelled to fulfil obligations originating under international law', and former Article 10 EC on the principle of loyal cooperation between Member States and the European Union. On the basis of a teleological approach, the Czech constitutional judges went on to identify the constitutional norm's most consistent interpretation of

100 As it did, instead, according to the Czech judges, the provision of the corresponding Article 23(4) of the Slovak Constitution which, prior to the constitutional revision of 2001, made express reference to the ban on extradition of Slovak citizens.

the implementing act, as well as of Framework Decision 2002/584, to the Polish Constitution.

It is not surprising then, that the Court managed to find constitutional grounds for almost all the problematic dispositions of the Framework Decision. Noteworthy in this respect was the legislative omission which had induced the German Federal Constitutional Court to declare the framework decision's implementing law unconstitutional and void, that is to say, the non-acceptance under national regulation of the possibility, pursuant to Article 4(7), to enhance the domestic connecting factor and allow a legitimate rejection of an EAW request by the implementing[101] judicial authority. Actually, the said provision had not been taken into account by the Czech legislature either in the implementation of the Framework Decision. Nevertheless, according to the Czech Constitutional Court, the obstacle could be surmounted through the (extreme) application of the principle of consistent interpretation. It held in fact that notwithstanding the legislative omission, the Czech system could not afford to lose the citizens' trust in their own legal order; therefore, coming close to a *contra legem* interpretation of the relating provision, the constitutional judges concluded that any offence carried out within the national borders would continue to be prosecuted under domestic criminal law. In other words, under the same circumstances, the Czech constitutional authorities would most likely reject the request to execute a EAW.

Accordingly, it is plausible to infer that the Czech Constitutional Court, in its firm intent to reach greater consistency between Article 14(3) of the Constitution and the EAW Framework Decision, strained the literal content of both the constitutional dispositions and the domestic law under discussion. The argument was that whereas the constitutional norm had been interpreted as a mere ban on the surrender of a Czech citizen to the jurisdictional authority of another Member State, for the purpose of prosecution for a crime committed in that territory the grounds underlying the whole decision would have ceased, i.e. the equivalence in terms of fundamental rights' protection among EU Member States, reflecting also a substantive convergence of the various criminal statutes and procedures.

---

[101] As already stressed at the beginning, under Article 4(7) of the EAW Framework Decision, the implementing judicial authority may refuse to execute the EAW if it relates to offences which, according to the law of the executing Member State, have been committed in whole or in part in the territory of the executing Member State or in a place treated as such. It also permits refusal of execution where the offences were committed outside the territory of the issuing Member State and the law of the executing Member State does not allow prosecution for the same offences when committed outside its territory.

Unavoidably, this led to the acceptance by the Czech judges of the principle of mutual trust, rejected by their German judicial colleagues, in the criminal legislation of other Member States' legal systems, through the direct reference to the ECJ judgments in *Gözütok* and *Brügge*, which have been questioned by the 'sceptical' approach of the Karlsruhe judges.

Models of Conflict Settlement Between Interacting Legal Systems

In an attempt to provide a conceptual conclusive framework of the different approaches of the German, Polish and Czech constitutional judges, the three decisions appear to be the expressions of the respective courts' different ways of tackling the delicate issue of the relationship between EU law and Member States' constitutional legal systems.

With the ruling on the EAW, the German Federal Constitutional Court proved that it advocates a certain 'democratic statism', as defined by Mattias Kumm. This is, to state it more clearly, 'a normative conception of a political order establishing a link between three concepts: statehood, sovereignty and democratic self-government'.[102] Statehood and sovereignty[103] constitute, indeed, the *leitmotif* of the entire argument underlying the German judgment. A decision based on such cornerstones could not but lead to the annulment of the national implementation of the EAW Framework Decision, as well as, more generally, as has emerged from the decision's analysis, to the refusal of any idea to 'communitize' the European area which mainly reflects statehood and sovereignty among Member States: the cooperation in criminal matters entailed by the Union's third pillar. In such a state-oriented view of the European integration process, the Basic Law represents the supreme *grund norm* conferring validity on any other, internal or external, source of law, including European law, namely through the *Solange* jurisprudence's codification of Article 23 of the Basic Law.[104]

---

102 M. Kumm, 'Who is the Final Arbiter of Constitutionality in Europe? Three Conceptions of the Relationship between the German Federal Constitutional Court and the European Court of Justice' (1999) CML Rev 351, 366.

103 For a recent contribution on the primary role that sovereignty plays within the European scenario, which is characterized more and more by conflicts arising within legal orders, see A. Jakab, 'Neutralizing the Sovereignty Question' (2006) European Constitutional L Rev, 375.

104 With regard to the FCC decision, J. Baquero Cruz is also very critical when he stresses how 'the German Constitutional Court saw the case through the exclusive prism of the German Constitution, misinterpreting the framework decision'. See J. Baquero Cruz, *The Legacy of the Maastricht Urteil decision and the Pluralist Movement*, EUI working paper, 2007/13.

The focus on the concept of *Staatvolk*, giving rise to 'objective ethnic factors'[105] as legitimate grounds for the constitution's supremacy has, needless to say, further repercussions, beyond the relationship between Germany and the EU, on the horizontal dimension which connects the EU Member States. The most evident of these repercussions is the sense of poorly-hidden distrust, which permeates the entire judgement, of the other European legal systems' ability to secure an adequate level of rights protection. The sole guarantee left to the German citizen is the certainty of being, as far as possible, prosecuted, judged and eventually convicted by a domestic German court.

On the opposite side, upon a closer look, the Polish Constitutional Tribunal did exactly what the most extreme 'pro-Community activist' would ask for in the case of an irreconcilable conflict between the Constitution and EU law. Does the EAW Framework Decision clash with the constitutional norm of a Member State? The Constitution should be revised and, meanwhile, the annulled provision remains temporarily in force. EU law 1 – Constitutional law 0 and *game over*.

It is not by chance that a Polish scholar observed how the legislature's request to review the Constitution and the temporal limitation of effects of the decision proves that

> the Constitutional Tribunal in fact recognized the supremacy of EU law. [. . .] It thus accepted that the Constitution itself was no longer an absolute framework for control – if it hinders the correct implementation of EU law, it should be changed [. . .]. It seemed that in this judgment the Tribunal went further than the existing practice, it implicitly accepted the supremacy of EU law over constitutional norms.[106]

Upon a closer look, the two approaches considered herein (the German and Polish ones), while very different in their identification of which is the supreme legal source of reference (in the former, the Constitution, in the

---

[105] Judge Kirchhof, according to many, the 'mind' behind the Maastricht decision of the FCC in 1993, encompasses these factors within a common language, a shared culture, with common historical roots. See Kumm, 'Who is the Final Arbiter of Constitutionality in Europe?', 367.

[106] See K. Kowalik-Bańczyk, 'Should We Polish It Up? The Polish Constitutional Tribunal and the Idea of Supremacy of EU Law' (2005) German L J 1360–1361. Along the same lines, according to Angelika Nußberger, the judgment might seem to suggest that the tribunal denies the supremacy of EU law and is adopting a Euro-sceptical position, in fact, the opposite is true. See Nußberger. 'Poland: The Constitutional Tribunal on the Implementation of the European Arrest Warrant', 166.

latter, EU legislation), have something in common: both of them focus on identifying a supreme source of law. In other words, in both decisions, the game is played out on the field of sources-of-law based theory delimited by the identification of hierarchical, predetermined and unassailable relations among the norms involved. Correspondingly, such an idea of the relationship between EC law and national constitutional law is neither flexible nor open to comparisons. It is not flexible because it is determined by a clear-cut, 'once and for all' definition of these relations, which does not permit derogations and forces upon the judicial interpreters the solution for the relevant conflict settlement. It is not open to comparisons because of the tendency to solve conflicts by solely referring to the domestic constitutional landscape.

In this respect, it is worth noticing how both the Polish and German judgments: (1) did not recall relevant ECJ jurisprudence, (2) did not refer to decisions adopted by other European constitutional courts attempting to solve similar conflicts, and (3) never considered the possibility of a dialogue with the ECJ through a preliminary reference.[107]

Conversely, the three elements do converge in the Czech decision and represent specific and concurring clues to demonstrate that the Brno Court opted to play the game of conflict settlement between domestic and EU law in a field characterized by an interpretation-based theory[108] rather than a theory based on the hierarchy of sources of law, as it seems was favoured by their colleagues in Karlsruhe and Warsaw. The field chosen by the Czech Constitutional Court is characterized instead, from a substantive point of view, by the acceptance of the idea of constitutional pluralism as the paramount parameter for the settlement of constitutional conflicts,

---

[107] Actually, Warsaw's Constitutional Tribunal would not have been in the position to use the preliminary procedure's instrument provided for by Article 35 EU anyway, owing to the not particularly Euro-friendly attitude of the Kaczynski twins' government, which, needless to say, had not carried out the (optional) jurisdiction attribution declaration to the ECJ, as per the same article of the Maastricht Treaty. The awaited change of strategy promised by the Civic Platform's leader Donald Tusk, who won the last political elections in October, has yet to come.

[108] In Italy, one of the most extensive studies of this issue was undertaken by Antonio Ruggeri. Amongst his numerous papers dealing with this subject, see at least the following: A. Ruggeri, 'Prospettive metodiche di ricostruzione del sistema delle fonti e Carte Internazionali dei diritti, tra teoria delle fonti e teoria dell'interpretazione' (2002) Ragion Pratica, 63; Idem, 'Tradizioni costituzionali comuni e 'controlimiti', tra teoria delle fonti e teoria dell'interpretazione' (2003) Diritto pubblico comparato ed Europeo, 102. Such an axiologically-oriented view seems to share the reconstructive bases of MacCormick. See. See N. MacCormick, 'Beyond the Sovereign State' (1993) MLR 1;

while, as to methodology and procedure, it applies a dialogic and communicative theory of inter-constitutional law.

From a substantive point of view, the Czech Constitutional Court, although never fully abandoning basing its reasoning on the classical concepts of sovereignty, limited transfer to the supranational system and the 'counterlimits' doctrine, attempted to convey on an axiological basis, and without any idea of hierarchicalization between interacting legal systems, the ultimate rationale behind the EAW implementing national law, on the one hand, and the constitutionally protected values on the other. To sum up, the Czech judges found that the fact that the EAW Framework Decision does not always apply the double criminality requirement, and does not infringe the constitutional principle of legality in criminal law, as the absence of the latter rule does not affect the principle 'with regard to the Member States of the EU, which have a sufficient level of values convergence and mutual confidence that they are all states having democratic regimes which adhere to the rule of law and are bound by the application to observe this principle'.[109]

The process of ascertaining conformity of national rules implementing EU norms to the Constitution is not carried out through a strict application of the unassailable rule of EU law primacy over the whole domestic law, nor by assuming unconditioned supremacy of the Constitution over any other source of law, but rather with the objective of identifying the best solution to fulfil 'the ideals underlying legal practice in the European Union and its Member States'.[110] With regard to the second, methodology-based, aspect, the Czech Constitutional Court fits its reasoning within a much broader normative framework than the literal interpretation of a relevant constitutional parameter would have allowed. Through adopting verbatim certain quotes of European and comparative constitutional jurisprudence, far from giving evidence of 'constitutional arrogance', the Czech court has shown willingness to be part of that project of 'cooperative constitutionalism' which seems to represent one way out of the constitutional conflicts between the EU legal order and Member States' constitutional systems. Certainly, it is not the easiest road to take, but it is most likely the only one with a chance to strike the right balance between different but interconnected legal systems, and consequently to find 'harmony in diversity'.[111]

---

[109] Kumm, 'The Jurisprudence of Constitutional Conflict', 286.

[110] Ibid.

[111] See V. Onida, '"Armonia tra diversi" e problemi aperti. La giurisprudenza costituzionale sui rapporti tra ordinamento interno e comunitario' (2002) Quaderni costituzionali, 549.

A second consideration, already anticipated above, relates to the fact that, in the relationship between interacting legal systems, a growing distance is emerging between the (low) degree of openness towards EU law in the CEE constitutions and the more generous tendency to accept the mechanisms of European law in domestic law which CEE constitutional courts are currently showing. To clarify this, let us apply this consideration to the EAW saga. Upon an initial, 'static' reading of the relevant constitutional norms, it has been pointed out an ex-ante evaluation of the provisions of the EAW Framework Decision, as regards the binding obligation on the executing State, except for the cases strictly provided for, to surrender a national to the requesting Member State, appeared more in line with the German Basic Law regulating extradition than with the corresponding provision of the Czech Charter of Fundamental Rights.

More generally, while always maintaining the perspective of the relevant constitutional norm, it is evident that the 'sovereignist' nature of the CEE national constitutions, and specifically the Polish and Czech ones, left little room for their constitutional courts to demonstrate their pro-European 'enthusiasm', when compared with the flexibility theoretically allowed the German Constitutional Court under the Basic Law's relevant provisions, which has never been noted for having a marked 'sovereignty-focused' character (also in light of the historical context in which it took shape). Moreover, one should bear in mind that the 'European clause' introduced into Article 23 of the Basic Law upon the ratification of the Maastricht Treaty in 1993 further acquired the already existing predisposition of the German constitution to be influenced by European and international law.

Notwithstanding the advantage of the German legal system as to the interpretation of the relevant constitutional parameters as compared with the CEE legal systems, and especially the Polish and Czech ones, the 'leap' of the Warsaw and Brno Constitutional Courts, which has just been examined above, not only cancelled out this advantage, but also enabled Polish and Czech constitutional jurisprudence, despite adverse constitutional parameters, to accept the penetration of European law in domestic legal systems to a much greater extent than the German Federal Constitutional Court proved with its decision. In other words, this new season of European constitutionalism seems to be marked by a sense of 'exploration' in terms of new argumentative techniques and original judicial interaction between national and European courts, which follows novel 'off-piste' routes from those outlined by the interpretative routes suggested by applicable constitutional parameters. To simplify even more, what is emerging seems to be a constantly growing bifurcation between the static reading of the constitutional clauses in the interconnecting legal systems and their dynamic judicial interpretation by constitutional courts.

FINAL REMARKS ON THE JUDICIAL STYLE OF THE ECJ

In the previous pages we have seen the substantive efforts of the ECJ to adapt its judicial attitude to the new post-enlargement era. Nevertheless it should be pointed out that what seems to remain inappropriate is the ECJ's language towards the new judicial interlocutors. Especially with reference to the ordinary judicatures of the CEE Member States, the actual judicial style and the argumentative structure of the ECJ legal reasoning do not appear fully adequate.

As Mauro Cappelletti perceptively wrote: 'Unlike the American Supreme Court *and the European Constitutional Courts*, the ECJ has almost no powers that are not ultimately derived from its own prestige, [and the] intellectual and moral force of its opinions'.[112] With special regard to Member States' judicial interlocutors, the main factors at the heart of the ECJ's legitimacy still remain the clarity of the legal reasoning of its judgments[113] and the persuasive force of its arguments. This attitude strongly characterized the first years of the ECJ's case law, when the European judges applied to their legal reasoning, by way of a didactic methodology, 'a judicial style which explains as it declares the law'.[114] This is particularly true with specific reference to the procedure of Article 234 EC. It was not easy for the ECJ to induce national judges to feel confident about such a new and sophisticated tool of judicial conversation, but over years of 'courteous pedagogy',[115] they managed to persuade them.[116]

Apparently, with time, the ECJ's judicial style has progressively lost its original didactic and pedagogic character. The reasons seem easily identifi-

---

[112] See M. Cappelletti and D. Golay, 'Judicial Branch in the Federal and Transnational Union', in M. Cappelletti, M. Seccombe and J.H. Weiler (eds), *Integration Through Law*, Vol. 1 (Walter de Gruyter 1985) 333, note 281 (italic added).

[113] See Weiler, 'The Transformation of Europe', 2425

[114] F. Mancini, 'Attivismo e autocontrollo nella giurisprudenza della Corte di giustizia' (1990) Riv. Dir. eur, 233.

[115] Cappelletti and Golay, 'Judicial Branch in the Federal and Transnational Union', 333.

[116] In this regard, it should not be forgotten that the national courts have followed the instructions from Luxembourg even when these instructions have been against their constitutional mandate. It is enough to recall here the *Simmenthal* case, 'The culmination of the principle of direct effect and supremacy, in which the ECJ held that the Italian Courts simply had to defy Italian constitutional rules to the *Corte costituzionale*'. See Monica Claes, *The National Courts' Mandate in the European Constitution* (Hart, 2006), 4.

able: on one hand the national courts of first-generation Member States soon learnt to 'digest' the impact of the novelty of EC law over time, thus gradually reducing the need for the didactic and pedagogic approach. On the other hand, the growing case load combined with the difficulty of finding at the same time a compromise, a convincing and persuasive position in an enlarged ECJ, have become increasingly difficult tasks for the European judges. However, now, with 12 new CEE national judicatures that 'will have the time to learn more than the mere basics of Community Law',[117] the ECJ again needs to find a judicial style which explains, as well as states, the law and the persuasive strength of its arguments, which it has somehow lost. A good example of this evolution of the ECJ's judicial style is, in line with our research focus, the awaited decision of the ECJ regarding the EAW.[118]

Owing as well to the great interest aroused by the decisions of the German, Polish and Czech Constitutional Courts, there was a long wait for the ECJ's decision, which had been requested under Article 35 EU by the Belgian *Cour d'Arbitrage*, on the validity of the EAW Framework Decision, no. 2002/584. As the Advocate General, Dámaso Ruiz-Jarabo Colomer, stressed in his Opinion,[119] the referring Belgian court challenged the Framework Decision's compatibility with the EU Treaty on both procedural and substantive grounds. The first of these questions related to the legal basis of the European Council's decision. In particular, the referring court was unsure that the Framework Decision was the appropriate instrument, holding that it should be annulled because the EAW should have been implemented, instead, through a Convention provided by former Article 34(2)(d) EU. In this case, in fact, according to the Belgian court, it would have gone beyond the limits of former Article 34(2)(b) EU, pursuant to which framework decisions are to be adopted only for the purpose of approximation of the laws and regulations of the Member States. Secondly, the Belgian court asked whether the innovations brought by the Framework Decision regarding the EAW, even when the facts in question do not constitute an offence under the law of the executing State, were compatible with the equality and legality principles in criminal proceedings in their role of general principle of European law.

More specifically, the alleged infringement of the principle of equality would have been due to the unjustified dispensation, within the list of 32

---

117 Komarek, 'Inter-Court Constitutional Dialogue'.

118 Court of Justice, C-303/205, *Advocaten de Wererd VZW v Leden Van de Ministerraad*, 3-5-2007: curia.eu.int.

119 Opinion in *Advocaten de Wererd VZW v Leden Van de Ministerraad*.

offences laid down in the Framework Decision, with the double criminality requirement, which is held instead for other crimes. Conversely, the principle of legality would have been breached owing to the Framework Decision's lack of clarity and accuracy in the classification of the offences. It was the opinion of the Belgian court, in fact, that should Member States have to decide whether to execute a EAW, they would not be in the position to know whether the acts for which the requested person is being prosecuted, and for which a conviction has been handed down, actually fall within one of the categories outlined in the Framework Decision.

The Advocate General, in his Opinion, had no doubts about the high relevance of the preliminary request which should have been included, also in the light of the German, Polish, Cypriot and Czech rulings:

> . . . in a far-reaching debate concerning the risk of incompatibility between the Constitutions of the Member States and European Union law. The ECJ must participate in that debate by embracing the prominent role assigned to it, with a view to situating the interpretation of the values and principles which form the foundation of the Community legal system within parameters comparable to the ones which prevail in national systems.[120]

On a first reading, the ECJ's judgment is disappointing. The second reading does not give a much more favourable impression. It was opined, indeed, that the ECJ had failed to engage fully in undertaking the role of 'protagonist' assigned to it by the Advocate General and more harshly that 'the Court's decision may serve as an example of how judicial discourse should not be conducted, particularly when the issues at stake involve decisions of national Constitutional Courts'.[121] The ECJ refused to declare the EAW invalid and, consequently, to reset the balance carried out by the Council through the adoption of the Framework Decision between the exigency of enhancing cooperation in criminal matters and respecting the constitutional values of the Member States.

There can be little doubt that the ECJ steered clear of the role of leading protagonist, but given the constitutional tension of the inter-legal orders preceding the judgment, that could have been the right option if it would not have achieved that output through a succinct, not persuasive, cryptic and in some parts even apodictic reasoning in which comparative

---

[120] Ibid., paragraph 8. Of the same opinion is Alonso Garcia, *Justicia constitutional y Unión Europea* (Civitas, 2005), expressly mentioned by the AG in his Opinion.

[121] See D. Sarmiento, 'European Union: The European Arrest Warrant and the Quest for Constitutional Coherence', (2008) International J Constitutional Law, 171, 183.

arguments were unjustifiedly absent. The ECJ settled the dispute over the appropriateness of the Framework Decision as a legal instrument to govern the EAW by stating that EU Treaty provisions may not be interpreted as granting the sole adoption of framework decisions falling within the scope of former Article 31(1)(e) EUT.[122] It is true, the Court held, that the EAW could have been governed by a Convention as per Article 34(2)(d) EUT, but, at the same time, it stated that the Council enjoys the discretion to decide upon the appropriate legal instrument, where, as in this case, the conditions governing the adoption of such a measure are satisfied. The carte blanche, without further explanation, given to the Council in the choice of the appropriate legal basis to pursue the sensitive goal of enhancing the cooperation of the Member States in criminal matters does not seem the best strategic move in order to reassure the CEE national parliaments and judges about the European Union's commitment to the principle of legal certainty, so important in the constitutional structures of the post-communist legal orders. However, the more unsatisfactory and cryptic part of the reasoning is that related to contesting the alleged breach of fundamental rights by the EAW Framework Decision.

With regard to the alleged violation of the principle of legality, the ECJ operates an artificial translation of the playing field from the European level to the national level, arguing that Article 2 of the Framework Decision, which abolishes the requirement of double criminality from the list of 32 offences, does not itself harmonize the criminal offences in question, in respect of their constituent elements or penalties.[123] Consequently, even if the Member States reproduce verbatim the list of the categories of offences set out in Article 2(2) of the Framework Decision for the purposes of its implementation, the actual definition of those offences and the penalties applicable are those which follow from the law of the issuing Member State. The Framework Decision does not seek to harmonize the criminal offences in question in respect of their constituent elements or of the penalties which they attract (paragraph 52).

This is a clever but risky means of tossing 'the hot (constitutional) potato' back to the national courts. It is clever because the fundamental

---

[122] With regard to the progressive adoption of measures for the setting of offences and their punishments' constituent elements in matters relating to organized crime, terrorism and drug trafficking.

[123] Under Article 2(2) of the Framework Decision, the offences listed 'if in the (issuing) Member State the punishment or the custodial sentence incurs a maximum of at least three years' provision for surrender pursuant to a EAW, regardless of whether the acts constitute an offence in both the issuing and the executing Member State.

issue of the respect by European legislation of the fundamental principle of legality of the criminal offences and penalties suddenly becomes, and almost magically so, a matter determined by the law of the issuing Member State, which must respect fundamental rights and fundamental legal principles as enshrined in Article 6 EUT (paragraph 53).[124] It is risky because the ECJ's judicial attitude of 'washing one's hands of the problem' without further explanation does not exactly seem to be the right approach to foster the confidence of the national (especially of CEE) courts, so essential in the enhancement of the European area of freedom, security and justice, in the fundamental rights commitment of the European Union.

In response to the third argument concerning the alleged violation of the principles of equality and non-discrimination of the EAW, owing to the unjustified differentiation between the offences listed under Article 2(2) providing for the abolition of the double criminality requirement, on one hand, and all the other crimes where surrender is conditional on the executing Member State's recognition of the criminal liability on which the EAW is based on the other, the ECJ has played, in just one passage, that protagonist role the AG referred to in his Opinion. Such a 'regurgitation' of judicial activism', in the absence of a proper argumentative and persuasive basis, and in the light of the severe inter-constitutional perturbation which anticipated the ECJ ruling, makes the interaction between the European dimension and the constitutional one on this delicate issue even more problematic. The ECJ, in fact, in an attempt to justify the rationale behind the above mentioned differentiation, made an express reference to the *mutual trust* between Member States as an indispensable tenet at the heart of any third pillar action – an argument openly questioned, as noted above, by the German Federal Constitutional Court – thus stating that according to the classification as per Article 2 (2):

> The Council was able to form the view, on the basis of the principle of mutual recognition and in the light of the 'high degree of trust and solidarity' between the Member States, that, whether by reason of their inherent nature or by reason of the punishment of a maximum of at least three years, the categories of offences in question feature among those the seriousness of which in terms of

[124] Accordingly, the European judges did not miss the opportunity to stress how the principles of legality and non-discrimination fall within the 'supra-primary' parameters on the basis of which they ascertain the validity of an EC secondary law not only through the usual 'transfiguration' of Member States' constitutional principles into common constitutional practice first, and then EC law's general principles, but also by the express acknowledgement of these principles, by articles 49, 20 and 21 of the Charter of Fundamental Rights.

adversely affecting public order and public safety justifies dispensing with the verification of double criminality. (Paragraph 57)

In other words, the different treatment of persons suspected of having committed offences featured in the list set out in Article 2(2) of the Framework Decision and those suspected of having committed offences other than those listed is justified, according to the apodictic, cryptic and unpersuasive reasoning of the ECJ, by a presumption of the existence of mutual trust in the Member States for the guarantees provided by their respective criminal law. Furthermore the said presumption was heavily contested less than two years earlier by the most prestigious Constitutional Court in Europe, the Federal Constitutional Court of Germany. There was not a single word, instead, which could have been read as an answer to the constitutional objections raised in relation to the EAW by many constitutional courts in Europe. As has been correctly argued, 'the ECJ's sparse reasoning in the decision contrasts with the firm and outspoken approach of the national Constitutional Courts'.[125]

The lack of persuasive strength in the reasoning and the lost talent for pedagogical method are not the only facets of the ECJ's current style that hinder, in the current post-enlargement times, the communication between the European level and the domestic constitutional level. The EAW decision could in fact represent a (bad) model for speculation on the ECJ's need eventually to expand its legal reasoning equipment to include a method until now too dangerously disregarded: the comparative one. It is well-known that the ECJ has always been sparing in direct reference to Member States'[126] comparative law, leaving this 'delicate business' to the Advocate General's Opinion. Two reasons seem to support this choice. Firstly, in the early years, the ECJ devoted all its argumentative efforts to stressing the peculiar features of the 'new legal order', distinguishing Community law from national and international law. The absence of reference to comparative law in the ECJ's reasoning would be instrumental to that aim. Secondly, with the further enlargements and the risk of emphasizing

---

125 Sarmiento, 'European Union: The European Arrest Warrant and the Quest for Constitutional Coherence', 182.

126 P. Pescatore, 'Le recours, dans la jurisprudence de la Cour de justice des Communautés européenne, à des normes déduites de la comparaison des droits des Etat membres' (1980) Rev. in. dr. comp., 337; K. Lenaerts, 'Interlocking Legal Orders in the European Union and Comparative Law' (2003) ICLQ 873, 887ff. Perhaps the more direct and broad reference to comparative law may be found in one of the very first decisions of the ECJ. See Joined cases 7/56, 3/57– 7/57, *Dineke Algera and others v Common Assembly of the European Coal and Steel Community* (1957) ECR 39, paragraph 55–56.

references to certain legal orders to the detriment of others, the ECJ very quickly understood that the strategic reference to the 'common constitutional traditions' formula as a source of inspiration for European judges could have served to legitimize the European integration process in a more diplomatic way in the Member States' eyes.

Now the question is whether, after the latest enlargements to the east of 2004 and 2007, the time has come for the ECJ to take seriously the comparative law argument in its legal reasoning. In the past, it has been possible to justify the exclusive reference to the common constitutional traditions under the 'majoritarian activist approach' judicial strategy. Conversely, today, also in order to ensure a correspondence between the judicial argumentation level and the content-based level, in the light, on one hand, of the new value-based season increasingly committed to taking into consideration the single Member State's constitutional identity and, on the other, of the ever more heterogeneous national constitutional *humus*, the exclusive reference to the common constitutional tradition has seemingly become unsuitable. On the contrary, a more audacious recourse to the explicit comparative reference to Member States' law would serve a twofold purpose: enhance the judicial acceptance of the European legislation within the CEE Member States, thus providing a role model for their national courts,[127] as well as fit the growing tendency towards an effective interaction between the European legal order and the national ones.

CONCLUSIONS

In the attempt to rationalize and systematize, in the light of the case law above mentioned, the new more deferential post-enlargement season of the ECJ jurisprudence with regard to the Member States' constitutional dimension, it is possible to distinguish two groups of cases.[128]

A first group is composed of cases like *Schmidberger*, where the ECJ found a constitutional tradition which is considered as 'common'. This

---

127 M.J. Möllers, 'The Role of Law in European Integration' (2000) Am J Comparative Law, 679, 698.

128 For a different classification, see N. Shuibhne, 'Margins of Appreciation: National Values, Fundamental Rights and EC Free Movement Law' (2009) Eur L Rev 230; J. Gerards, 'Pluralism, Deference and the Margin of Appreciation Doctrine' (2010) Eur L J, 80; J.H.H. Weiler, 'Fundamental Rights and Fundamental Boundaries: On Standards and Values in the Protection of Human Rights', in J.H.H.Weiler, *The Constitution of Europe* (Cambridge University Press 1999), 102, 104.

first group has to do with balancing properly understood, since there it is up to the Court to balance two principles or two sources belonging to their legal order (the idea behind that is of conceiving national and supranational law as characterized by an overlapping zone). In a second group of cases (*Omega*, *Dynamic Medien*, *Sayn Wittgenstein*), the ECJ had to apply a constitutional principle which is specific to a single legal system. In the second group of cases there is something different because the ECJ cannot balance, with a principle of EU law, another norm formally belonging to another legal order (the national one).

A confirmation of this distinction could be found in the wording of Article 6 of the EU Treaty (pre-Lisbon Treaty): while paragraph 2 referred to the common constitutional tradition, the third paragraph, instead, referred to the national identity, thereby treating them as two distinguished concepts.

It is only in the second group of cases that the post-enlargement constitutional sensitivity of the ECJ acquires the form of a strategic use of the margin of appreciation doctrine[129] in order to foster the constitutional tolerance of the single Member State.

If this is the main consequence of the new importance the ECJ seems to give to enhancing the Member States' margin of appreciation in its post-enlargement jurisprudence, it is worth pointing out two further aspects connected with the said main consequence. The first aspect has to do with the further amplification of the discretion given to 'local decisions' such as those connected to the notions of public order and morality where the ECJ seems willing to emphasize, more than in the past, the need for a certain margin of appreciation in favour of Member States.

The said amplification clearly emerges from reading a 2009 judgment of the ECJ,[130] in which the question arose of whether it was possible to justify, on the basis of moral and cultural values, domestic measures restricting the free circulation of services. The ECJ stated that:

> In that context, as most of the Member States which submitted observations to the Court have noted, the legislation on games of chance is one of the areas in which there are significant moral, religious and cultural differences between the

---

[129] For a recent in-depth analysis of the difference between the notions, similar but not overlapping, of margin of appreciation and margin of discretion, see M. Forowicz, 'State Discretion as a Paradox of EU Constitutionalisation: An Introduction to a Functional Analysis', paper presented at the Max Weber Programme's Lustrum Conference, 8 June 2011, Florence, European University Institute.

[130] ECJ C-42/07, *Liga Portuguesa*, 8-11-2009: www.curia.europa.eu.

> Member States. In the absence of Community harmonisation in the field, it is for each Member State to determine in those areas, in accordance with its own scale of values, what is required in order to ensure that the interests in question are protected. (Paragraph 57)

The second aspect which should be pointed out is the enhancement, in the reasoning of the ECJ, of the already present tendency to return expressly to the judicial technique that characterizes the application of the margin of appreciation in the jurisprudence of the ECtHR. It suffices to recall, in this respect, a recent judgment[131] that dealt with a possible violation of the freedom of expression, in which a Danish citizen posted information in the Internet about a medicine whose advertising was prohibited under Danish law. It is obviously a judgment of the ECJ, but to all intents and purposes it sounds just like the reasoning of a ECtHR judgment. For its parameter of reference in fact, the ECJ used the protection of the freedom of expression as provided for by Article 10 of the ECHR and as interpreted by ECHR jurisprudence.

After mentioning these provisions, the ECJ took over the standard of evaluation applied by ECHR jurisprudence confirming that:

> whilst the principle of freedom of expression is expressly recognised by Article 10 of the European Convention for the Protection of Human Rights and Fundamental Freedoms, signed in Rome on 4 November 1950, and constitutes one of the fundamental pillars of a democratic society, it nevertheless follows from the wording of Article 10(2) that freedom of expression is also subject to certain limitations justified by objectives in the public interest, in so far as those derogations are in accordance with the law, motivated by one or more of the legitimate aims under that provision and necessary in a democratic society, that is to say justified by a pressing social need and, in particular, proportionate to the legitimate aim pursued. (Paragraph 26)

If it is undeniable that, from the analysis carried on above, a new constitutional sensitivity of the ECJ is emerging, which, compared with the new post-enlargment aggressive approach of the ECtHR, seems to have caused a trend towards the convergence of the self-image of the two European Courts with regard to the impact of supranational law toward the Member States' legal orders, it is however very important not to reach hasty conclusions.

On the one hand, with regard to the ECHR dimension, it has emerged in the first section of this chapter that the ECtHR seems, between the end of 2010 and the beginning of 2011, to have changed its previous approach

---

131 ECJ C-421/07, *Damgaard* [2009] ECR I-2629.

by showing, in the recalled decisions *Lautsi 2* and *A, B and C v Ireland*, a new deference for the constitutional domestic values of the single Member State, even when those values are not shared by the majority of the contracting States.

On the other hand, in relation to the EU dimension, it must be pointed out that, in the last years, the case law of the ECJ has been characterized not only by a path toward a new constitutional sensitiveness, but also by an opposite trend which seems to have brought a more intrusive penetration of EU law in the Member States' legal orders and, more generally, a wider, *praeter legem* to the domestic application of EU law.

There are at least four relevant expressions of this trend. First of all, besides the new deference towards the constitutional values of the Member States, shown by judgments mentioned above, such as *Omega, Dynamic Medien* and *Sayn-Wittgenstein*, there is a group of cases which goes in the opposite direction and disregards the domestic constitutional preferences. It is enough to recall, in this regard, the *Michaniki* judgment of 2008.[132] Despite the emphasis of the Advocate General, Miguel Poiares Maduro,[133] on the obligation upon the EU to respect the constitutional identity of the Member States, the ECJ did not take due consideration of Article 14(9) of the Greek Constitution, pursuant to which the contractor, even if financially independent of the relative agent, is nevertheless required to prove that he has acted independently, on his own account and in his own interest. Even if the Greek referring judge asked the possibility to interpret as not exhaustive the list of grounds for excluding contractors provided in

[132] ECJ C-213/07 [2008] ECR I-9999.

[133] See the Opinion of Advocate General Maduro of 10 August 2008. In particular he remarked that 'It is true that the European Union is obliged to respect the constitutional identity of the Member States. That obligation has existed from the outset. It indeed forms part of the very essence of the European project initiated at the beginning of the 1950s, which consists of following the path of integration whilst maintaining the political existence of the States. That is shown by the fact that the obligation was explicitly stated for the first time upon a revision of the treaties, a reminder of the obligation being regarded as necessary by the Member States in view of the further integration provided for. Thus, Article F(1) of the Maastricht Treaty, now Article 6(3) of the Treaty on European Union, provides that "the Union shall respect the national identities of its Member States". The national identity concerned clearly includes the constitutional identity of the Member State. That is confirmed, if such was necessary, by the explanation of the aspects of national identity put forward in Article I-5 of the Treaty establishing a Constitution for Europe and Article 4(2) of the Treaty on European Union as amended by the Treaty of Lisbon. It appears, indeed, from the identical wording of those two instruments that the Union respects the national identities [of Member States], inherent in their fundamental structures, political and constitutional.'

Article 24 of Directive 93/37, the ECJ concluded that the list must be considered exhaustive. The consequence of such a conclusion is self-evident: the relevant provision of the Greek Constitution is to be considered, according to the ECJ, in contrast with EU law and the national judge has to put aside the former in order to favour the application of the latter.

Secondly, in its most recent case law, the ECJ seems ever more determined to isolate the European constitutional courts and to bypass their mandate to a centralized constitutional judicial review by inviting the national common judges to pursue an ever more decentralized assessment of the conformity of their national law with European law. We refer to the *Mangold*[134] and *Kücükdeveci*[135] judgments[136] in which was established the direct application of non-self-executing directives due to the circumstance that the said directives have given a specific expression to a general principle of EU law (the principle of non-discrimination on grounds of age).[137] It is not a coincidence that, in reaction to *Mangold*, the former president of

---

134 ECJ C-144/04, 22-11-2005.

135 ECJ, C-555/07, 9-1-2010.

136 F. Fontanelli, 'General Principles of the EU and a Glimpse of Solidarity in the Aftermath of *Mangold* and *Kücükdeveci*' (2011) European Public Law, 225; S. Peers, 'Supremacy, Equality and Human Rights. Comment on *Kücükdeveci* (C-555/07)' (2011) Eur L Rev, 849; G. Thüsing and S. Horler, 'Case C-555/07, *Seda Kücükdeveci v. Swedex*, Judgment of the Court (Grand Chamber) of 19 January 2010' (2010) CML Rev, 1161; A. Wiesbrock, 'Case Note – Case C-555/07, *Kücükdeveci v. Swedex*, Judgment of the Court (Grand Chamber) of 19 January 2010' (2010) 11 German L J 539; M. Payandeh, 'Constitutional Review of EU Law after *Honeywell*: Contextualizing the Relationship between the German Constitutional Court and the EU Court of Justice' (2011) 48 CML Rev, 9–38; V. Sciarabba, 'Dopo Mangold la Corte di giustizia torna sul rapporto tra principi generali, direttive e norme interne' (2010) Diritto pubblico comparato ed europeo, II; idem, 'La sentenza Kücükdeveci e le prospettive della giustizia costituzionale europea': www.gruppodipisa2010.it, in www.europeanrights.eu and in www.astrid-online.it.

137 More precisely, in *Mangold* the ECJ stated that 'It is the responsibility of the national court to guarantee the full effectiveness of the general principle of non-discrimination in respect of age, setting aside any provision of national law which may conflict with Community law, even where the period prescribed for transposition of that directive has not yet expired' (paragraph 78). In *Kücükdeveci* the ECJ, beside the reference to the general principle of non-discrimination, also named the directive expressly by stating that 'it is for the national court, hearing proceedings between individuals, to ensure that the principle of non-discrimination on grounds of age, as given expression in Directive 2000/78, is complied with, disapplying if need be any contrary provision of national legislation, independently of whether it makes use of its entitlement, in the cases referred to in the second paragraph of Article 267 TFEU, to ask the Court for a preliminary ruling on the interpretation of that principle' (paragraph 56).

the Convention on the Future of Europe wrote an article with the telling title 'Stop the European Court of Justice'.[138]

Thirdly, the ECJ case law has recently enhanced the already existing tendency of European law to go beyond its scope of application as provided in the Treaties. For instance, with regard to the scope of application of the provisions related to European citizenship, a telling example of the above mentioned trend is the *Zambrano* judgment.[139] In this case[140] the reference to the status of citizen of the Union plays a prominent role that differs somewhat from earlier decisions in the same field.[141]

In particular, this status is presented as the real source of the rights and duties conferred on to EU citizens and to their family members. The consequence is that the status in itself has to be protected in order to protect the rights attached to it. These rights refer to the rights of citizenship (movement, non-discrimination, social integration) but one can also see a reference to the fundamental rights protected under the Charter and the ECHR. If taken seriously, the combination of citizenship and fundamental rights would have far-reaching effect in the broadening of the scope of application of EU law.[142]

---

138 R. Herzog and L. Gerken, 'Stop the European Court of Justice', http://euobserver.com.

139 ECJ C 34/09, *Gerardo Luis Zambrano v. Office National dell'Emploi*, 8-3-2011, in www.curia.eu.int.

140 As already characterized the ECJ judgment, C-135/08, *Rottmann*, 2-3-2010, in www.curia.eu.int.

141 See C-184/89, *Grzelczyk* (2001) ECR I-6193; C-413/99, *Baumbast* (2002) ECR I-7091; C-148/02, *Garcia Avello* (2003) ECR I-11613.

142 See L. Azoulai, 'A Comment on the Ruiz Zambrano Judgment: A Genuine-European Integration' in www. http://eudo-citizenship.eu/citizenship-news/457-a-comment-on-the-ruiz-zambrano-judgment-a-genuine-european-integration. See also the powerful Opinion to the case given by Advocate General Sharpston: 'The Court has a number of difficult and important choices to make. What precisely does Union citizenship entail? Do the circumstances giving rise to the national proceedings constitute a situation that is "purely internal" to the Member State concerned, in which European Union ("EU") law has no role to play? Or does full recognition of the rights (including the future rights) that necessarily flow from Union citizenship mean that an infant EU citizen has a right, based on EU law rather than national law, to reside anywhere within the territory of the Union (including in the Member State of his nationality)? If so, ensuring that he can exercise that right effectively may entail granting residence to his third country national parent if there would otherwise be a substantial breach of fundamental rights.

At a more conceptual level, is the exercise of rights as a Union citizen dependent – like the exercise of the classic economic "freedoms" – on some trans-frontier free movement (however accidental, peripheral or remote) having taken place before the claim is advanced? Or does Union citizenship look forward to the future, rather

Finally, another group of cases that go in the same direction of enhancing the risk of conflict between the European legal order and the constitutional values of the domestic legal orders is that in which the ECJ has shown the clear attitude of jeopardizing the principle of national *res iudicata* in order to ensure the uniformity of interpretation. The problem of the equilibrium between the need for interpretive uniformity and the respect for the principle of *res iudicata* was tackled by the ECJ in the *Kühne & Heitz* case.[143] There (with regard to administrative decisions), the ECJ clearly expressed its preference for overcoming the national *res iudicata*, where the applicable national law allows it. This reference to national autonomy (suggested by the *a quo* judge himself when raising the preliminary question) seems to mitigate the strong acceleration of the ECJ's interpretive uniformity. In *Kapferer*,[144] the ECJ answered a preliminary question raised by the *Landesgericht Innsbruck* (Austria) in *Rosmarie Kapferer v Schlank & Schick GmbH*. The *a quo* judge expressly proposed the possibility to extend the *Kühne & Heitz* principle to the case of *res iudicata* in a judicial decision. The ECJ highlighted that:

> It should be added that the judgment in *Kühne & Heitz*, to which the national court refers in Question 1(a), is not such as to call into question the foregoing analysis. Even assuming that the principles laid down in that judgment could be transposed into a context which, like that of the main proceedings, relates to a final judicial decision, it should be recalled that that judgment makes the obligation of the body concerned to review a final decision, which would appear to have been adopted in breach of Community law, subject, in accordance with Article 10 EC, to the condition, inter alia, that that body should be empowered under national law to reopen that decision (see paragraphs 26 and 28 of that judgment). In this case it is sufficient to note that it is apparent from the reference for a preliminary ruling that that condition has not been satisfied.[145]

The *Kapferer* doctrine seemed to resolve the issue. Yet, a few months after that decision, the ECJ dealt with another interesting case, *Lucchini*.[146] In

than back to the past, to define the rights and obligations that it confers? To put the same question from a slightly different angle: is Union citizenship merely the non-economic version of the same generic kind of free movement rights as have long existed for the economically active and for persons of independent means? Or does it mean something more radical: true citizenship, carrying with it a uniform set of rights and obligations, in a Union under the rule of law in which respect for fundamental rights must necessarily play an integral part?'

143 ECJ C-453/00, *Kühne & Heitz* [2004] ECR I-837.

144 ECJ C-234/04, *Kapferer* [2006] ECR I-2585.

145 *Kapferer*, paragraph 23.

146 ECJ C-119/05, *Ministero dell'Industria, del Commercio e dell'Artigianato*

Lucchini the ECJ, following the Opinion of Advocate General Geelhoed, concluded that:

> Community law precludes the application of a provision of national law, such as Article 2909 of the Italian Civil Code, which seeks to lay down the principle of *res iudicata* in so far as the application of that provision prevents the recovery of State aid granted in breach of Community law which has been found to be incompatible with the common market in a decision of the Commission which has become final.

As Giuseppe Martinico has elsewhere[147] argued, the impression is that one can explain the final conclusion reached in *Lucchini* by the fact that the contested decision was issued *ultra vires*. Indeed, as the ECJ itself recalled, the challenged decision had been adopted on a subject of undisputed Community competence, given that national courts 'do not have jurisdiction to give a decision on whether State aid is compatible with the common market'.[148] As Advocate General Geelhoed said, the principle of *res iudicata* cannot permit the persistence of a judicial decision which amounts to a clear violation of the simplest separation of competences between the EU and the Member States.[149] *Lucchini* seemed to be an extraordinary judgement, unlikely to set a precedent on the point; broadly speaking, the judicial autonomy of the Member States did not seem to be put in doubt. However, a few months before the time of writing, in *Cartesio* the ECJ 'has opened the possibility for national Courts to make references and maintain them, even if they are quashed on appeal by a superior Court on points of EC law'[150] thus jeopardizing the 'national judicial autonomy' of the states.[151]

---

v Lucchini SpA [2007] ECR I-6199. About *Lucchini* see: X. Groussot and T. Minseen, '*Res Judicata* in the Court of Justice Case-Law: Balancing Legal Certainty with Legality?' (2007) Eur Constitutional L Rev, 385.

[147] See G. Martinico, 'Constructivism, Evolutionism and Pluralism' (2009) King's Law Journal, 309

[148] Case C-119/05, *Lucchini*.

[149] 'In short, the key question is whether a final judgment which came about in the circumstances referred to above, which, as is evident from the previous point, may have serious implications for the division of powers between the Community and the Member States, as this results from the Treaty itself, and which would also make it impossible for the powers assigned to the Commission to be exercised, must be considered inviolable. To my mind, that is not the case', Opinion of A.G. Geelhoed in *Lucchini*, delivered on 14 September 2006.

[150] D. Sarmiento, 'The Silent Lamb and the Deaf Wolves. Constitutional Pluralism, Preliminary References and the Role of Silent Judgments in EU Law', paper presented at the conference 'Constitutional Pluralism in the European Union and Beyond', held at St Anne's College, Oxford, 20–21 March 2009. 'Where rules of national law apply which relate to the right of appeal against a decision making

Even more recently the ECJ has shown an evident aggressiveness towards the national procedural autonomy; hence some authors have described this ambit as a sort of 'paradise lost'[152] and the *Elchinov*[153] case is an another link of this chain. In the *Elchinov* case, the ECJ seems to continue its battle against the national judicial hierarchies and emphasize that the preliminary ruling mechanism should be seen as characterized by a direct and privileged cooperation between the *a quo* judge and the ECJ without any intermediation. The Luxembourg Court has stressed the fact that a national court has to have the 'widest discretion in referring matters to the Court if they consider that a case pending before them raises questions involving interpretation of provisions of European Union law, or consideration of their validity, which are necessary for the resolution of the case' (paragraph 26).

In this case the ECJ 'saved' the *Cartesio* and *Rheinmühlen* doctrines, not taking into account the revolutionary proposal of Advocate General Cruz Villalón, who had said in his powerful Opinion: 'It does not appear to be necessary also for a lower court to consider it possible to disregard its internal hierarchical organization in order to preserve the effectiveness of European Union law, since, inter alia, an individual who holds rights conferred by European Union law may now bring an action for liability for judicial acts'. In his Opinion, the Advocate General showed

---

a reference for a preliminary ruling, and under those rules the main proceedings remain pending before the referring court in their entirety, the order for reference alone being the subject of a limited appeal, the second paragraph of Article 234 EC is to be interpreted as meaning that the jurisdiction conferred by that provision of the Treaty on any national court or tribunal to make a reference to the Court for a preliminary ruling cannot be called into question by the application of those rules, where they permit the appellate court to vary the order for reference, to set aside the reference and to order the referring court to resume the domestic law proceedings.' C-210/06, *Cartesio*, Judgment of 16/12/2008.

[151] 'Cartesio raises many questions about the degree of interference that the ECJ is willing to inflict on national judicial autonomy, but it is clear from its wording that national Courts that engage in a preliminary discourse with the Luxembourg Court are protected from most appellate intrusions of superior domestic Courts. When the ECJ states that a revocation or an amendment from the appellate jurisdiction is a matter that the inferior court 'alone is able to take a decision on', it is conferring on the said Court a power to disregard a judgement delivered by an appellate Court, on a case that will eventually return to that same jurisdiction when the judgements of the ECJ and the referring court are dictated', Sarmiento, 'The Silent Lamb'.

[152] D.U. Galetta, *Procedural Autonomy of EU Member States: Paradise Lost?* (Springer 2010).

[153] C-173/09, *Elchinov*, www.curia.europa.eu.

more deference towards the national legal structures and stressed the new 'instruments' offered by EU law[154] to the national citizens after *Traghetti del Mediterraneo*[155] and *Köbler*.[156]

In this respect the ECtHR, bound to the provision of Article 46 of the ECHR, which leaves free the contracting States to decide for themselves how to conform to the ECHR obligations, has never identified the reopening of a proceeding as a compulsory measure to be taken by the condemned State. As in fact the ECtHR itself has stated: 'Where it finds that an applicant has been convicted despite a potential infringement of his right to participate in his trial, *the most appropriate form* of redress would, in principle, be trial *de novo* or the reopening of the proceedings in due course and in accordance with the requirements of Article 6 of the Convention' (paragraph 86).[157]

Along the same lines, it has been noted that 'Contracting states are not under an obligation to introduce review proceedings before national courts; such proceedings may, however, be very useful and considerably facilitate the execution of a decision of the European Court of Human Rights'.[158] Despite the lack of an obligation in this sense, in almost all the

---

[154] 'Thus, after the Supreme Administrative Court had referred the case back to the *Administrativen sad Sofia-grad*, and that court has given judgment dismissing the action, Mr Elchinov would have the right to bring proceedings for liability against the State for infringement of European Union law. In the course of those proceedings, the competent national court could seek a preliminary ruling from the Court of Justice concerning whether, in accordance with its case-law, there had been a manifest error of law. If the infringement were confirmed, the referring court would give judgment and would make reparation to the applicant, in short, in the same terms as it would have done under the *Rheinmühlen I* case-law. Finally, in the event that the court did not uphold the action for liability, it is appropriate to point out that the alternative remedy of an action for failure to fulfil obligations would still be available, which the individual could, by means of a complaint, request the Commission to bring. In contrast to the situation in the 1970s, it is possible to assert today that European Union law has reached a level of maturity which allows it to ensure its own practical effectiveness before the courts of the Member States with a lesser degree of involvement in the autonomy of national courts than that which indubitably results from *Rheinmühlen I*. That is why the time for reconsidering that case-law appears to have arrived'. Opinion in *Elchinov* by Advocate General Cruz Villalón (30–31).

[155] ECJ C-173/03, *Traghetti del Mediterraneo* [2006] ECR I-5177.

[156] ECJ C-224/01, *Köbler* [2003] ECR I-10239.

[157] *Somogyi, Somogyi v Italia*, ric. 67972/00. On the same line, ECtHR, 24-3-2005, *Stoichkov v Bulgaria*, ric. 9802/02 and 1-3-2006, *Sejdovic v Italia*, ric. 56581/00.

[158] P. Leuprecht, 'The Execution of Judgments and Decisions', in J. Macdonald et al. (eds), *The European System for the Protection of Human Rights* (Kluwer 1993), 791, 792.

Member States,[159] there is provision, in normative or in judicial terms, to reopen (in general, criminal) proceedings because of a Strasbourg decision that contradicts the national *res iudicata*.

The point has already been underlined by those who have spoken of 'a quiet revolution in European procedural law'.[160] It would be inappropriate, however, in this regard, to compare the cooperative attitude shown by the Member States towards the ECtHR with the sharp national reactions which have followed, for instance, in Italy[161] and in Spain,[162] decisions of the ECJ calling into question the constitutional principle of *res iudicata*. If, in fact, the *res iudicata* scenario is a physiological situation in the ECHR mechanism, in the light of the requirement to exhaust internal remedies and, consequently, the lack of possibility to reopen a national proceeding risks depriving of any *effet utile* the protection afforded by the ECtHR, the same could not be said in relation to its Luxembourg counterpart. In this case, in fact, the ECJ could be invested with the national case at an earlier stage, making the *res iudicata* scenario a hypothesis external to the physiology of the judicial review system envisaged in Luxembourg.

---

159 Italy, 113/11.
160 Keller and Stone Sweet,704.
161 C-119/05, *Lucchini*; ECJ C-2/08, *Fall.*Olimpiclub, 3-9-2009.
162 ECJ C-40/08, *Asturcom Telecomunicaciones*, 6-10-2009.

7. Conclusions

In the light of the outputs of the research presented in this book, it is possible to conclude, with regard to the supranational scenario, that there is a growing trend in the more recent case law of the ECJ and the ECtHR. Indeed, the two European Courts seem to have involuntarily started to converge in terms of their 'idea' of the domestic effects of EU law and the ECHR in the legal orders of the Member States of the two supranational organizations.

In this respect, it has been argued in the previous chapters that the above mentioned trend of convergence finds its roots in the two opposite ways in which the two European Courts have reacted to the challenges emerging from the enlargement of the European Union and of the Council of Europe towards Eastern Europe. In fact, on the one hand, the ECtHR has opted for an acceleration of judicial activism according to which the Strasbourg judges have started to amplify the direct and indirect effect of their case law on the domestic legal orders; on the other hand, the ECJ seems to have privileged, since the great enlargement of 2004, the appraisal of national constitutional values even of single Member States.

Against this background, our hypothesis is that the ECJ's recent attitude to the exploitation of EU primacy, combined with the opposite tendency of further centralization of the adjudicatory powers favoured by the ECtHR, seems to have reduced the distance between EU law and ECHR law with regard to their relation with domestic law. First of all, absolute, radical supremacy no longer seems to be a cornerstone of EU law, and the ECJ is more and more committed to (working on) a self-restriction of the principle of primacy when it comes to the protection of the fundamental principles of one or more Member States.[1]

Second, the progressive self-perception of the Strasbourg's Court's constitutional role has led to the consequence of increasing the acknowledgement of the (relative) primacy of the European Court of Human Rights' interpretation of national law. Beginning with the reaction of the ECtHR

[1] The best answer to the 'counterlimits doctrine' of the 'old' European Constitutional Courts.

to the enlargement we have seen that, since the end of the Cold War, the Council of Europe has experienced a dramatic increase in the number of members. In 1989, the Council of Europe was an exclusively Western European organization with 23 Member States. By 2007, its membership had grown to 47 countries, including almost all the former Communist states of central and Eastern Europe.

Our assumption is that the ECtHR has reacted to the Council of Europe's enlargement to the east with a more explicit understanding of itself as a pan-European constitutional court, as a result of both the exponential growth of its case load and the realistic possibility for it to ascertain systemic human rights violations in CEE countries. This has implied a shifting away from an exclusively subsidiary role as 'secondary guarantor of human rights' to a more central and crucial position as a constitutional adjudicator.

Against this background, and with regard to the new 'season' of a centralized judicial activism of the ECtHR, the further relevant question has been whether (and in the case of a positive answer, in which direction) the ECJ has somehow developed a new judicial sensitivity after the 2004 and 2007 enlargements. The addition of 12, not always homogeneous, constitutional identities seems in fact to entail that the ECJ's exclusive reference to the concept of common constitutional traditions is starting to become progressively less suitable.

Bearing these considerations in mind, our answer to the research question identified above is that the ECJ seems to have reacted to the change in a pluralistic identity-based direction, of the dynamic nature of constitutional tolerance. In particular, the European judges seem to have understood that if the majoritarian activist approach had been partially able to convince the Germans and Italians when they were 'invited' to obey the European discipline in the name of the peoples of Europe, the same 'invitation' would have proven much less successful when applied to Estonians or Hungarians.

The post-2004 era has called, then, for a new *ad hoc* judicial strategy to combine with the pre-2004 majoritarian activist approach. After all, what new Member States need to be reassured about seems to be that even if, with regard to those national values relating to a peculiar constitutional identity to protect, they found themselves in a minority or isolated position, the European judges would not sacrifice them on the altar of the majoritarian-activist approach. It does not seem a coincidence, indeed, that some months after the 2004 enlargement, the Court stated, against an exclusively majoritarian logic, for the very first time, that 'it is not indispensable in that respect for the restrictive measure issued by the authorities of a Member State to correspond to a conception shared by all Member

States as regards the precise way in which the fundamental right or legitimate interest in question is to be protected'.[2]

The appraisal by the European Courts at supranational level of the approximation between the domestic effects of EU law and ECHR law needed, as was done in the first part of the book, to be combined with a comparative analysis rooted in the national dimension, in order to verify, on the basis of the points outlined in the introduction, the way ordinary and constitutional judges treat EU law and ECHR law.

In the next few pages, some of the most important distinguishing features of national judicial treatment of ECHR and EU law in Europe will be underlined through a select number of references to national experiences. The importance of focusing on internal judicial interpretation and application of supranational laws is very well captured by underlining that 'despite the different quality of the EU and the ECHR supranationalism, one common denominator is the role of the judge'.[3]

The first relevant element that emerges from the analysis carried out is the constantly growing bifurcation between a static reading of the relevant 'European' and 'international' clauses present in the constitutions, which was pointed out in the introduction, and their dynamic judicial interpretation by constitutional courts. In other words, this new climate of European constitutionalism seems to be marked by the need to search for new argumentative techniques and original judicial interaction between national and European courts, by following new 'off-piste' routes with respect to those indicated in the national constitutions.

In this regard, among the many examples that one can find in the various chapters, the Scandinavian case is particularly significant with respect to EU law and the Czech and Italian experiences are relevant to ECHR law. With regard to EU Law, one simply has to quote Carl Lebeck, who underlined that 'all Scandinavian countries regard EU law from a formal perspective as only a matter of international law, which is clearly not the case insofar as one looks to the case law involving these legal orders'. In relation instead to the ECHR, Michal Bobek and David Kosař have pointed out that 'the Czech "Euro" amendment adopted in 2001 clarified that the ECHR does not have a constitutional rank, because all

---

2 ECJ C-36/02, *Omega* [2004] ECR I-9609, paragraph 37.

3 V.P. Tzevelekos and S.E. Vetsika, 'Report on Greece', in G. Martinico and O. Pollicino, *The National Judicial Treatment The National Judicial Treatment of the ECHR and EU Laws. A Comparative Constitutional Perspective* (Europa Law 2010), 224, 227.

international treaties, including international human rights treaties, "only" enjoy the application priority'.[4]

What was clear reading the new constitutional parameter was evidently not so clear to the Czech constitutional judges given that, in a much disputed decision of 2002, they concluded that international human rights treaties have *retained* their constitutional status. Indeed, however, what clearly emerges from the analysis of Bobek and Kosař is that the Court constitutionalized, for the first time, international human rights treaties, including the ECHR.[5]

The same aim, underlying the above mentioned Czech decision (i.e. that of not losing the competence to decide on conflicts between the ECHR and domestic statute law), has been pursued by the Italian Constitutional Court. Indeed, although Article 117 of the Italian Constitution seems to put European Union law and ECHR law on an equal footing by stating that 'legislative powers shall be vested in the State and the Regions in compliance with the Constitution and with the constraints deriving from the EU legal order and international obligations', the Constitutional Court, in 2007, opted, as we have seen, for a diverging approach by upholding the para-constitutional nature of EU law and underlining the sub-constitutional character of the ECHR.

As the Czech and Italian cases thus demonstrate, the 'off-piste' routes followed by constitutional judges with regard to the applicable constitutional parameters are often due to their fear of having to abdicate from their privileged position of final arbiter of the protection of fundamental rights in a critical sphere where the constitutional dimension encounters the supranational dimension.

Returning then to the supranational dimension, it is common knowledge that, with regard to the domestic effects of the decisions of these two European Courts, the ECJ judgments are widely recognized as having *erga omnes* effects of *res intepretata*, while Article 46 of ECHR limits the effects of ECtHR judgments to the Contracting State condemned in Strasbourg. In the previous chapters attempts have been made to show how, more recently, the Strasbourg Court has tried to amplify the indirect effect of its case law, with the aim of extending the obligation to abide by its judgments to states that were not directly involved in the decision.

This idea is supported by Nikolas Kyriakou when he notes that 'the

---

4 M. Bobek and D. Kosař, 'Report on the Czech Republic and Slovakia', in Martinico and Pollicino, *The National Judicial Treatment of the ECHR and EU Laws*, 117, 133.

5 Bobek and Kosař noted that, in fact, the international human rights treaties had *never* had constitutional status before.

Strasbourg Court's case law has attained a de facto *'erga omnes'* effect, as *Opuz v Turkey*[6] illustrates'.[7] In particular, in that case, the ECtHR specified that it will consider 'whether the national authorities have sufficiently taken into account the principles flowing from its judgments on similar issues, even when they concern other States'.

By looking to the national dimension, the generally applicable rule seems to be that according to which the majority of the general reforms adopted by the national political and administrative powers has only followed decisions against their own Member State, confirming the self-perception that the Strasbourg decisions only have *inter partes* effects. Among the relevant exceptions in this regard, it is worth underlining the very open attitude[8] towards accepting the indirect effect of Strasbourg case law in the Netherlands, where, as Elaine Mak remarked, 'changes of national law have also been induced by ECtHR judgements concerning other states'[9] and in Slovenia, as it has been pointed out.[10]

The Netherlands is also one of the few Member States that has granted the *erga omnes* effects of *res iudicata* to the decisions of the ECtHR. By contrast, it is well known that such an effect is only widely recognized in Europe with regard to the decisions of the ECJ as, *inter alia*, the Italian experience demonstrates.

With regard to the attitude of national ordinary judges in the case of conflict between EU law and the ECHR, on the one hand, and national law, on the other, the first premise is that, at supranational level, the two European Courts are not asking the national judges to do the same thing. Indeed, whereas the ECJ has established that EU law has to be applied in the domestic legal orders instead of national law so as to guarantee the

---

6 *Opuz v Turkey*, 2009, paragraph 163.

7 N. Kyriakou, 'Report on Cyprus', in Martinico and Pollicino, *The National Judicial Treatment of the ECHR and EU Laws*, 150, 157.

8 . . . which is not surprising looking at the extreme openness of the Constitution with regard to international law.

9 See E. Mak, 'Report on the Netherlands and Luxembourg', in Martinico and Pollicino, *The National Judicial Treatment of the ECHR and EU Laws*, 301, 310.

10 In particular it has been noted that is '[. . .] entirely undisputed that regarding the interpretation of the European Convention on Human Rights, the opinion of the European Court of Human Rights is decisive. Such interpretation is not formally binding on the Constitutional Court, however in reality it must nevertheless be respected considering similar subsequent cases if the Court does not wish to risk Slovenia being found in violation before the European Court of Human Rights. [. . .] The Constitutional Court is naturally not restricted to cases in which the European Court of Human Rights decided on the basis of applications from Slovenia, although the Court pays particular attention to them'. C. Ribičič, 'Položaj slovenske ustave po vključitvi v EU' (2006/25) Pravna praksa, 29–30.

effet utile and the very existence of EU law, the ECtHR has never, at least not with the same emphasis, requested the national judges to set aside the national statutes in contrast with the ECHR.

Having said this, the analysis carried out demonstrates the fact that, in many cases, it is the constitutional mandate of the ordinary judges that obliges them to treat the two sources of supranational law differently. In fact, in the majority of European states characterized by a system of centralized constitutional justice in which international law is granted a supra-legislative status, the power to evaluate the conformity of a national law with ratified international treaties is reserved to constitutional judges.[11] This means that an ordinary judge who ascertains a conflict between the ECHR and a national statute is constitutionally obliged to raise the issue of constitutionality before his or her own Constitutional Court. On the contrary, it is common knowledge that, under the pressure of the ECJ, constitutional courts have granted ordinary judges the power to derogate from their constitutional mandate with regard to the application of EU law. Indeed, they can put aside national laws that are in contrast with EU law. Furthermore, as underlined in the previous chapters regarding Italy, the Italian Constitutional Court has reacted to those 'subversive ordinary judges' that have started to treat the ECHR like EU law.

In this regard, and as seen above, one should underline the judicial creativity of the Czech Constitutional Court, which insists on retaining the power to have the last word in cases of conflict between the ECHR and national statutes despite a constitutional parameter which says exactly the opposite. Worth noting, in this respect, is Poland, which deviates from the general judicial trend underlined above. Indeed, as Krystyna Kowalik-Bańczyk clearly underlined, even though the Polish Constitutional Tribunal has repeatedly stated that the ECHR can be directly applied by domestic courts, the Convention is not used in this manner by the majority of Polish courts which prefer to apply the method of consistent interpretation.[12]

Romania is another interesting case. In fact, as Ioana Raducu has pointed out:

> if from a strictly constitutional point of view, national court's mandate is primarily bound to obey national provisions as long as they are not declared incompatible with the Constitution, the doctrine unanimously upholds that the article 11 and 20 of the Constitution implies that the national judge's mandate

[11] France, and to some extent, Portugal, Spain and Belgium, as will be underlined below, represent a notable exception in this regard.

[12] K. Kowalik-Bańczyk, 'Report on Poland', in Martinico and Pollicino, *The National Judicial Treatment of the ECHR and EU Laws*, 326.

is to give precedence to the ECHR provisions as interpreted by the ECtHR over domestic law.'[13]

Among the few systems of centralized constitutional justice which allow ordinary judges to set aside a national law that is in contrast with international law, is that of France. As outlined by Maria Fartunova, according to this principle the conventionality control is granted to the ordinary judges who consequently apply the same rules for settling contrasts between ordinary statutes and ECHR law and EU law respectively. There is a similar situation in Luxembourg where, in case of conflict between domestic legislation and the ECHR, the courts usually give precedence to the Treaty.

In Belgium, the ordinary courts directly apply the ECHR and EU law in case of contrast with national statutes, because, as Patricia Popelier pointed out, 'the Constitutional Court has no competence to review Acts of Parliament directly to international or supranational law, but it does so indirectly via the Articles 10 and 11 of the Constitution'.[14]

With particular regard to the ECHR, the Court has been very keen not to centralize the control of '*conventionalité*' by stating that 'ni l'article 26 par. 1 de la loi spéciale du 6 janvier 1989 sur la Cour d'Arbitrage, ni aucune autre disposition, constitutionnelle ou législative, ne confère à la Cour de pouvoir de statuer à une disposition d'une convention internationale. En tant que la question invite à un control direct au regard de la Convention européenne des droit de l'homme, la Cour n'est pas compétente pour y répondre.'[15]

The same does not apply to Portugal and Spain. Indeed, even if in Portugal the Constitution itself, and in Spain much less equivocally the case law of the Constitutional Tribunal, would entitle the common judges to put aside the national law in contrast with the ECHR, the judges do not use this possibility, preferring instead to apply the method of consistent

---

[13] I. Raducu, 'Report on Romania', in Martinico and Pollicino, *The National Judicial Treatment of the ECHR and EU Laws*, 369, 372.

[14] P. Popelier, 'Report on Belgium', in Martinico and Pollicino, *The National Judicial Treatment of the ECHR and EU Laws*, 81, 89.

[15] Cour d'Arbitrage, Decision 25/200. Interestingly enough, in the Belgian experience an expression of the convergence trend between the domestic impact of the EU and ECHR legal orders is given by a recent intervention of the legislative power in reaction to a clear position of the Belgian Constitutional Court. When, in fact the Constitutional Court clarified that it would have considered itself competent to decide on the preliminary reference related to the constitutionality of EU Treaties or the ECHR, 'the law maker deprived the Court of its jurisdiction to answer to preliminary references concerning an Act of assent to a EU Treaty or to the European Convention of human rights or a Protocol'.

interpretation or to raise the issue of constitutionality before their own constitutional court.

In brief, as it is shown by the judicial practices in the Baltic States, Bulgaria, Poland, the Czech Republic, Slovakia, Romania, Portugal and Spain,[16] in centralized systems of constitutional review consistent interpretation is acquiring a growing importance among the tools at the disposal of the ordinary judges so as to avoid conflict between the ECHR and EU law, on one hand, and the national law, on the other. In decentralized systems of constitutional justice the interpretative tool of consistent interpretation is instead already now, by far, the one most privileged by the ordinary judges. The Scandinavian experience is very significant in this regard because as it has been pointed out, with specific reference to the ECHR, 'the role of consistent interpretation has over time evolved from being a matter of presumption that national law is consistent with the requirements of the ECHR, to that national law as far as possible should be made to conform with the ECHR'.[17]

With regard to the two European countries where there is no constitutional review (United Kingdom and the Netherlands), the fact that Dutch judges, who cannot ascertain the contrast between national law and the Constitution, are entitled to put aside the national statutes conflicting with ratified international treaties has obviously had the effect not only of reinforcing the ECHR as a 'shadow Constitution' but has also brought about a convergence in the judicial treatment of the ECHR and EU law in the Netherlands.

As far as the United Kingdom's experience is concerned, when it is not possible for judges to interpret primary and subordinate legislation in a way which is compatible, respectively, with Convention rights and EU law, the solution that is adopted is quite different. As Cian Murphy pointed out, 'unlike national law found to be contrary to EU law, law incompatible with the Convention is not disapplied or declared invalid. A declaration of incompatibility does not affect the "validity, continuing operation or enforcement" of the law, nor does it bind the parties before the Court. Instead, a procedure is provided to allow Parliament to fast-track an amending bill.'[18]

---

[16] It should also be emphasized that the Spanish, Portuguese and Romanian Constitutions expressly provide that they must be interpreted in the light of the International Declaration of Human Rights.

[17] C. Lebeck, 'Report on Scandinavian Countries', in Martinico and Pollicino, *The National Judicial Treatment of the ECHR and EU Laws*, 389, 418.

[18] C. Murphy, 'Report on the UK and Ireland', in Martinico and Pollicino, *The National Judicial Treatment of the ECHR and EU Laws*, 478, 488.

Still with regard to the UK, even if a cooperative judicial attitude emerges in the attempt to interpret primary and secondary legislation, as requested by the Human Rights Act, 'so far as it is possible to do so, in a way which is compatible with the Convention rights', recently, nevertheless, objections have been raised with respect to the very activist period of the ECtHR. It is worth recalling the fierce criticism, mentioned in the introduction, formulated by Lord Hoffmann when he underlined that:

> the fact that the 10 original Member States of the Council of Europe subscribed to a statement of human rights in the same terms did not mean that they had agreed to uniformity of the application of those abstract rights in each of their countries, still less in the 47 states which now belong. . . . The Strasbourg court has no mandate to unify the laws of Europe on the many subjects which may arguably touch upon human rights.[19]

It would be difficult to find a better expression of the feeling of betrayal,[20] which is quite widespread among the founding Member States of the Council of Europe, with respect to their original expectations of the role and the limits of the European Court of Human Rights and the recent period of judicial activism.

These expectations were clearly underlined by Lord Hoffmann himself some years ago when he pointed out that 'when we joined, indeed, took the lead in the negotiation of the European Convention, it was not because we thought it would affect our own law; but because we thought it right to set an example for others and to help to ensure that all the Member States respected those basic human rights which were not culturally determined but reflected our common humanity'.[21] It should not then be surprising if, as the more recent case law of the Italian Constitutional Court shows, resistance has emerged in the old Member States with respect to the European Court of Human Rights' new self-perception as a pan-European Constitutional Court.

This resistance, as emerges from the analysis carried out in the book, has been weaker in the Central and Eastern European (CEE) Member States, not only because as late comers they did not have any illusions that the ECHR would only be a 'normal' international treaty and that the ECtHR would have acted as a normal international court, but also because, as

---

19 Lord Hoffman, 'The Universality of Human Rights' [2009] LQR 416.

20 The point was first raised by W. Sadurski, 'Partnering with Strasbourg: Constitutionalisation of the European Court of Human Rights, the Accession of Central and East European States to the Council of Europe, and the Idea of Pilot Judgments' [2009] Human Rights L Rev 397.

21 Lord Hoffman, 'Human rights and the House of Lords' [1999] MLR 159.

Sadurski has underlined, 'if there is a domain in which concerns over national identity and accompanying notions of sovereignty are obviously weak in Central and Eastern Europe it is in the field of protection of individual rights'.[22]

If those are among the main reasons which can explain the cooperative attitude of the CEE Constitutional Courts to Strasbourg, the same cannot be said with regard to the attitude of the CEE ordinary judges towards supranational law in general. In comparison to the constitutional judges of this area, who are in general quite open 'to the partisans of the transition and to the innovative spirits',[23] the ordinary judges are, even if much less than before, 'still enslaved by textual positivism'.[24]

While the CEE Constitutional Courts, as third-generation constitutional courts, were born into a flourishing international human rights jurisdiction, the ordinary judges, especially in comparison with their colleagues in the West, are still very deferential to the literal interpretation of the law and are thus not exactly in a mood for dialogue[25] with the European Courts. In other words, they are more keen on keeping a good relationship with their hierarchically superior colleagues, if not with the political powers.

As emerges, for example, in the Polish and Czech-Slovak experience, the constitutional courts have tried to indicate to the ordinary judges a path towards emancipation, especially with regard to their role of European judges and the immediate application of EU law and the dialogue, through the preliminary reference procedure, with the ECJ.[26]

However, equivocal indications to the ordinary judges may come from

---

22 W. Sadurski, 'Constitutionalization of the EU and the Sovereignty Concerns of the New Accession States: The Role of the Charter of Rights', in *EUI Working Paper Law*, n. 11/03, www.iue.it/PUB/Law03-10.pdf.

23 L. Sólyom, 'The Role of Constitutional Courts in the Transition to Democracy: With Special Reference to Hungary' (2003) International Sociology 136.

24 Z. Kühn, 'Words Apart, Western and Central European Judicial Culture at the Onset of the European Enlargement', Am J Comparative Law, 549.

25 G. Martinico, 'Preliminary Reference and Constitutional Courts. *Are You in the Mood for Dialogue*?' *in* F. Fontanelli, G. Martinico and P. Carrozza, *Shaping Rule of Law through Dialogue. International and Supranational Experiences* (Europa Law 2009).

26 As has been stated 'The Czech Constitutional Court and the Slovak Constitutional Court have also declared themselves ready to function as *de facto* enforcers of the last instance ordinary courts' duty to submit a request for a preliminary ruling, similar to the approach elaborated in the case law of the German Federal Constitutional Court and the Austrian Federal Constitutional Court'. See Bobek and Kosař, 'Report on the Czech Republic and Slovakia', 127.

the extremely 'ECHR friendly' attitudes of some CEE constitutional courts that, on one hand, invite the ordinary judges to go beyond the black letter of the law and make use of their hermeneutical powers, while on the other hand, urging them to deprive themselves of the margin of appreciation by declaring, as the Slovak Constitutional Court recently did, that the case law of the ECHR and ECtHR represents 'binding interpretative guidelines for interpretation and application of statutory rules on the relevant aspects of the right to a fair trial'.[27]

As far as the issue related to the convergence between the domestic impact of EU law and the ECHR is concerned, the Baltic States could be declared the champions in this regard (besides the symmetry underlined with respect to ordinary judges' national mandate in France, Luxembourg, Poland, Belgium and the Netherlands). Indeed in a recent analysis it has been pointed out that 'the jurisprudence of the Constitutional Courts (and the Supreme Court of Estonia) clearly demonstrates the convergence of views towards the ECHR and EU law as special sources of supranational legal orders'.[28]

According to research carried out, it seems much more difficult to identify the same trend in Slovenia, Slovakia, the Czech Republic, Portugal, Greece, Germany and Austria, where the ECHR and EU law mechanisms are still understood to play different roles and have a different scope and objective.

Pal Sonnevend[29] has raised an interesting point when, after stating that neither the judiciary nor legal scholarship seem to support any trend towards convergence between the domestic impact of ECHR law and EU law, he goes on to underline that 'it is to be expected, however, that such convergence will rather follow from EU law itself and this may lead to a different approach at national level'.

With regard to the Irish and British experiences, the fact that EU law and the ECHR are incorporated in different ways in both jurisdictions means that there is little scope for convergence without much greater judicial activism. In the Nordic countries, as Lebeck stated, there is convergence in the sense that both ECHR and EU law tend to take precedence over national law and that both work as a substitute for constitutional judicial review. Formally there is no convergence, but practically there is certain convergence, and in both cases it seems possible only because of

---

27 Judgment of the SCC of 19 December 2001, I. ÚS 49/01, available at http://www.concourt.sk.

28 I. Jarukaitis, 'Report on Baltic States', 202.

29 P. Sonnevand, 'Report on Hungary', in Martinico and Pollicino, *The National Judicial Treatment of the ECHR and EU Laws*, 251, 265.

the long tradition of 'pragmatism' in relation to constitutional issues that is characteristic of the Nordic countries.[30]

In Romania, as Ioana Raducu pointed out, there is, according to legal scholarship, a consensus 'on the idea that the ECHR and EU law should converge in the national judicial treatment. However, the practice still presents inconsistencies in applying the ECHR and EU standards.'[31] The same asymmetry between legal scholarship and the judiciary can be found in Spain, where Aida Torres Perez underlined that:

> on the whole, from a scholarly standpoint, it is increasingly the case that the impact of both systems upon constitutional structures is the object of combined research projects. Indeed, the judiciary tends to be at the core of legal analysis which addresses the interaction between legal systems. Judicial practice, however, is more divergent towards ECHR and EU law.[32]

In Italy, as we have seen, the convergence suggested by the Constitution, following the amendment of 2001, is denied by more recent case law of the Italian Constitutional Court, which is concerned about the risk of losing its role as final arbiter for the protection of national fundamental rights. The trend that is emerging in many European countries for the constitutional court to have the last say on the adequate standards of protection of fundamental rights when there is a conflict between the national legal order, on the one hand, and the ECHR and EU law, on the other hand, does not imply a devaluation of the role played by national ordinary judges. On the contrary, while constitutional courts have the last say, the ordinary judges have the first. Indeed in many cases the first say may also be the last say, if the ordinary judge is successful in his/her attempt to solve the contrast between national and supranational law by using the tool of consistent interpretation.

In this respect, consistent interpretation, being the privileged interpretive technique of nearly all the jurisdictions examined, is the real *trait d'union* between the domestic impact of the two European legal orders. Perhaps one could consider this as the first (judicial) stone in the construction of a unitary theory of supranational law.

---

[30] Lebeck, 'Report on Scandinavian Countries', 435.

[31] Raducu, 'Report on Romania', 387.

[32] A. Torrez Perez, 'Report on Spain', in Martinico and Pollicino, *The National Judicial Treatment of the ECHR and EU Laws*, 457, 473.

Index